F*CK IT! LET'S PIVOT

AN ENTREPRENEURS GUIDE TO SURVIVING AND THRIVING IN A CRISIS

Includes Stories from Real-Life Entrepreneurs
on Pivots that Turned into Profit

MICHAEL SIERVO

F*CK IT! LET'S PIVOT
AN ENTREPRENEURS GUIDE TO SURVIVING AND THRIVING IN A CRISIS

iUniverse books may be ordered through booksellers or by contacting:

iUniverse
1663 Liberty Drive
Bloomington, IN 47403
www.iuniverse.com
844-349-9409

Additional Credits
Design Cover: JM Acuna
QR Codes and Pivot Web Designer: Jm Acuna
Photographer: Jesse Tomayo

ISBN: 978-1-6632-3511-4 (sc)
ISBN: 978-1-6632-3512-1 (e)

Print information available on the last page.

iUniverse rev. date: 02/16/2022

This book is dedicated to the brave entrepreneurs and business people who have taken the plunge to follow their dreams—and the supportive family, friends, and community along the journey. Your path is never easy, yet you show courage by acting with faith during times of adversity. Continue to have courage during difficult times. You got this.

Michael Siervo

Disclaimer: Whether it's a pandemic, a recession, a crisis, or any event that throws you off your goals, life will always blindside you with adversity. This book isn't about the pandemic. Shit happens. Acknowledge it, learn from it, and then adjust accordingly. This book is about the pivot and how you can shift your mindset in business to one that thrives rather than survives, regardless of the changing environment.

CONTENTS

Introduction.. xi
- Looking Out While Being Locked Down...............................xi
- How to read this book: The Setup xiii
- Who this book is for xvi

PART 1: LET THE JOURNEY BEGIN

Chapter 1: It's All in the Footwork: The Pivot 1
- Let's get technical: formal definition of pivot 2
- Lesson 1: The devil is in the details..............................4
- Lesson 2: Master the pivot..5
- Pivoting in business..6
- How I pivoted..10

Chapter 2: History Doesn't Repeat Itself, But It Does Rhyme.. 15
- Certainty? Benjamin Franklin was only partially right......21
- How I pivoted..24

Chapter 3: Never Waste a Good Crisis 28
- How I pivoted..33
- How I pivoted..35

Chapter 4: The Future Is Here ... Time to Adapt 37
- To pivot or not to pivot?...41
  - Should I put my head down and keep grinding away?...42
  - Should I shift direction and pivot?............................43
  - Should I cut my losses and shut it down? 44

- Deciding whether to pivot permanently.................................45
- How I pivoted.. 46
- How I pivoted.. 49

Chapter 5: Teaching Old Dogs New Tricks 53
- Changes in the Education System: Going Online 53
- COVID-19 and the New World of Distance Learning 56
- Everyone Learns Differently: Style and Formats................. 58
- How I pivoted..61
- How I pivoted.. 66

PART 2: OLD DOORS CLOSE, NEW ONES OPEN—SIDE-HUSTLING IN THE GIG ECONOMY, SALES, AND WINNING THE MENTAL GAME

Chapter 6: The Rise of the Gig Economy.................................73
- What is the Gig Economy and why does it matter to you? 73
- Old excuses don't apply here—no excuses, just pivot!........75
  - Lack of Resources 76
  - Lack of Knowledge 77
  - Lack of Time 79
  - Lack of Confidence.. 80
- Fear is a lie! 80
- How I pivoted.. 82

Chapter 7: Who Is in the Gig Economy? 93
- Pivot and expand at a fraction of the cost............................ 96
- How I pivoted.. 98
- How I pivoted.. 100

Chapter 8: The Entrepreneur Mindset.....................103
- Fail Forward; Fail Often.. 105
- How I pivoted.. 107
- How I pivoted..111

Chapter 9: "Me" Incorporated..**113**
- The Future Belongs to the Competent.................................. 115
- Take Charge of Your Income.. 115
- The 7 Rs to Pivoting Your Career...................................... 119
- How I pivoted.. 125

Chapter 10: You Are the Brand!.......................................**128**
- Be like Mandela.. 131
- Creating the Brand 132
- Why are you here?... 134
- What makes you different? 136
- Sho Sushi: Winning and Prevailing through Pivoting..... 136
- What's that You Said? I Can't Hear Your Voice! 139
- Why Should I Believe You?.. 142
- How I pivoted.. 144

Chapter 11: Getting Social with Social Media....................**148**
- Facebook: The Godfather of Social Media........................ 154
- YouTube: Seeing is Believing 156
- Instagram: A Picture tells a Thousand Words.................... 158
- LinkedIn: It's about linking up....................................... 159
- ClickFunnels: One click away from conversion 161
- Can't forget this notable mention................................... 164
- Five Essential Social Media Tips for the Business Pivot.. 165
- How I pivoted.. 168

Chapter 12: Sell or Die—Why You Need to Learn to Sell **176**
- Just Learn to Sell: Network Marketing............................. 180
- How I pivoted..181
- The Sales Myth.. 184
- Five key reasons why selling is so important.................... 184
- Ten Quick Tips to Improve your Sales Skills 189
- How I pivoted.. 193

Chapter 13: Plan to Succeed **198**
- Statistics for small businesses to consider in 2022 and beyond 199
- How I pivoted..204

Chapter 14: Think Pivoting Is Necessary? Prove It! **209**
- The Trend is your Friend 210
- The pivot must not undermine the intent of the company... 215
- The pivot must be sustainable................................. 215
- How I pivoted..217

Chapter 15: Pandemic Pivot Strategies....................................**220**
- Six Simple Pivot Strategies.................................... 221
- How I pivoted.. 229
- How I pivoted.. 232

Chapter 16: This Won't Be Your Last Crisis **235**
- Nine things you need to focus on during a crisis............... 236
- How I pivoted..244
- How I pivoted..248

Chapter 17: Conclusion Life Is About Endless Beginnings....**251**

Resources and Book Recommendations 257
- Books that feed my brain.. 257
- Podcasts that inspire me... 258
- Apps that make my life easy 259

About the Author 261

Acknowledgement **263**

INTRODUCTION

Looking Out While Being Locked Down

*You never know how strong you are, until being
strong is your only choice. —Bob Marley*

So, THERE I WAS, EITHER GLUED TO THE TELEVISION OR TRAPPED
in this vortex of newsfeed regarding the pandemic. Although I
remember living through the first case of SARS in Toronto, Canada,
this was a completely different animal. Airplanes were grounded.
Restaurants shut down. People were forced to hunker down in their
homes, not knowing what would happen next.

I remember seeing empty shelves in the grocery store as the
community braced for an apocalyptic scenario worthy of an HBO
series. Toilet paper rolls trumped gold bars and became the next hot
commodity. I guess when we are stuck in our homes, there's nothing
to do but sit on the toilet and scroll through social media.

Headlines graced every newsfeed and referred to this pandemic as
the worst since the Spanish flu. Not only did this pandemic kill people,
it murdered people financially. Many felt the economic disaster would
echo the Great Depression. No one knew what was real or what was
an exaggeration. I remember standing on the floor of the New York
Stock Exchange in 2008 wondering if this was the end of society as
we know it. This time felt different.

Close to a year after COVID-19 was declared a global pandemic,
as death tolls continued to rise, the hardest hit was not the health of
global citizens but the financial health of people. The truth is, we
still don't know what lies ahead. Mentally and financially, the world

suffered and continues to suffer. For many, it feels like they've been in a 12-round title fight with someone two weight classes above them.

The knockout punch hit the economic lifeblood of any society—the small-business owner. The smaller business owner didn't have the deep pockets to ride out months of closed doors while continuing to pile up expenses. Even as governments provided stimulus and subsidy, much of this was a financial Band-Aid that would only temporarily stop the bleeding. Businesses failed. They shut their doors permanently and contributed to the downward spiral of mental illness and financial despair.

As I saw this happening, I dreaded opening the mail. Bills piled up. Calls from banks and landlords continued. I stopped answering my phone when I saw unknown numbers. The financial hardship hit many people, including me. My other businesses and income streams were creating just enough income to cover the hemorrhaging from other highly sensitive businesses, such as my restaurants.

As a multi-property real estate investor, I was banking on the concept that my real estate would generate passive income or be a source for refinancing. Unfortunately, that plan didn't work. Where I live, my real estate properties took a massive hit, so the equity I had in them wasn't nearly as much as it had been prior to the pandemic. That nice, juicy nest egg I thought would help me weather a storm wasn't prepared to ride out a full-blown economic tsunami. In desperation, I remember selling a property to cover expenses, only to suffer a 20 per cent loss. Ouch! That one hurt.

At the height of this pandemic, I did whatever I could to survive. I went all-in on what I knew would make money, and out of necessity created other income streams to stay afloat. While staying locked down, I remember seeing my wife post random stuff from our house that we didn't need on Facebook Market.

One thing I learned from sales guru Grant Cardone is that there is nothing beneath you when it comes to generating money to put food on the table. *Sell something or die*, he would champion. And that's just what I did. I used resources and skills such as sales, business creation, networking, digital marketing, and so on to add a few extra income streams to my portfolio.

I couldn't help but think about my business colleagues who invested their entire life savings only to see it vanish in a matter of months. I was lucky, but how many people around the world were not? How many hard-working entrepreneurs held on and are still holding on by a thread? This book is for those who haven't lost hope.

I can't promise some mystical pill to create a massive windfall. Nor do I profess to solve all the economic problems we face. But I will highlight the mindset needed to survive, the maneuvering needed to execute a plan, and the stories of some creative entrepreneurs who came out stronger than before. I am not a business guru with a magical formula to fix your financial woes. If I was, I'd be on a beach sipping piña coladas while doing Zoom calls. What I am is a straight-up entrepreneur who got hammered by this pandemic and saw hope when many may have lost it.

The lessons and stories are things I personally did, read, or saw first-hand that inspired me to continue pushing forward. The stories written by others are their unfiltered words and experiences. The culmination of all of this is not just additional income streams but an overall maturity, sense of gratitude, and perspective that I believe can help you regardless of the fastball to the head that life throws at you.

Change is inevitable. If it's not COVID-19, it's some other crisis that will hit you when you least expect it. This book is meant to build resiliency so that you have the best fighting chance to survive and thrive in any economic situation.

How to read this book: The Setup

This book has two parts. Part One will focus on a brief history of business and some fundamental insight needed before pivoting. Now, it might seem odd to start off with a history lesson but believe there's some value in it. You may already be a seasoned businessperson or someone considering entering the world of entrepreneurship.

Regardless, I felt it would be useful to establish a frame of mind and historical perspective so that we know how we got here in order to know where we're going. As it is often said, history doesn't always repeat itself but it sometimes rhymes. Success leaves clues, so hopefully history can help guide us.

In addition, before moving on to more tactical concepts and ideas in Part Two, we will consider what I believe to be a vital part of any successful journey: the mental game and the execution plan. If you want to play the game of life, you need to have a winning mindset. Every entrepreneur goes into battle expecting to win. You may have a solid plan that you are willing to execute. It's only when we get knocked down that reality sets in and we must decide whether this is a winnable battle.

The great Iron Mike Tyson once said, "Everybody has a plan until they get punched in the mouth." Well, this pandemic punched many of us in the mouth. I don't care what contingency plans you had in place; I don't think anyone was truly prepared for this fight.

Here's what I believe: it is a winnable battle. But just like David and Goliath, you're not going to win this battle on a level playing field. You need to change your strategy. The fact is that despite the doom and gloom we read in the news headlines, many businesses have thrived over the last year or so and will continue to ride this momentum well into the future.

Part Two focuses on simple, executable ideas and concepts that anyone can do. Entrepreneur or accidental side-hustler, welcome to the gig economy. Get familiar with this term, as it's going to be around for some time. In fact, it's been around for years, but many of us never thought to participate in it—until now. This section opens the world of the pivot and how this pandemic has created opportunities to make money.

There is an oft-cited quote (actually, a misquote) attributed to Charles Darwin which states, "It is not the strongest of the species that survives, nor the most intelligent that survives. It is the one that is most adaptable to change." It is the entrepreneur, part-time side hustler, stay-at-home parent, retiree, corporation, or person working smart to get ahead who survives rather than slides down the slippery slope COVID-19 or any crisis for that matter has created. We will discuss what some average people have done to ensure their survival through their ability to adapt.

Finally, you don't have to believe me when I tell you that there are opportunities. Who am I to position myself as the subject-matter expert of business pivots when I admit that I took a kick to the economic balls from a pandemic bully that doesn't play fair? Throughout this book, I will share stories written by real-life people about their experience, insights, and success tips during this pandemic. I have been fortunate to have several local business owners from all walks of life share how they have successfully pivoted. Seeing is believing, so let's see the pandemic through their eyes and in their words.

Throughout the book, you'll see QR codes that will make this journey interactive. You'll be able to watch videos and hear from the business owners themselves on how they pivoted their business and their tips on moving forward.

This book can be read cover-to-cover or selectively. In fact, when I wrote this, it wasn't meant to be read chronologically, as it is a compilation of ideas, observations, stories, and best practices that I have seen during this pandemic. Throughout the book, you will read stories that perhaps describe your situation, your thoughts, and your feelings, and hopefully provide guidance moving forward. The tips shared in this book have been proven successful by real small-business owners to help you

- generate additional revenue
- save on expenses
- open new opportunities
- gain mental clarity
- grow more confident in moving outside your comfort zone
- uplift your spirit
- give you that little push to say, "This isn't working. Fuck it. Let's pivot."

Don't have time to read all of it? No problem. The idea is to find ideas that resonate with you. I promise you that this book is filled with them.

If you have a rock-solid foundation of the entrepreneurial mindset or don't feel like learning about the history of business, then jump right to Part Two. However, I may have a bias that there are some great tips and reminders in Part One that can be transferred into other aspects of your life. Mindset is key. Without winning the mind game, you'll eventually lose the execution game in the end.

> *Progress is impossible without change, and*
> *those who cannot change their minds cannot*
> *change anything.* —George Bernard Shaw

Who this book is for

> *We cannot solve our problems with the same thinking*
> *we used when we created them.*—Albert Einstein

If you are reading this book, you could be a business owner, a momtrepreneur, an employee worried about the status of your job, or simply someone who wants to be prepared for the uncertainty that lies ahead. I won't profess to know everything, but this book includes ideas, strategies, concepts, and stories that have worked for those brave small-business owners who took the plunge into the uncertain world of entrepreneurship. It includes real pivot strategies that helped people get through some seriously scary times.

In fact, you don't need to have a business. This book is for anyone who acknowledges that the world as we know it has changed and continues to change. By mentally and intellectually preparing yourself for whatever comes, you will give yourself a fighting chance to twirl that slingshot and slam Goliath right between the eyes. Of course, you'll need to first know what a slingshot is and how to use it. That's what this book is about. It's a start for you to increase your odds of survival.

PART ONE
Let the Journey Begin

I think a hero is an ordinary individual who finds strength to persevere and endure in spite of overwhelming obstacles.—Superman

CHAPTER 1

It's All in the Footwork: The Pivot

THIS BOOK IS CALLED *F*ck It! Let's Pivot: An Entrepreneur's Guide to Surviving and Thriving in a Crisis* because there will be many times in your life where you are smacked in the face with a crisis and are forced to make some life-changing decisions. It's going to happen, and it's happening right now. You can either throw up your hands and give up, or find that inner courage and say, "Fuck it. Let's pivot!" It's that moment in poker when you push in all your chips and say, "To hell with it, I'm committing to this move and will live with the outcome." The thing is, when pro poker players make that move, it's a very well calculated and strategic move that just has the theatrics of pushing all your chips in.

A pivot describes a shift in direction or angle. In life, you're constantly shifting, adjusting, redirecting, adapting, and changing based on whatever this unrelenting world has to throw at you. Like it or not, thispandemic gave us the biggest pivoting opportunity in our lifetime. Let's be real here: no one really wanted this pandemic to happen (quiet all you conspiracy theorists, this isn't that kind of book). However, it really forced us to make some big changes as our world was ripped out right from under us. *Change or die* is what went through many of our minds as the shit hit the fan, so to speak. Before we dig deeper into this, let's first take some time to explore just what the heck a pivot is.

> *Pivoting is not Plan B. It is changing*
> *the strategy without changing the vision*
> *of Plan A.—Michael Siervo*

1

Let's get technical: formal definition of pivot

According to the Merriam-Webster Dictionary, *pivot* means

> **1:** a shaft or pin on which something turns

> **2a:** a person, thing, or factor having a major or central role, function, or effect

> **b:** a key player or position *specifically* : an offensive position of a basketball player standing usually with back to the basket to relay passes, shoot, or provide a screen for teammates

> **3:** the action of pivoting

> **4:** an adjustment or modification made (as to a product, service, or strategy) in order to adapt or improve

For me, the best way to think about a pivot is in sports. I love sports due to the competitive nature and the need to constantly adjust to changing situations. It's unpredictable—so thinking on the fly and pivoting is always happening. The momentum can swing in the favour of one team or the other at any given time. Therefore the pivot is important if you want to win the contest. This is equally true if you want to win in life as well.

Now in sports, the concept of pivoting from one direction to another is crucial as you try to outplay your competition. Let's take one of my favorite sports, for instance. In the game of basketball, pivoting is exceptionally crucial, as it is the basis of one of the most fundamental violations in the game. If you drag or move your pivot foot, you can easily be called for travelling. If this happens, the other team gets possession of the ball along with the opportunity to score a goal. The only way to win games is if you score more goals. If your opponent has the opportunity to score a goal on you, that's a possibility of losing the game. Simple, right?

If you've ever watched basketball like I tend to do, there are so many tiny violations that may or may not be called by the referee. It's such a fast-paced game, you can't blame the referees when they miss a call here or there. With elite athletes whizzing back and forth across the court with each possession or bodies battling all over the place for positioning, it's really easy to miss these calls.

Imagine if one of these calls was made during a crucial moment in a championship game. Imagine the countless one-point victories because of a single game-winning shot. We tend to focus on that last shot to determine the outcome of the game. But think about one blown call that might have given the other team possession earlier in the game. We don't think about that. We focus on the final seconds rather than the moments that got us to that final moment. It's a tough job being a referee because whether you make a call or not, one team isn't going to like it.

> *"I wanted to have a career in sports when I was young, but I had to give up the idea. I'm only six feet tall, so I couldn't play basketball. I'm only 190 pounds, so I couldn't play football, and I have 20/20 vision, so I couldn't be a referee.—Jay Leno*

Lebron James, arguably the greatest basketball player of our generation, has won four NBA Championship rings. As great as he is, he's notorious for traveling violations. If he was called for travelling in a handful of these crucial games, would he have won all those rings? Would his legacy be the same? Who knows? What I'm trying to get at here is that sometimes the smallest miniscule details can sway victory or defeat without ever being noticed. In business, this is equally crucial. The pivot can be such a small tiny adjustment or a massive corporate upheaval. The pivot is the ability to change direction without changing the vision. As in sports, that vision is to win.

Lesson 1: The devil is in the details

The tiny decisions we make in life can either lead us to greatness or lead us to being forever remembered for losing the game. Just ask former Michigan State Fab Five legend and NBA great Chris Webber about his time-out call during the 1993 National Championship. With the game on the line and 11 seconds left to play, he gets away with travelling while the referee's back is turned. He dodges a turnover, runs up the court, and calls a time-out. The problem is that his team didn't have a time-out available, which put them in violation. This effectively lost the game for them. You can watch this legendary moment to relive the impact of how missing a small detail can cause you to lose it all when everything is on the line.

Be aware of the details when making decisions. Life doesn't always have an obvious referee making a call on the play regarding each and every decision you make. We don't always have someone overseeing us to make sure we play by the rules and win the game properly. Changing trends, new technologies, crises, threats, opportunities, or new regulations can change the dynamics of the playing field and thus impact the outcome of your game. Be aware. The tiniest details can mean a world of a difference.

The second and probably best analogy I can think of when it comes to a pivot is in boxing. As you can see on the front cover of this book, there's a boxer punching this bag draped in money. In boxing, the pivot is among the most critical things to master. Your footwork can prevent you from getting your clock cleaned with a right hook to the jaw or position you on an angle to throw a punch that your opponent doesn't see coming.

In boxing, the pivot is one of the most often overlooked aspects of the game. The main reason is that on the face of it, the pivot is not a glamorous skill. It doesn't offer the potential for a highlight reel explosion of punches to end a contest like Manny Pacquiao highlights on YouTube. Nor does the pivot catch the eye like evading attacks using slips and ducks, the way Floyd Mayweather would do as opponents looked foolish swinging at the air in frustration.

To leverage my boxing analogy, if I want to leave you with one takeaway, it is that the pivot is the single most versatile skill a boxer uses, providing options to unlock many opportunities. If you're in close range to an opponent who is strong and powerful, he may use that advantage to push you back. The pivot allows you to cancel this strength by deflecting the line of attack without having to retreat. Now you are free to unleash some short-range shots without having to enter your opponent's wheelhouse.

Let's say, on the other hand, that you're fighting a skilled boxer who is superior as a counter-puncher. He feels comfortable and is effective at retreating. You can run around the ring and chase him only to be caught with an unsuspecting left hook to the side of your head. Knockout!

Here, you can use the pivot to maintain the centre of the ring. Pivoting allows you to follow your opponent without chasing. It prepares you for an inevitable attack. In essence, you are now controlling your environment by using the simple yet fundamental footwork of the pivot.

There are so many ways to use the boxing analogy to explain the pivot, as it essentially gives you more options. In life, the more options you have, the better it is when shit hits the fan and you need to adjust. It's easy to coast in life and take whatever comes, but if you really want to function in a state of excellence, you need to focus on the details, know your options and execute with force.

When you pay attention to detail, the big
picture will take care of itself.—George
St. Pierre, UFC Hall of Famer

Lesson 2: Master the pivot

Mastering the pivot in boxing is fundamental to opening up your options, positioning yourself for both offensive and defensive opportunities, and controlling the situation instead of the situation controlling you. In business, these lessons also hold true. You will be faced with opponents who want to take what you have (sorry, Tax Man, but you're in this category as well). Competitors will come out with new technologies, or the economic environment will change, and you will need to decide to either play offense or defense, to be proactive or reactive.

Play into the game plan of the opponent or change the game entirely. Understanding the importance of the pivot can make the difference between being economically knocked out or raising your hand in financial windfall when the bell rings.

Sometimes the best way to throw a punch is to take a step back.—*Morgan Freeman,* Million Dollar Baby

Pivoting in business

I read a quote in Forbes Magazine that said "To *pivot* means to fundamentally change the direction of a business when you realize that current products or services aren't meeting the needs of the market. The main goal of a pivot is to help a company improve revenue or survive in the market, but the way you pivot your business can make all the difference."

At the time of this writing, the world is in massive flux (well, with fast-paced technology and innovation, it seems like it's always in flux). Technology has changed the way consumers receive and search for information and seemingly unending time-wasting distractions on social media. Even something as obvious as getting older needs to pivot.

Senior citizens are living a lot longer than ever before, with healthy habits and improvements in modern health care. According to statista. com, in 2015 there were about 417,000 centenarians worldwide. This is expected to grow to 3.7 million, according to PewResearch.org. The health care system has to pivot and find ways to address this growing and inevitable strain on the system. And then, if you're a healthy senior citizen like my mother, Alicia, you need to find new things to do in retirement if you're going to keep yourself busy with all those extra years of life.

We are in a global pandemic, which requires us to adapt and change the way we think and live. This is a crisis that has never been seen before—a pandemic so great that not one single country in the world has come out unscathed. Businesses have been crippled, and many will never open their doors again. Combine a global pandemic alongside massive disruptors such as Amazon, the demand for online shopping has crushed many brick-and-mortar businesses. You can now buy anything from clothes to toilet paper to diapers online without ever leaving your house. This isn't just Amazon, but many businesses are going online out of necessity. If not, these businesses will die. The International Monetary Fund estimates that the global economy shrunk by 4.4 per cent in 2020. The organization described the decline as the worst since the Great Depression of the 1930s.

Despite the development of new vaccines, many are still wondering what recovery could look like if and when it comes. We are waiting for things to get back to normal. But will it ever be like it once was? It's like waiting for the typewriter or the cassette tape to come back. While it may never come back, I have seen a rising demand for analog vinyl records, with their crisp sound appreciated by audiophiles such as myself. The old becomes new, and for some businesses, the cycle begins again. They just need to be able to pivot once the trend comes back in their favour, if ever.

On the other hand, imagine a world without Netflix. It was only a few years ago that people watched movies by physically renting them from a Blockbuster only to return them a few days later for their neighbours to watch. If you're a Gen Z, you probably have no clue what the typewriter, cassette tape, or Blockbuster even are. But that's OK, because in this new world, you likely won't ever have to go through the hassle of rewinding your cassette tape with your pencil or renting DVDs and VHS tapes in your lifetime.

As mentioned sometimes the old becomes new again for a who new demographic. The vinyl record has made a bit of a comeback along with overalls and loud colours. However, if you are a betting man, I'd bet that Blockbuster isn't coming back anytime soon, or at least not in this parallel universe. However, you can ride the trend of the comeback if you can spot the opportunity and pivot accordingly.

So I've titled this book *F*ck It! Let's Pivot.* Why did I name it this way? For one, it sounds cool; but also, if you are not able to pivot and alter your business, you will go the way of the typewriter, cassette tape, blockbuster, VHS, dot-matrix printers, or any other business that disappeared from the face of this earth. This book is here to help.

I originally called this book *The Post-Pandemic Profit Plan.* However, I could have easily called it *The Pre-Pandemic Profit Plan.* Even before this pandemic occurred, the idea of pivoting your business was imperative for survival. Eric Ries, entrepreneur and author of *The Lean Startup*, defines a business pivot as a "structured course correction designed to test a new fundamental hypothesis about the product, strategy, and engine of growth."

Pivots do not need to be dramatic. Making minor adjustments to a message or communication to clients or employees is a pivot. Sometimes a pivot has more strategic implications, such as shifting focus to different segments and verticals or completely changing channel partners.

All those businesses I mentioned are dinosaurs because they **didn't** pivot. The dinosaurs were giants that walked the earth and ruled the land. They were massive creatures that seemed immovable. But just like us with the Great Depression, the Financial Crisis of 2008, and COVID-19, they didn't see it coming.

Let's face it, a giant *Tyrannosaurus rex* and his short arms couldn't do jack shit when a huge meteor hit the earth, but perhaps those businesses I mentioned could have. They might still be around if they were able to foresee their doom. They might have looked different, but they could have future-proofed their business to withstand any type of economic meteor heading their way. Expect the worst and hope for the best, but always be willing to change. Just like my boxing analogy earlier, the pivot would have allowed Blockbuster to see the threat coming and buy Netflix when it could. Blockbuster could have bought Netflix for $50Million but they thought it was a joke. Who's laughing now?

Change is inevitable. The pivot is necessary to address that inevitability. Here is what I truly believe and have seen first-hand: this pandemic has accelerated the speed with which technology and other advancements will be embraced by society as a whole. It was coming no matter what. That meteor or asteroid was rocketing through space regardless of what anyone on Earth could say or do. You can believe in the 1998 movie *Armageddon*, but Bruce Willis isn't getting on a spaceship to blast that asteroid before it hits Earth. Call the pandemic The Great Accelerator if you may but the technological revolution, among other trends, was well on its way regardless.Now it's been accelerated by multiple years sooner

Be fearful when people are greedy and be
greedy when people are fearful.—Warren
Buffet, world's greatest investor

I believe in the Warren Buffett quote above. For years, we have been fattening up our bellies with a historic bull rally in the stock market. Companies, regardless of whether they were profitable or not, were flush with cash as investors continued to plow money into the stock market. However, as one stockbroker once told me, when there is blood in the streets, there is opportunity.

And there is a lot of blood in the streets right now. In any crisis, there is opportunity. The deeper and more disruptive the crisis is, the greater the opportunity. The current crisis is as deep and disruptive as any I've seen in my lifetime.

If you are reading this book, perhaps you are going through some changes in your business. It may be teetering on survival, or perhaps you are just getting into the world of entrepreneurship and want to explore opportunities ahead. Regardless of where you are in your entrepreneurial journey, there is something in here for you.

I will walk you through the importance of understanding the ever changing world we live in, preparing our mindset to take on the pivot, and determining if and how you can pull off this pivot. We will look at the importance of branding and sales, potential new trends afoot, and the importance of coming up with a simple execution plan to put this all together. Change can be scary, but it is necessary. Get ready to pivot. Rather than spare change, let's make some profit.

The secret to change is to focus all of your energy, not on fighting the old but building the new.—Aristotle

How I pivoted

Donny Wong, CEO and Founder of BOOOST CBD and NOMAD Properties

"They're rolling *tanks* through the city, man!"

My business partners could clearly see what I was raving on about. The little WhatsApp video I sent them showed the military rolling into the streets of Wuhan, completely locking down the city and province.

While the rest of the world was being told this was nothing to worry about and that the "China virus" was just a little cold, we weren't so sure.

Soon, Italy would be ravaged by the virus, and all major European countries would follow. Germany, UK, Greece, France, the list goes on. In the span of just a few weeks, countries would restrict travel, and borders would be completely closed to the world—devastating our short-term-rental business.

As many entrepreneurs felt the chaos of COVID, a few industries took the biggest kick in the teeth, with hotels and travel hospitality being #1. Our business landed smack dab in the crosshairs. It was truly a bittersweet moment. On one hand, we had just reached a major milestone—$1,000 per day in revenue. At $30,000 per month, we would be on pace to double or triple our previous year. And then it all went to zero.

At the time, our business was built on *rental arbitrage*, which meant we rented our clients' properties and in turn rented those properties back out to global travellers for higher nightly rental rates. This isn't such a great model when the entire world bans travel. You know what's also not great? Knowing you have responsibility for your clients' mortgage payments.

We were now stuck with over $13,000 in monthly hard expenses and zero income. *Plus* the cancellations of all our bookings for the entire year. From $250,000 to zero.

Our team had an emergency meeting. Our ensuing conversation broke down into three parts:

1.   How to stay alive

     - **Cut all salary.** No one was getting paid, but we made every effort to help each other apply for the CERB payments (Canada Emergency Response Benefit). We kept each other up to date and helped each other apply, ensuring everyone had a lifeline.
     - **Protect the clients.** The #1 rule we decided right away was that we weren't going to abandon our clients. Meaning, there was no way in hell we were going to just give them back their keys and leave them high and dry. We contacted all our clients individually and let them know exactly what was happening and what our game plan was for each one. It wasn't a mass email. It was one client, one phone call. We also made it a point to call them *first*.
     - **Stop the bleed.** We had one looming disaster upon us: our monthly $13,000 expense, which accounted for upcoming rent on our portfolio. We needed an answer

11

fast. Paying $13,000 out-of-pocket would essentially sink us the very next month. Game over.

2. Re-strategize

- **Assess strengths, weaknesses, opportunities, and threats (SWOT).** We took a real hard look at our business. It's easy to romance and defend your ideas on a normal day, but when faced with disaster, that all goes out the window, and objectivity wins over *everything.* Driven by the need to protect our clients, we identified SWOT. This gave us a North Star to operate from (save the clients!) while visually narrowing down our next moves and potential threats along the way. (Spoiler alert: the "threats" column was long.)
- **Recalibrate.** After spilling our entire company onto a sheet of paper, we narrowed down two main goals: save the clients and get rid of our monthly hard costs. That would give us enough runway to get through the next twelve months. But how do you magically cut out $13,000 of monthly costs? Pivot!

  In our SWOT analysis, we identified one single opportunity that would enable us to save our clients: finding long-term renters for each property. There were two major issues with this:

  o We had only done that once. We didn't understand the market and therefore couldn't guarantee results, as we could on short-term rentals.
  o Long-term rentals were almost 10 times *less* ROI. Meaning we would essentially be doing free work for the next 12 months.

Although these problems were valid, we decided it was more important that we hyperfocus on our goals and company values to guide us.

3. Execute

    We now had a plan to help our clients. It was a stretch, but we knew there was a high chance of success. We also figured that if we could call each and every client with a solution, we could renegotiate our contracts with them, freeing up our commitment to rents (so long as we could find long-term tenants) and erasing $13,000 of monthly expenses. *Voila!*

In the end, our clients were very happy that we engaged them with solutions and candid feedback about the situation. We didn't sugar-coat anything (I've never been one to hide from our mistakes). And as always, we delivered on our promise, finding long-term tenants for each and every single one. Not a single one of our clients lost a single month of rent, ensuring they had one less thing to worry about during the pandemic of 2020.

As for us? We didn't make much money during 2020, but figuring out how to market, position, operate, and execute long-term rentals completely reshaped our company and gave us an entirely new service offering going forward. It equipped us with new skills and the ability to take a 10,000-foot view of how to position ourselves, what products we wanted to bring to market, and how it fit our overall strategy. The pandemic forced us to break our business model, and now we hyperfocus on the key performance indicators that matter—ones that ensure a strong and healthy company in *any* market condition. Our company now runs on a monthly operating expense of just five hundred dollars (from $13,000 to $500!). Also, our clients trust us more than ever—a win-win for everyone.

In summary:

- *Stick to your values.* Now is the time to double down on what you believe in. Operating from your core values means sticking to them and showing the world what you stand for. It makes decision-making easier and blocks out the noise during critical situations where multiple options are present.
- *Keep it simple.* Simplify everything. Cut the fat. Go back to the core offering. Forget the fancy stuff. The simplest solution is often the best (especially during a crisis).
- *Fight like hell.* I have a saying that goes, "It's probably gonna get a lot worse before it gets better." Make sure you prepare yourself for a *fight*. While the world said it would be a 15-day lockdown, we were prepping for a 12-month war. (A lot of people actually got angry at me when I told them to prepare for a year-long lockdown back in March 2020.) How you prepare yourself matters a *lot*. You need to show up every single day ready for battle and fight like hell.

Donny Wong
Co-Founder of Nomad Property
Management

CHAPTER 2

History Doesn't Repeat Itself, But It Does Rhyme

If history repeats itself, and the unexpected always
happens, how incapable must Man be of learning
from experience. — *George Bernard Shaw*

WHEN I WAS YOUNGER, I ALWAYS FELL ASLEEP IN HISTORY CLASS. I know there are many of you reading this who can relate. However, after reading that quote from our good friend George Bernard Shaw (nice job, George, you've made it to twice in this book so far), I feel like it's describing me as I wiped my drool while the teacher says class is dismissed. As a grown-ass man, I wish I'd paid a bit more attention during history class. Perhaps not so much to understand the details of the War of 1812 or how Magellan was killed in Cebu, Philippines, but to become more conscious and aware that history can sometimes repeat itself and that success leaves clues.

Therefore, I want to spend some time going back in a time machine to search for clues. Worst-case scenario, you'll be enlightened by the rich history of entrepreneurship and business.

The idea of receiving something of value from someone else for something of perceived value to someone else has been around for decades. Heck, it's been around for centuries. Whether it was travelling months across the ocean to distant lands in order to find the spice route or trading beaver pelts for bear meat, exchange meant progress. It meant people could expand their options, leverage someone else's expertise, and improve their overall lifestyle. This was and is the essence of business and entrepreneurship.

Now, I am sure that some caveman or ancient tribesperson traded a pile of grain for primitive tools or weapons. Everything was up for exchange if you could convince the other person that what you had was worth exchanging for what they had. Business was and is the backbone of the advancement of modern-day society. Throughout the centuries, business has evolved. We exchange time, money, expertise for things that we believe will improve our lives. As expected, humans progress, evolve, and try their best to be as efficient as possible. I used to tell my mom that laziness is the mother of efficiency. I'm still trying to find an efficient way to clean my room. Even as I write this, NFTs (Non-Fungible Tokens) and cryptocurrencies are being exchanged as a more efficient transfer of value. I know this space is still in its infancy however if you're reading this book 10 years from now, I'm predicting that the idea of exchanging digital contracts or currency won't sound as bizarre as it may sound now. Who knows, you may be reading this on a beach somewhere in the metaverse.

> *I will always choose a lazy person to do a difficult job ... because he will find an easy way to do it .—Bill Gates, billionaire philanthropist*

With the speed of 5G technology and the constant creation of faster and more efficient ways of living our life, how we exchange goods in the form of commerce will drastically change. Quite frankly, this can scare the crap out of the average person or the newbie entrepreneur. The world is moving at a neck-breaking speed, and we must look back on history to find a road map. While history may not necessarily repeat itself, it certainly rhymes. Understanding the brief history of business will provide gems of knowledge to prepare us for the new era ahead. Business has always been about getting ahead and generating a profit. If you're not making profit and creating wealth, you are a charity. This is no different today.

The prevailing paradigm of business over the last century is shifting. What was a simple barter or exchange is the past is much deeper than ever before. Before the advent of money, people would simply trade something they had for something they wanted. "Hey, that's a sweet beaver pelt. Wanna trade that for my bushel of wheat?" Done deal. Now it's much more complicated, as the level of exchange and negotiation can be done between you and someone in a remote area thousands of miles away. The world isn't limited to local trade anymore, and the world is now your oyster. Slurp it up.

Over the next decade, we will see the nature of businesses change due to external and internal factors. I have never seen a time such as this where governments and capital markets are so closely intertwined. Factors such as the environment, government regulation, political unrest, and human rights policies demand faster solutions to satisfy consumer appetite and the desire of people to have their items now.

The fact that Amazon can deliver an item in the matter of a few hours is insane. Comedian Ronny Chieng had me in stitches with his Amazon Prime joke: He says people are so spoiled in America, "land of the free and land of never leaving your house." This was even before the pandemic. Eventually, people will be so lazy that Amazon Prime's same-day delivery is too slow. "Forget Amazon Prime," he says. "It's too slow. We need Amazon Now: Two-hour delivery. Prime Now. In America, there should be no lag from the time between when I press the buy button until the item is gently placed in my hand ... Prime Now! ... Send it to me before I want it!"

It's a hilarious skit, but there is truth behind it. It highlights how consumerism and buying has changed. But don't be alarmed; this change has happened many times before. In fact, the idea of what a business is has evolved profoundly through a series of what we can see as definite eras. We see it so rapidly as Internet speeds allow us to download anything in seconds. It usually takes anywhere from 40 to 50 years for this evolution to be fully adopted.

There is typically a company or technology that changes the game as we know it. Today, companies such as the FAANG stocks (Facebook,

Amazon, Apple, Netflix and Google) would fall in that category. And don't forget Tesla. Tesla produced approximately 400,000 electric vehicles in 2020, while Toyota, Volkswagen, Daimler, and Honda built 26 million cars, and yet Tesla's company valuation exceeds that of the four other companies combined. It just shows that this period in time is rewarding future innovations before they even happen.

Speaking of automobiles, in the past, it was Ford Motor Company and its invention of the horseless carriage that was the disruptive force that changed the business landscape. For you young folk reading this, before cars were zipping around on electric batteries, people used a horse and carriage to get by.

> *If I had asked people what they wanted,*
> *they would have said faster horses.—*
> *Henry Ford, automotive visionary*

Prior to Charles Babbage inventing the very first computer in 1822 (yes, 1822!), humans wrote messages on paper, and some countries taught addition and subtraction with an abacus. Prior to watching Netflix on a cell phone or keeping up to speed with what's going on in the world via social media, people gathered around the radio to listen to the news. Similar to life, one thing that is constant in business is change. Its evolution is an excellent predictor of what lies ahead. We need to get ahead of the curve and foresee the trends to help us determine or predict a future pivot.

The pivot happens more often than we think. The moment entrepreneurship became a thing, businesses learned how to adjust as new negotiations came out of the blue. Some of the earliest recorded forms of entrepreneurial exchange happened in ancient Greece. Business first took modern form back then. Money, markets, and entrepreneurial businesses began coming together in the early sixth century BC. Entrepreneurial businesses vied to sell their wares in public markets to the populace at large. Who knows what was being exchanged in ancient Greece, but I'm sure bartering for olive oil, the newest pair of sandals, or the latest trend in flowing togas was a cause of economic negotiation.

In the eighth century BC in India, early organizations called *shreni* were the first firms that could independently enter into contracts or own property. They had a right to an agreed exchange, property, or task. Essentially, this meant that they could sue and be sued. Funny how this practice has stood the test of time.

In 960 AD, China saw the advent of gunpowder, printing presses, the first paper money, the first business partnerships, and joint stock companies that resemble the modern capital structures we see today. Things were booming. Beginning in 1500 AD, government-backed firms like the Dutch East India Company and British East India Company began building global trading empires, floating stocks and bonds on new exchanges as their goods floated around the world. Their tea trade alone reshaped the world map. Cinnamon from Sri Lanka and Cassia from China found its way to the Middle East through the Spice Route. Pivots galore happened as new iterations and business structures popped up with each new industry.

By about 1790, the Industrial Revolution was underway. And with all that tea to brew, firms like Wedgwood found ways to standardize processes once done by hand. Artisans who used to make one whole teapot at a time now focused on making parts of it. It was the company, not one person, that made the pot. Lots and lots of pots, in fact.

Let's not forget the branding and marketing that they needed to sell them to an emerging breed of consumers. Advertising and branding started to become an integral part of the business process. It became about efficiency and how to get more people to know about what you did and get it into their hands.

Every 40 to 50 years, businesses would evolve with mind-blowing concepts and inventions. In the 1830s, US railroad companies became the first truly modern management organizations. Since large companies expanded so rapidly, management became a career. And by the 1960s, those managers were running the growth of conglomerates and monopolies that eventually became titans in the world of commerce. Ownership of businesses and a share of wealth meant the world of business was no longer reserved for individuals or oligarchs.

At the time of this writing, I work with a company that invented the very first mutual fund. Investing was reserved for the ultrawealthy until a company in Boston called MIT (Massachusetts Investment Trust), now MFS (Massachusetts Financial Services), invented the idea of selling fractions of a share to people. This was the first mutual fund.

Imagine if that pivot never happened? No one would have access to the stock market, and wealth would be generated for those who were able to participate in the market. Now regular people could participate in the business by virtue of the stocks if they could afford a share, ETF (exchange-traded funds), or mutual funds to get a one basket of investments in one product.

My business partner Andrew Haukedal and I always talk about how something as simple as the mutual fund transformed the world of investments. In fact, according to *Smithsonian* magazine, the mutual fund was one of the top 50 most influential inventions that changed the modern economy. Heck, who knows, if it wasn't for the mutual fund, Andrew and I would be working for oil barons in a field somewhere!

Pivots happen in every business. Your business pivot can have unintentional consequences that benefit more people than you imagine.

Now back to the Great Depression. Not only were business models changing, but with the Great Depression in the late 1920s and the turmoil of the 1970s, society as a whole had a new way of thinking. Consumer tastes and preferences empowered the buyer like never before. Companies pivoted to cater to their finicky demands. Donna Summer, big Afros, and bell-bottom pants were cool. Music was funky, and disco was rocking the airwaves. People wanted more tacky outfits and psychedelic fashion.

But in terms of business, they also wanted to unlock the value trapped in companies by making sure investors and managers shared the same interests. This was the impetus of the social entrepreneur. These were entrepreneurs that did business and used capitalism for good. It also included companies that did their best to provide profit to their shareholders while still doing what's right for the planet. We will get into why this is important in Part Two of the book.

Certainty? Benjamin Franklin was only partially right

Now that we have exited the telephone-booth time machine circa *Bill and Ted's Excellent Adventure*, we arrive at today. If you were born after the 1990s, that *Bill and Ted's* reference went way over your head. Google it. It's essentially a young Keanu Reeves time traveling in a telephone booth to save the world. Oh, how many of us wish Keanu could save the state of the world now. Anyway, I digress.

> *Nothing is certain except death and*
> *taxes.—Benjamin Franklin*

Benjamin Franklin, one of the Founding Fathers of the United States of America, said that in 1789. But Big Ben was only partially right. Yes, death and taxes are a certainty in life. However, he forgot one other certainty: change. Life, people, the economy, business, music, even the number-one top trending movie on Netflix will change. Change is not only certain, but it's inevitable.

Since the dawn of the Industrial Revolution, businesses have entered a new era roughly every 50 years. That's a great factoid to drop at a cocktail party. But if you're an executive, small-business owner, consultant, organization, charity, or simply someone who wants to get ahead in life, you don't need numbers to tell you that a new era is beginning again.

Why, you ask? Because you feel it. The language, the consumer preference, the way we consume information, and something as simple as how people express their feelings is changing. You can communicate without even saying a word. Heck, you don't even have to write a word. Emojis and cartoon characters are the way we express ourselves. I feel like I'm an ancient Egyptian when I mention to a Gen Y that the pound sign on a phone isn't a hashtag.

Sadly, the pandemic has created a grim reality for many. Sometimes change isn't good for everyone. On the BBC website, the unemployment rate worldwide is staggering. Although the stock market whipsawed from a massive pullback that saw close to 20 per cent evaporate in a few months to rebound higher than it was prior to the pandemic, many people around the world feel the real pain. Unlike paper losses seen on a trading account, people saw real losses as their customers stopped walking through the door.

Many countries, such as the US and Canada, saw unemployment almost double during this time. Most countries were in a recession by the start of 2021. The only major economy to grow in 2020 was China at 2.3 per cent. The economy is predicted to grow by 5.2 per cent in 2021 due to the rapid growth in India and China, forecasted to grow by 8.8 per cent and 8.2 per cent respectively. Commercial flights remain well below normal levels as planes sit idle in hangars.

The hospitality sector has shut its doors worldwide, as millions of companies have gone bankrupt and jobs have disappeared. Global tourism is crumbling. Many analysts believe that international travel and tourism won't return to the normal pre-pandemic levels until around 2025. Retail foot traffic for shopping saw a massive drop. Just walk through Chinook Centre in Calgary or Eaton Centre in downtown Toronto at the height of the pandemic; it was like a ghost town. At the time of writing, we are approaching a third lockdown in Canada. This means many businesses will once again take a hit.

In the US, foot traffic is down 20 per cent year over year. Canada is down 65 per cent, as people aren't leaving their homes. The UK and Germany are like barren deserts, as they are down 78 per cent and 97 per cent respectively. It is insane to think that a country's retail foot traffic is almost non-existent.

It's not all doom and gloom though. Where there are losers, there are winners. The rise of pharmaceutical companies has created massive wealth for timely investors with extra cash. Moderna is up 715.5 per cent, and companies like Amazon, Zoom, and those that leverage online and social media have benefitted. I have been around long enough to see the tech wreck and Y2K fiasco and the great recession in 2008. Winners then are no longer winners now. Just ask Nortel, Blackberry, and Blockbuster. Change is inevitable.

The secret of change is to focus all of your energy, not on fighting the old, but on building the new.—Socrates

So, what will the firm of the future look like? No one can say for sure. But we believe some trends are clear. Technology will allow companies to achieve scale and retain customer intimacy. Power will shift from professional managers to the experts who deliver to those customers. Education won't necessarily come from Ivy league schools but from experienced whiz kids from Silicon Valley. Companies will own only those assets critical to their mission and rely on external ecosystems to manage the rest.

Business teams will reach across time zones, cultures, language, and skill sets as the world becomes smaller. Investors won't just invest in companies; they'll also invest in social projects. Employees will change jobs regularly if they don't find a company that represents their values. Sure, they need money, but they won't stick around if the job doesn't align with what they believe in. Every company will have two engines: the one that powers today's profits and the one that will generate the profits of tomorrow.

The dawn of a new era is upon us if not already here. If there's one thing that this pandemic has taught us, it's that the only certainty in life is uncertainty. If history repeats itself, it shouts loud and clear that there's only one thing to do during times of change, and that is to pivot. Are you ready to pivot and profit on this post-pandemic planet?

The past is something that cannot be changed. However, by understanding things that cannot be changed and viewing them as lessons that can impact change, our past and present can foretell the future.—Michael Siervo

How I pivoted

John Sheard, Hons BA, LLB, Partner at Sheard Law PC

In an empty office on a cold spring morning, the electronic chime of the fax machine gave way to the click and whirr of gears pulling its paper through the drum. Soon there was a stack in the tray. Nobody was there to read it, and the message sat for days in an office locked down from the virus.

On that morning, the legal world was starting to wake up to a new reality, incorporating the progress and innovation of the new millennium. While the courts scrambled to decide what came next, the cloud systems and remote work capability implemented at Sheard Law PC in the years leading up to the pandemic allowed uninterrupted continuity of workflow. This technological push in a conservative professional sector exposed the shortcomings of a more traditional model of work. As the courts shut down and work moved into the home, the cloud-based enterprise-level file management and storage system began to shine like never before.

In the early days of the pandemic, the abrupt revelation that "traditional" procedures could no longer continue injected a current of uncertainty. While the Sheard Law systems remained at the ready, the court issued notices cancelling all hearings, deferring them in ways previously unheard of. Clients called asking what would become of their cases. It remained difficult to predict how everything would unfold. The signal was clear: the systems were in place—it was now time to tweak the service delivery.

The law changes slowly, and so too can the institutions that dispense it: courts and lawyers. For many firms, the pandemic caused an existential crisis that required immediate action. If firms and institutions were to adapt, they needed to catch up to the rest of the business world, to move online, and to take advantage of technology as a core element of their being. No longer could the idea of online document submission be a quaint and experimental alternative to standing in long lines or paying professionals to physically attend court to hand documents over to counter staff.

As the weeks turned into months, the lawyers at Sheard Law PC gradually began to get a sense of how the justice system would adapt to the ongoing pandemic. Gradually, guidelines issued with respect to new ways to identify clients, to sign documents, and to interact with clients changed accordingly. Meetings moved to Zoom, which in turn began to change the nature of the meetings themselves. Rather than looking at each other face to face, the lawyer and client would now both be focused on a document through a shared screen, enabling more efficient revisions in real time.

These small tweaks allowed further efficiencies that would not have been possible without the new allowances for remote work. Sheard Law PC embraced these changes and enhanced its service delivery on the sound infrastructure platform implemented in the years before the pandemic.

With nobody in the office, new solutions became necessary throughout the legal profession. Soon, cords were cut, and faxes were redirected to an email address, bypassing the machine entirely. Their numbers dwindled as the government introduced rules to finally put email on the same footing as fax for legal service of documents. The government expanded its pilot project to allow lawyers and the public to file documents through an online portal. The courts began using email for document filing.

Little by little, the court system creaked back into action on computer screens across the province. The judge who previously loomed over the proceedings on a robust bench under a coat of arms was now one of perhaps many squares on a Zoom call. Long commutes disappeared and wait times with them. Matters seemed to proceed toward justice as they always had, albeit a bit faster and on an actual schedule.

At Sheard Law PC, client intake forms were further updated in accordance with new policies and guidelines. Welcome emails now came with instructions about how to work remotely with a lawyer from beginning to end. Armed with new permissions and licence to count on electronic signatures for documents, remote commissioning of affidavits, and the ability to email the final result to the opposing party, the solicitor-client interaction shifted more in three months than it had in three decades. Sheard Law PC was prepared for this new status quo based on innovations it had implemented long before the pandemic began.

Having the correct infrastructure, hardware, and technical expertise in place allowed adaptation to the challenges of the pandemic era with nimble confidence. The fact that these systems existed allowed largely uninterrupted service even as the pandemic evolved in new and previously unanticipated ways.

While traditional firms scrambled to adjust to the new work environment, Sheard Law PC continued in its service delivery with minimal disruption. The ability to do this came not from how it reacted to the crisis but rather from the flexibility early adoption of technology provided.

The common idea of a law firm may still involve opulent brown leather couches, shelves stacked with dusty old law reports, files about to spill over the edge of an antique desk, and storage rooms full of banker's boxes. The cloud offered Sheard Law PC the opportunity to move away from this model. Having done this before the pandemic struck gave Sheard Law PC a significant advantage when the same changes were forced upon other firms that had chosen not to adapt.

By the time the pandemic arrived, Sheard Law PC was already presenting clients with a clear, uncluttered workspace, enabling lawyers and staff to work from anywhere while still preserving the security of highly sensitive documents. The early adoption of technology generated efficiencies proactively. These only grew stronger as the pandemic revealed the need to evolve. This approach allowed a seamless transition when the time came to pivot into the new reality. Evolving in a way that embraces and implements innovations remains an ongoing process, and the new reality of business and work has only underscored its importance.

The firms able to adapt to the new reality of service delivery have discovered that pandemic-induced innovations have dramatically improved efficiency. Those who have not adapted so willingly are now perhaps reopened but are still waiting for the fax machine to ring ...

John Sheard
Partner, Sheard Law PC
www.sheardlaw.com

CHAPTER 3

Never Waste a Good Crisis

Never let a good crisis go to waste.—
Winston Churchill

THAT FAMOUS LINE WAS SPOKEN BY WINSTON CHURCHILL IN THE 1940s. There is some speculation that Churchill said it in his meeting with Stalin and Roosevelt that first brought up the formation of the United Nations, but there is no actual confirmation of that other than it sounds like something Churchill would say.

A similar quote was used by Rahm Emanuel, and the thought was also in Saul Alinsky's *Rules for Radicals*. When Rahm Emanuel used the quote, he took it one step further to explain what he meant: "Never let a serious crisis go to waste. And what I mean by that is that you have an opportunity to do things you think you could not do before."

I love Rahm's comment, as it makes absolute sense, especially during this crisis. The reality is that the comments from Winston Churchill and Rahm Emanuel both essentially mean that in a crisis, there is opportunity. It sounds so cliché, but many politicians, including Al Gore and John F. Kennedy, have alluded to this phrase in their campaign speeches: the Chinese word for crisis consists of two characters, one of which means *danger* and the other *opportunity*.

Although this pandemic hurt many people physically, mentally, and financially, if you're an optimist like me, you're trying to find a positive spin to it. For example, families are spending time together; there's less travel time to and from work; stimulus injections along with lowered consumer spending have boosted up North American savings rates; and industries such as health care, education, food, and technology have experienced advancements out of necessity.

From my personal experience and from data shared among many, citizens from around the world are accessing much-needed health care without ever stepping foot in a doctor's office. For instance, my father, who is diagnosed with Parkinson's disease and early stages of dementia, has been meeting with his doctor on a regular basis using online conferencing services. More and more countries are embracing the concept of telemedicine to access patients in a much more efficient way. Doctors have been collaborating remotely with specialists around the world to help diagnose complex cases.

About the education system, you can easily access courses and professors without ever leaving your home. The cost savings to students will allow them to graduate without massive financial burdens as they enter the workforce. This increases the opportunity for upward mobility in society. I believe so much in education— not necessarily the traditional forms of education, but education in general. I personally believe that education is the great equalizer and can pull people out of poverty. In my opinion, educating and learning from experience is all part of any meaningful pivot.

Technology and remote learning will allow this levelling of the playing field to potentially equal out or at least help tilt the socio-economic scales somewhat. This positive outcome doesn't necessarily come at the expense of schools. The lower cost for students allows increased admission rates, which ultimately increases profit for the universities. I am so intrigued by the changes in education that I spend all of Chapter 5 on the subject.

This is true even for more mature industries, such as the food and grocery industry. The rise in delivery services has allowed food to reach more and more people. People who were homebound prior to this pandemic now have access to fresh food. In addition, there has been a movement to support local businesses as a sense of community increases. Some farmers have even created delivery options to bypass the middleman by going straight from farm to table. Farmers now have opportunities to expand their customer base rather than relying solely on the traditional distribution channels of grocery stores.

Behind many of these positive outcomes are technology and the adoption (or forced adoption) of new ways of doing business. Again, if you can't adapt, you'll be left behind in this ever-changing environment. Technology and communication were already scaling at a rapid pace as countries like India focused on providing high-speed Internet, free banking, and streamlined identity tracking of citizens through a single Unique Identity Number called the Aadhar. (Imagine having your bank account, social security number, health care number, and driver's license all on one card). 5G towers continue to pop up in major cities where I live in Canada. The ability to download anything in seconds is amazing, as entertainment and the thirst for new social media content increases while people try their best not to go crazy staying at home.

The online gaming industry has exploded, and companies like EA Sports, Capcom, Take-Two Interactive, and pretty much any company able to provide online entertainment will benefit. I knew that there was this subculture of gamers growing, but I had no clue that eSports would be what it is today. My introverted gamer friends are like rock stars in this community!

It's not just the popularity but the amount of money gamers are making that blows me away. According to statista.com, N0tail (Johan Sundstein), JerAx (Jesse Vainikka), and ana (Anathan Pham) have made more than $6 million USD as of March 2021. You're talking professional-sports-type income without even have to do push-ups or 5 a.m. wind sprints in the gym. That is insane!

I can go on and on about how the crisis has opened up opportunities, but going back, the other word that makes up the definition of crisis is *danger*. We are experiencing dangerous times. While we are blessed here in North America, the US maintains a strong lead on the number of deaths and infections at over 25 per cent. Many young people have moved back in with their parents, as they don't have enough job seniority to survive job cuts. Stress levels of parents have increased, as they must wear multiple hats simultaneously as they work remotely, cook food for the family, babysit a crying newborn, and ensure that their kids are actually following their online classes.

What is also alarming is the change in behaviour pre- and post-pandemic. I had a conversation with a friend of mine about what beer we have been drinking during this pandemic. We listed off several interesting brands of beer and compared which craft brewery was the best. I paused for a second and said, "This is weird. I'm not much of a beer drinker, and here I am drinking at least a few bottles of beer while I binge-watch Netflix."

The shocking trend (this could be positive or negative depending on whether you are the seller or consumer) is that dangerous industries have profited from this pandemic as consumer behaviours have changed. Here are a few alarming statistics from CNN, CNBC, New York Times, and NPR comparing behaviours from April 2019 vs. April 2020:

- online alcohol sales—UP 250 per cent
- handgun sales—UP 50 per cent
- restaurant reservations—DOWN 60 per cent
- airline travel—DOWN 80 per cent

The fact that restaurants are either closed, limiting the number of patrons, or only catering to online orders, while gun sales and alcohol are spiking, is alarming. Unemployment has been rising (40 million jobs were destroyed in 10 weeks during the start of the pandemic in the US). Stress levels and mental illness are increasing due to the uncertainty. I have attended or hosted more mental-health events within my corporation than I have ever done in my life.

The stress and anxiety are real and need to be addressed. Cyberbullying is on the rise, as kids are online more hours of the day. With gyms closed and people on lockdown, obesity is increasing. Personally, it blows my mind that gyms are closed. To me, they are an essential service that provides more benefit than most people imagine. You will read a few stories of how the fitness industry has pivoted—in many cases, for the better.

In future chapters, I will discuss the topic of sales and how vital this skill is in order to pivot. Those who can master sales in this new digital, socially distanced world will really shine. Let me give you an example of a pivot that has occurred in my own business.

Typically, I am on the road meeting clients face to face. Whether it's breakfast, lunch, dinner, happy hour drinks, sporting events, or hosting a social event, my life is in front of people. Behind the scenes are my team members, Andrew Haukedal and Kit Lui. They help create proposals, support the client relationship, send marketing material, invite people to my events, send emails on my behalf, update my calendar, and really just keep me organized so my head doesn't explode. My role as the leader has historically been in the spotlight. I am the face of my business and have owned the client relationship.

However, this pandemic has allowed me to pivot and rethink that model. Rather than owning that relationship with the client, I've empowered my team more than I ever have in the 20 years I've been doing this.

Firstly, where my assistant would be more of a support and admin role, she now joins me on virtual social events and even comes out of her shell to say a few words. She is a lovely and sweet person who most of my clients would never have had the opportunity to meet. Clients get to know her and in fact ask about her periodically.

Secondly, my business partner Andrew would typically be on the phones answering calls, booking meetings, and doing analysis. Because all my meetings are done virtually, I can invite him to join me on joint Zoom calls. This would never have been possible if I was having a lunch meeting with a client. It would be so awkward to crack open my iPad and have him virtually join us while we munch on some fancy steak from Hy's! That's just cruel.

Now Andrew is fully engaged in the meeting and has an equal voice during each call. Where most people in my position would feel threatened by having another salesperson on the call, I am not. I love it. It allows me to mentor him as he gains real-life sales experience for the next chapter in his career.

You would think that the client experience has suffered as we are socially distanced. It has not. Clients truly get to see a team-based, high-service, client-centric model while building more of a personal relationship with every member of my team. If you ask several sales executives in my position, some will want to keep the spotlight. I disagree. The spotlight is meant to be shared, and it has proven how amazing all members of the team can be when given the chance to shine. As a result, 2020 was a record year, and 2021 is on pace to eclipse that.

There are countless stories of simple yet effective pivots, such as allowing your assistant to be more engaged in virtual meetings or embracing true collaboration and teamwork. It takes time to adjust and trust those around you when things seem so uncertain. At this juncture, it is difficult to say if the good outweighs the bad. However, it is fully in our control to ensure that this crisis does not go to waste. It is up to us to create a positive outcome in the future.

How I pivoted

Valen Vergara, CEO of Activation Energy

Pivoting all starts with the right psychology. That is why you must believe in pronoia in times like these. It is the opposite of paranoia.

Paranoia is the acceptance that the universe is working against you. *Pronoia* is the acknowledgement that the universe is working in your favour. Paranoia is thinking that everything is against you; pronoia is thinking that everything is *for* you. Without this paradigm shift, you will likely not stand a chance against *any* pandemic.

Personally speaking, I had no choice but to initiate this type of transcendent thinking. *Adapt or die*, as they say. Two of my major companies are event- and networking-based. If I did not pivot, I would have lost my footing and fell flat on my face. Like most businesspeople as of recently, I had to pivot into the online economy or be left behind.

I immediately sprung into action against a lot of resistance and pulled my offline events and attempts at navigating around restrictions and moved fully online, leveraging virtual conferencing, telephone meetings, and video-communication platforms. It was the right move, and things are better than ever. If I hadn't acted fast, I would have been left in the dust.

This is where *activation energy* comes in. When you have an idea, it takes about five seconds for your brain to come to a halt and start making excuses. Make excuses or create results in moments of conflict. The choice is in your hands.

When unprecedented turmoil happens, it causes a drastic cycle of change. Implementing changes during such periods can be daunting and make you feel insecure. This is the formula to respond swiftly and ensure you are making the right decision for your business and even your life:

1. **Start a campaign.** Create a profitable idea. Do market research. Make sure there is a high demand. Is there competition? Do a SWOT analysis (Strengths, Weaknesses, Opportunities, Threats). Will your offering be a one-time commission or recurring?
2. **Get traffic and attention.** Test your offering on a small scale for little to no money. Use free surveys to see if your deliverables are getting positive feedback. Make sure to capture your client leads. Always build a list and customer base whenever possible. And make use of CRM (customer relationship management) software.
3. **Track ROI (Return on Investment).** Always know your numbers. Traffic stats. Visitors. What is your cost per visitor? This should be tracked online and offline! Lead conversion percentage. Sales conversion percentage. Use tracking software and technology.
4. **Are you scalable?** Test-offer with multiple different sources. If it is profitable, do a rollout. If it is not, you must course-correct

and test other offers in different formats. Disqualify what is not working right away and quantify which ones are working. Go as large as you can as fast as you can with the offerings that are winners.

If you follow and move forward with the above, it is safe to say you are now ready to pivot in any environment.

Valen Vergara, CEO of Activation Energy
www.velenvergara.com

How I pivoted

Nathan Newman, CEO and founder, UNTITLED Champagne Lounge and The Derrick Gin Mill

My business at its core is hospitality excellence, with a compelling focus on meticulous customer service and exceeding patrons' expectations. This is executed through our modernist approach to an innovative and interactive cocktail and food experience. It is further inspired by an attributed comprehensive mood setting, which provides a desired environment for socializing.

When news of the pandemic first hit, truthfully, I was ignorant and foolishly believed that my business would not be affected. It was the weekend of March 13th when I realized I was wrong and we were in tremendous trouble. We had over 300 reservations that weekend; however, we were dismayed to have served only 100 guests once the weekend concluded. On Monday, March 16, after pacing around my condo for hours, I made the unthinkable announcement: *temporary closure*. At that time, I sincerely did not know if *temporary* would turn into *permanent*.

The day after I made the announcement, the government mandated that all businesses close and invoked a state of emergency. This inexplicably gave me a sense of relief and, in a strange way, assured me I had made the right decision. I knew the next steps for me would be a series of uncomfortable conversations, beginning with my landlord. I was remarkably fortunate to have an understanding and compassionate landlord. After our meeting, I felt bullish about re-opening. In fact, I felt so bold that I believed there could be further potential to notably benefit from this situation. Recognizing our landlord's current position of weakness and uncertainty, I started to put together a modest proposal to purchase the property. After some dialogue and careful consideration, we made a deal that concluded with us being our own landlord.

Two months passed before the government flirted with the idea of re-opening, and nearly three months before we got the official OK to safely open our doors. After meeting with my management team followed by my staff, I was elated and excited that my team felt safe enough to open up and invite guests into our elaborate spirit and food oasis. With the uncertainty of guest traffic, we adopted a focused mentality on being productive, not busy. We successfully made the venue safe, and when we opened our doors, we *were* busy—as busy as we could be considering all of the imposed restrictions.

Lockdown #2, next chapter: This lockdown was less exasperating. We knew what to expect, and we knew we were secure with our lack of landlord and our market share of regular customers. This is when I made the personal time to establish a plan to construct complementary businesses within our new building.

What lessons were learned? Always focus on the solution and avoid being consumed by undesirable circumstances.

Nathan Newman, CEO and Founder
UNTITLED Champagne Lounge and
The Derrick Gin Mill
www.untitledyyc.com www.thederrickyyc.com

CHAPTER 4

The Future Is Here …
Time to Adapt

The best way to predict the future is to
create it.—Abraham Lincoln

THE FUTURE IS AN INTERESTING CONCEPT. IT IS THE TIME AND space that is yet to happen and will happen immediately after the thing that just happened. With that concept in mind, it can almost feel as if we are trying to catch up and chase down the future. If we believe in the wise words of Abraham Lincoln, then there is no greater time in history to do it than now.

The future is not something we *enter*; it is something we *create*. The amazing thing is that the pandemic puts a microscope on our actions, as we are more conscious than ever about how it will impact the future. What we post, what we say, what we buy, where we go, and who we associate with all play a role in shaping it. Now more than ever, data on our preferences, tastes, and biases are recorded digitally to shape a more catered approach to us.

As humans, any crisis tends to be a wake-up call to a certain extent. This wake-up call, however, impacts the way we see technology, health care, government, and each other. It is all intertwined, as the world is more interconnected than ever before. It is important to understand how these services are created and what mediums are at our disposal.

Gary Vaynerchuk, who is one of the greatest social media experts of all time, predicted the importance of Facebook, Twitter, Instagram, Snapchat, LinkedIn, and TikTok. He was way ahead of the curve before social media became the influential movement we see today. After graduating from college in 1998, Gary took charge of his father's liquor store, Shoppers Discount Liquors, and launched online sales through YouTube. His story is well documented all over the Internet, as he grinded for years pumping out video after video without any viewers. What started out as Wine Library TV has exploded into multiple business ventures, such as the media giant VaynerMedia. He is worth over $200 million as of 2020 and has predicted that he will buy the New York Jets within his lifetime.

Gary is an example of a man who has courage, belief, and the insight to be forward-thinking. If you've ever heard him speak, he constantly champions entrepreneurship for the simple reason that now is the best time to start a business. This thing called the Internet has changed the way consumers think and behave. Conversely, it gives forward-thinking businesses and entrepreneurs access to broader markets than ever before, with intel on how and what they will buy. By getting ahead of the curve, not only can you benefit from trends, but you can form the trends to come. Rather than being reactive to the current environment (such as a pandemic), you can become a game-changer.

What you pump out on social media or anywhere on the Internet forms preferences, tastes, and ideas that can impact your future revenue. The great thing is that there is no shortage of people who can consume your content. The Internet has opened up so many opportunities, from homemakers creating YouTube channels about homeschooling to seven-figure coaches selling their training to people on the other side of the world. The opportunities are endless. This pandemic has accelerated the entrepreneurial movement and has forced fence-sitters to get off the fence and take the entrepreneurial plunge. Gary was correct then, and he's correct now. The future is created by the actions (or pivots) you take today.

> *There has never been a better time in the*
> *history of time, than right now to start*
> *a business.—Gary Vaynerchuk*

Consider this: Last October 2020, there were almost 4.66 billion people who were active Internet users. This encompasses more than 59 per cent of the total global population. With the vast majority of people in developed countries and many developing countries having a supercomputer in the palm of their hands, mobile computing will be even more impactful. Mobile Internet users account for 91 per cent of total Internet users as of the beginning of 2021.

Michio Kaku, the physicist and popular author, put it like this: "Today, your cell phone has more computer power than all of NASA back in 1969, when it placed two astronauts on the moon." It is mind-blowing to think we have that much computing power in the palm of our hand. If you watch Joe Rogan's 2018 interview with Elon Musk (I love that interview, by the way), Elon straight-up says that the cell phone is an extension of ourselves. We are cyborgs, and we don't even know it. The opportunities are endless, as you can pivot into whatever trending sector can make you a quick buck without much risk or investment.

Now, I don't know if Gary Vaynerchuk predicted that the Internet would be this big, but he didn't waste time riding the wave when it came. Just like a surfer who is sitting after missing a huge wave, he knows that there will always be another one. Thankfully, the Internet ocean has been generating more and more waves for entrepreneurs to ride. These are not just baby waves, but massive waves created by business and consumers. It's like the Internet is one of those man-made wave pools, and the supervisors are cranking up the fun.

Many would enjoy watching poolside as the fun factor is cranked up. There's no problem enjoying being on the sidelines. However, if you are a business owner, you can't afford to be sitting poolside while the family shares stories about how much fun was had in the pool. Entrepreneurship is not a spectator sport, and if you plan on pivoting in any crisis or pandemic, you need to know what the heck is going on first-hand and what trend will impact your business.

What I'm trying to say is that if you are a business owner and have yet to embrace the digital economy, you might as well lower your expectations of any meaningful success. Unless civilization turns into a dystopian world like *Mad Max: Beyond Thunderdome*, digital is the place to be.

I mentioned in the introduction that this pandemic was a Great Accelerator. What this pandemic has done is accelerated what was already going to happen by three to five years. Senior citizens who would never have imagined ordering their Earl Grey breakfast tea from Amazon are checking to see if their Prime memberships allow them to receive their goodies on the same day. Personal trainers who are stuck doing face-to-face training sessions or have zero digital presence will lose out to the many personal trainers doing face-to-face sessions via Zoom. And even that space is not disruption-proof. Peloton is taking off, and it's no longer just a company with an expensive exercise bike. It's a whole new hip community of sweaty go-getters motivating each other on new interactive machines. Connections are being made despite being locked in our homes.

The digital world is here. It has always been here, but it is now staring right in our face like a meteor about to hit the earth and wipe out those poor short-armed *T Rexes*.

As I mentioned in my example with my own team, many large companies have decided to create virtual working environments. Not only is it efficient and at a low cost for companies, but overall happiness has increased in many professions. The time and cost of travel from the suburbs into a downtown office is gone. Companies have realized that working remotely is a successful business model.

> *If you want to be more productive, you need to*
> *become a master of your minutes.—Crystal Paine*

Thanks to the pandemic, many of you just got some extra minutes added to your day. Time to find ways to master that. Here's a simple life tip: if you don't have a LinkedIn profile, get one. It's crucial if you want to network with other businesspeople. If you like social media, then cut out some of your screen time looking at cat videos and beef up your LinkedIn profile. It's not only the connections that you can spend your time on, but it's doing yourself a favour and paying for the upgraded account.

Want to master your time? LinkedIn has thousands of amazing online courses that take anywhere from 20 minutes to a few hours. Believe me, this is time well spent. I mentioned how much I believe in education. Well, in the next chapter, we'll discuss how online learning is time worth spending in front of your screen. LinkedIn has certified courses just Lynda.com or Edx.com. Heck, spend some time on YouTube, and you'll see what the future holds.

To pivot or not to pivot?

Throughout this book, we focus not on the causes of the pivot (everyone knows we have gone through a global pandemic and will likely go through other catastrophes in life) but on the ways to pivot. However, you may feel that pivoting is such a big decision that you would rather ignore the noise and friend away. In most cases, I would agree and say yes. Focus on the things that you can control and ignore the news, social media, and other noise that distracts you from your goals.

I remember talking to this entrepreneur who designed a cooling vest for hikers. As global warming continues to increase the temperature, a cooling vest makes sense. He started off with ice packs that you insert. Then he found a way to add a small air-conditioning unit to keep the coolness consistent. Then he added outlets to plug in your smartphone. He has been tweaking this product for five years and has been funding it on his own. He has never made a single sale, nor has he inspired an investor to fund him.

I am always supportive of people who are chasing their dreams, but you haven't made money in five years, it's time to stop grinding and pivot. This entrepreneur has essentially allowed competition to flood his market before he even had a chance to defend it.

After speaking to this entrepreneur, I reminded him of the obvious: his time, effort, and capital are crucial assets that he's wasting away. Sometimes progress is better than perfection. Can you guys relate? I didn't want to discourage him, but I gave him some honest realities to ponder before he decides his next move.

You will never get the time back that you have already invested. Is it worth wasting more time? Your resources are depleted. Will this product recuperate all the money and resources invested? Think about the time value of money and whether the product is capable of generating a return on investment enough to become profitable. Lastly, are your supporters still on board? Loved ones and family members can easily be dragged into an entrepreneur's vision. Many are excited initially about the prospect of creating the next iPhone or great invention. However, over time, this energy can fade. Are your supporters still excited?

Given these harsh realities, you are faced with three questions to answer. How you decide will determine your future.

Should I put my head down and keep grinding away?

This is such a difficult one. While everyone around you may be losing hope, you must see a clear vision that it can work. When Elon Musk had numerous failures and was on the verge of bankruptcy, he put his head down and continued to push forward without being deterred. All entrepreneurs will get knocked down. That's the name of the game. However, many survive simply because they never gave up. Marc Benioff evolved Salesforce.com by introducing other consumer trends to the platform but never shifted away from making software accessible, simple to use, and ideal for businesses.

Before doing a major course correction, consider small correctional changes, such as tweaking a product, changing a marketing strategy, or increasing sales capacity. The first recommendation is to focus and stay the course.

Should I shift direction and pivot?

Although this is the premise of the book, that doesn't mean it is always the best idea. I believe that a major pivot must only be considered when you have exhausted all other options. A pivot can be expensive, lengthy, and emotionally draining, so consider whether any of the following are true when deciding that now is the time to pivot:

- Your company is trying its best but consistently losing market share to the competition.
- You have too much concentration risk on one product or service. Losing this one product would wipe out the majority of your revenue.
- Your product is not resonating with the market, or there is not a market for your product at all.
- Your business model and company philosophies have changed
- Your company is not progressing and has hit a plateau.

If these describe you, then it's time to pivot. Keep in mind that this can be done in multiple ways, so don't throw out all your marketing material and pitch decks just yet. We'll go deeper into several real-life examples and case studies of how businesses have pivoted throughout this book. We often feel that a pivot is a monumental shift; however, just as in boxing, it could be a subtle adjustment in footwork that gives a puncher a chance of winning.

Here are some examples of smaller pivots that might not seem minimal yet can make a major impact:

- **Focus on a different customer set.** No one set out to invent sticky notes. Dr. Spencer Silver, a chemist at 3M Company, was trying to invent a super-strong adhesive. Instead, he invented a super-weak one that left no glue residue behind. That accidental invention shifted the company's focus from customers looking for strong adhesive to temporary notepads.

- **Turn one feature of a product or process into a product on its own**. The company Tiny Speck created a game called Glitch. After launching this game, they found that the concept wasn't viable, and it became a flop. However, the internal communication tool that was used to communicate between the Canada and US offices turned out to be a viable venture on its own. In 2014, this messaging platform was successfully launched as its own product. You may have used it to communicate with your teams before. It's called Slack!

Should I cut my losses and shut it down?

This is a tough one. The last thing an entrepreneur wants to do is call it quits. As an entrepreneur, you have big dreams and goals. You have gone the other way from conventional wisdom and ventured away from the Man. Calling it quits is like admitting failure. Or worse, proving to your doubters that they were right.

The reality is that now is not the time for a pity party. Your ego will get you in more trouble than you already are. Sometimes, there are no more steps you can take, and the responsible thing is to cut your losses. Burning through your savings as time ticks away is financially, intellectually, and emotionally irresponsible. Before giving up too soon, though, you must ask yourself the following questions:

- What's my time horizon? How much time do I have left to live?
- How much capital do I have left to keep this going?
- Can I raise more capital to fulfill a need that resonates with customers?
- Is there a need at all, or has that window passed?
- Am I too early? Late? Or is my timing off?
- How confident am I that my product or service will be a winnable market?

- What is my opportunity cost? What am I giving up chasing this dream? Is it worth it?
- Am I able to provide a reasonable rate of return for my investors, or is this simply an ego-driven passion project?

These are exceedingly difficult decisions to make during a crisis, and each must be made without decision-remorse. When you are at this fork in the road and your business, livelihood, health, and family are teetering on implosion, it's time to dig deep and decide whether you need to make some changes and push forward, execute a well-thought-out pivot, or cut your losses and shut it down. As I mentioned before, you do not want to have decision-remorse. Amazon founder Jeff Bezos calls this "investigate everything" process the "regret-minimization framework."

Explore all options, plausible solutions, and outcomes so that you know that you are confident that the direction you are going is the right one, not the one that everything thinks you should go in. As my father would always tell me, measure three times and cut once. Once you decide, go forward with full effort.

Deciding whether to pivot permanently

Suppose that after weighing the three options mentioned above, you decide to pivot. During times of crisis, when a pivot is necessary for survival, speed is of the essence. You must avoid wasting time, energy, resources, skills, connections, and capital. You must determine if the pivot is aligned with the vision and mission of your business. It can be a scary thought that change is about to happen.

I've been wearing the same raggedy track pants and sweatshirt because it feels comfortable. They have holes in them, but I still wear them. If you're like most people, change can be unsettling, especially if it is permanent. The idea of permanently throwing away my high school sweatshirt saddens me, but I know at some point in time, it will disintegrate after one spin cycle in the wash.

How do you decide whether your pivot will be a permanent change or something temporary? During a crisis, ask yourself if any of the pivotal changes made during this crisis

- identify weaknesses to help you become more effective
- save you capital and resources
- create efficiencies
- improve your client experience and add value to the relationship
- create competitive advantages
- enhance and boost productivity
- create new opportunities that can be monetized
- improve the culture, morale, and long-term vision of the company

If you said yes to most of these points above, then it's time to throw out the metaphoric highschool sweatshirt and pivot. Go and buy a stretchy high-quality zip up Lululemon top or whatever brand suits your need. Whatever the decision may be, change will impact your business at some point in the future whether you like it or not. Having these basic questions and ideas to guide your thought process well in advance can save you time, stress and give you a sense of control.

Change is inevitable. Even models that have stood the test of time are now accepting their fate and either pivoting into this new world or closing up shop. For example, a business model as old as the education system has been forced to adapt. The transition has not been without hiccups, but even old dogs need to learn new tricks. We'll discuss this in the next few chapters.

How I pivoted

Brian Morales, Business Development Executive at Nimbly Market

As the world descended into COVID chaos, my business did too. My part-time job in the travel industry and my separate travel company closed their doors as promptly as the international borders. With all the forward momentum coming to a crashing halt, it would have been easy to default into survival mode. But armed with Ricco and Ailene's experience, distilled to nothing but essential values, we carefully imagined our grandest mission—a company that propped up small businesses.

I met Ricco and Ailene Dela Torre—who equally met a drastic drop in their former network marketing company revenues—to develop a new company that can impact the business community in a big way. That's how Nimbly Market was born: an online marketplace to shop inside your community. For consumers, it's an ultra-accessible neighbourhood shopping platform. For small-business shops, it creates an instant online presence with e-commerce and local delivery. It's all-new territory for us: new skill sets, new demographics, new technology. But the most challenging barrier was me.

A decade working at the same company had grooved a routine that was tough to undo. Job security and corporate benefits kept me safely inside a nine-to-five habit. An attachment to the title of "founder and director" of a travel company kept my ego (falsely) inflated. It was a black hole of comfort, the gravity of which was difficult to overcome. Luckily, the pull of a black hole *can* be overcome with the proper escape velocity and a new source of gravity—or, in this case, a world-changing global pandemic and a new worthy mission to gravitate toward.

Gone was the notion of a title. Nimbly Market didn't have that luxury. Ricco, Ailene, and I wrote fancy titles on our business cards to get us through the door, but the reality was we did everything: sales, marketing, copywriting, graphic design, videography, supplier relationships, hard labour, delivery, and food preparation, among other things. That's the magic of having unlimited time but a limited budget. We got creative. We're not boxed into job descriptions.

We kept opening doors to creative opportunities with near-reckless abandon, ignoring the legacy of "stay in your lane" attitudes. We had to. We're developing a start-up company with a business clientele slow to adapt to new technology. We met new partners, explored new industries, made new connections, and expanded our ideas. It served us well!

One conversation with our online jeweller about creating our company got us on CBC News and a shoutout from Alberta's premier on Twitter. Another discussion with our grocers and suppliers pushed us to develop our in-house brand of D.I.Y. Meal Kits that now sit proudly on the shelves of Asian specialty stores in Calgary after less than two months. As I write this, we're working with a former news writer on a breakout show for our marketing department!

I can remember clear as day that three months after our soft launch of Nimbly Market, after a couple of weeks of selling and now pivoting into the marketing side of our company, Ricco said, "We can adapt our plan, but we won't adapt our mission." That carries so much heavy gravity.

**Brian Morales, Business Development
Executive
Nimbly Market
www.nimblymarket.com**

How I pivoted

Daria Venkova, CEO and Head Business Consultant at Purley A&D Consulting

Give Yourself Permission to Pivot

While working on my undergraduate degree, I had convinced myself that the only thing that would bring me happiness was getting into medical school to become a plastic surgeon. I would not consider any other career path, and my happiness ultimately became dependent on this future achievement. It was a shared sentiment that occupied the minds of many of my fellow students in my bioscience faculty, making it more difficult to recognize how flawed this thinking was.

Following my undergrad degree, I decided to pursue a one-year master's in biomedical technologies. The way I saw it, it would give me a leg up during my medical school applications. The program combined fundamentals of business development in the context of scientific innovation and its commercialization process, and insight into the prospects of the newest technologies in health care. This is where my beliefs about my career first got challenged, eventually leading me to a turning point.

About halfway through my master's, I got an opportunity to begin volunteering my time at a point-of-care diagnostic start-up, Creative Protein Solutions (CPS), where I was able to apply the newly obtained business acumen from my master's to develop an operational plan and begin pitching the company at various start-up events. After completing my master's, I became the company's CEO, overcoming several major obstacles in the company.

From the opportunity to communicate with investors and potential partners and customers to continuously identifying forthcoming obstacles and coming up with solutions to solve them, seeing milestones being reached because of my work has made me feel in my element in a way I have never felt in my life before. I took this opportunity as a stepping stone, but by matters of fate, it turned into my primary career path of becoming a businessperson in biotech.

Over the next two years of working in that start-up, I decided that entrepreneurship was my true calling, and I could see myself doing this for the rest of my life. Initially, thoughts of second-guessing remained. Did I fail myself? Did I get off track and give up the ultimate dream? For a period of time, I would ruminate on these thoughts— things had shifted so fast that it was difficult to apply sheer logic when deciding how I felt about this change. One thing that was certain was that I was applying myself by doing what I enjoyed every day, and the outcome of my work could help thousands of farmers and animal owners around the world provide better care to their animals. The feeling of reaching milestones provided a sense of accomplishment, purpose, and ultimately happiness. Life was happening in real time, and I no longer felt that I was putting it on hold for what could have been another six to eight years.

I left my job at CPS just before the end of 2020 to start my own consulting company, Purley A&D Consulting, with a focus on the biotechnology, health care, and agriculture sectors. During my master's, and in the two years spent working in a start-up, I have come across a myriad of early-stage companies stemming from an academic background with potentially life-changing innovations, but not necessarily the perspective or the right human resources to bring their innovation to market.

It's a well-known statistic that about nine out of ten start-ups don't make it. In the context of health care, every failed start-up means that thousands of people are denied a solution that would have improved their quality of life or longevity. Comparably, ensuring success of even a single start-up will make an impact on an otherwise disadvantaged population for many years to come, and every successful project by our team at Purley A&D Consulting does exactly that.

Keeping this in mind is what gives me the drive to excel at my work today as the CEO and head business consultant of the company. I may not ever be a doctor or a surgeon, but my career still revolves around helping thousands of people benefit from modern medicine and technology, and that is the sort of impact I am proud and eager to contribute to the world.

As part of a pitch competition prize during my CPS days, I got an opportunity to attend Tim Draper's five-week entrepreneurship program in Silicon Valley. One of many hands-on exercises we did there was relying on communication from our teammates to race through a busy street while completely blindfolded. Tim told us afterwards that being an entrepreneur and starting your own company often feels like being blindfolded, and the feeling of being in the dark figuratively was quite accurately evoked through its physical enactment. One must overcome the feelings of doubt and fear and trust one's team to be able to move forward. This particular experience stuck with me and has resonated with me in the past couple of years more than ever, especially in the unpredictable environment in the context of the COVID-19 pandemic.

At CPS, we had to deal with several COVID-19 related changes. Investors became more cautious with their funding, university labs shut down for indefinite periods of times, and farmers were cautious about inviting people for animal testing. We had to become creative and make unconventional decisions—one of which included me delaying my salary for five months. Despite experiencing these hardships, moving forward with Purley A&D Consulting, my co-founder and I ultimately saw it as an opportunity. With most if not all aspects of business being run virtually, there is no longer a reason to limit the business to a local region—biotech innovation is happening globally, and that means we can help solve problems for start-ups all around the world.

Only one third of the companies we're working with now are in Calgary, where I reside, with the rest spread across other parts of Canada, the USA, and Europe. For companies like ours that provide strategic support that can be implemented from anywhere in the world, the pandemic has accelerated acceptance of the notion that collaboration can happen cross-border, which opens the doors to many more opportunities.

It can be difficult to pivot or accept change when there's weight tied to the initial plan and all the work and sentiment that has gone into getting there in the first place. In my master's program, we were taught that knowing how to "fail fast" is an essential part of creating a successful start-up. Multiple business books speak of the concept of testing various models before committing to a single one and being ready to pivot as a way to maintain flexibility and adapt to change.

Pivoting is a recurring and a natural part of any business, but when you are pivoting your entire career or when you're a solopreneur or stand in an executive position, pivoting becomes a more personal process. The reality, however, is that just like in our businesses, we need to give ourselves permission to change as people in accordance with our environment and new knowledge in order to thrive. It took an opportunity spontaneously presenting itself for me to realize that I have skills as an entrepreneur and a passion for entrepreneurship, and I am grateful for the ways in which this allowed me to change and grow into a new person. Change on a business level first happens on an individual level of the people who make the calls and being able to recognize change as part of personal growth in today's rapidly changing and unpredictable environment is part of being a successful entrepreneur.

Daria Venkova
CEO and head business consultant at Purley A&D Consulting
www.purley-consulting.com

CHAPTER 5
Teaching Old Dogs New Tricks

*Learning is not the product of teaching. Learning is
the product of the activity of learners.*—John Holt

DURING THE PANDEMIC I HAD AN OPPORTUNITY TO SPEND TIME
with my nephews. I felt that as we hunkered down together, I would have
a chance to spend uninterrupted time with them. I flew to Toronto to
spend 2 months working remotely. It was perfect. I would work hard and
spend some much-needed quality time during my break. Interestingly
enough, that wasn't the case. Expecting the kids to be running around, I
was instead met with a surprising silence. As I looked around the house, I
realized that like me the kids were focused on working remotely. Remote
education was definitely something that wasn't around when I was a kid.
For decades, the concept of kids sitting attentively in class while learning
their ABC's was how we learned. Although home schooling has been
around for some time, the pandemic took it to new level. In this chapter
I will go through some interesting trends in the way education is being
taught. Not only does this chapter shed some light on an antiquated
system that is going through flux but as potential pivoters, I hope it helps
you be cognizant as to how you can absorb and learn new skills to help
you make educated decisions as you pivot.

Changes in the Education System: Going Online

As mentioned in previous chapters, I want to highlight education
as an example that even time-tested institutions must evolve and adapt

in order to address the changing needs of the world. Even an old dog can learn new tricks—meaning you are never too old to change. This pandemic has turned regular citizens into entrepreneurs even after the age of 40, 50, 60, and sometimes 70. I have met countless seniors who took online courses and upgraded their technological skillset to navigate this new world. Age is but a number, and this pandemic has shown that it's about mindset and the willingness to change out of necessity, survival and curiosity.

Don't believe me? According to "Status of senior entrepreneurship in Canada" from the Economic Development Office of Mississauga (2018), 30 per cent of the total number of start-ups were founded by people aged 50 and above. This could be due to the fact that they got let go during an economic crisis and pivoted into business for themselves, or perhaps they were bored in retirement. In any case, you are never too old to learn new things and pivot.

Another positive that has come out of this pandemic is that more and more people are seeking education. They are using this time to strengthen their skill sets, add new ones, and train themselves to think outside of their comfort zone. How people are willing or forced to learn is something worth looking into.

Knowledge is a huge industry. Everyone has something to say and wisdom to bestow. The field of education has opened opportunities not only in the traditional form of education (such as schools) but also in learning that can be shared throughout the entire world. I have always said that education is the great equalizer. There is a desire for people to grow outside of their current situation and, for many, lift themselves out of their current economic situation. Education is key, and the pivots involved in this area alone are worth mentioning.

> *You can't teach people everything they need to*
> *know. The best you can do is to position them*
> *where they can find what they need to know*
> *when they need to know it.—Seymour Papert*

Since this chapter is about education, expect to see more statistics than in previous chapters. Consider the following:

- Among nearly 3,000 colleges in the United States, only 10 per cent had plans to offer their instruction completely online for Fall 2020, with the remaining 34 per cent of institutions intending to run classes primarily online, 21 per cent in hybrid format, 23 per cent primarily in person, and 4 per cent fully in-person.
- The online learning industry is projected to pass $370 billion by 2026. Think about alternative platforms such as Masterclass or MindValley that provide non-traditional ways to learn relevant and timely curriculum.
- 20 per cent of college students whose classes were moved online during the pandemic indicated it was a major challenge to find a quiet place for online instruction. Imagine living in a house where the college student struggles to concentrate while they hear their kid brother screaming in the room next door. Coffee shops are packed when businesses are allowed to be at full capacity and the quite tree in the park doesn't have an outlet to charge your laptop.
- 33 per cent of post-secondary-school administrators indicate they will continue to offer both remote and online course options even after their campuses have reopened and normal operations resume.

COVID-19 further exposed what most parents of students already know: how the education system in the US fails to adequately serve students. Elon Musk has even been quoted as saying "Colleges are basically for fun and to prove you can do your chores. But they are not for learning." I may not entirely agree with Elon as his argument is limited to rich countries with abundant alternatives to a university degree. Some skill such as nuclear physics, medicine, and neuroscience, can only be learned through a standard college education. I do give him credit as he challenged the traditional school system by creating his own school Ad Astra, which in Latin means "to the stars". Regardless, I get his point that the merits and weight that the formal education system had on determining success isn't what it once was. Unsurprisingly, in 2019, the education industry indicated the *lowest* adoption rate (17 per cent) of data analysis and data-driven features in designing instruction and optimizing learning outcomes. With the sudden and extensive shift to online learning, universities and colleges are looking to technology to streamline operations and boost flagging enrollment numbers.

During the pandemic, 42 per cent of students indicated that staying motivated was a major problem for them in completing coursework online. As convenient as it is for some students, the temptation to jump on social media, play an online game, or do something aside from listening to the professor is much higher in this environment.

Online learning can be a lifeline to those who have obstacles, such as geographical distances or physical disabilities.—Paul Levinson

COVID-19 and the New World of Distance Learning

It is estimated that the COVID-19 pandemic has disrupted more students and schools than any other event in history, with nearly 1.6 billion students affected worldwide. As much as I have and will champion online learning, there are some serious issues and drawbacks that need to be addressed. The socio-economic skills gap could potentially increase by more than 30 per cent due to COVID-19, as technology isn't as equally distributed globally. Think about the rural areas in remote places in the world that do not have stable internet access, power or access to computers. This is slowly changing, as the pandemic has accelerated the need to adapt faster.

Globally, actions taken to improve connectivity and facilitate distance learning have included the following:

- subsidized or free Internet access (60 per cent)
- subsidized or free devices (42 per cent)
- access available through mobile phones (63 per cent)
- access available through landline (28 per cent)
- no action taken (11 per cent)
- hiring additional teachers to support remote learning (33 per cent among mainly upper-middle and high-income nations)
- additional training and instruction for teachers regarding remote learning (66 per cent)

In education, technology can be a life-changer, a game changer, for kids who are both in school and out of school.—Queen Rani of Jordan

Among the poorest countries, 40 per cent did not support at-risk students, including children with disabilities, refugee and displaced children, and female students, who are often expected to shoulder domestic chores. In addition to traditional computer-based online learning, many countries utilized delivery methods such as TV and radio broadcasts for students. Remote learning modalities among nations varied:

- Lower-income nations utilized online platforms and take-home materials the least (64 per cent) and instead relied on television (92 per cent) and radio (93 per cent) broadcasts.
- Higher-income nations utilized online platforms the most (95 per cent), using television (63 per cent) and radio (22 per cent) the least.
- Only 27 per cent of low-income countries reported television instruction as having been effective.

The loss of learning could result in a reduction in average learning levels for all students worldwide and an increase of students with low levels of achievement due to dropping out of school, with a 25 per cent increase in students falling below the baseline level of proficiency needed to participate in future learning or to function in society. Approximately 15 per cent of students in Western Europe and North America are without Internet, compared to nearly 80 per cent in sub-Saharan Africa. Shameless plug coming - This is why during the pandemic I created The Kind Project which focuses on raising money to build libraries and computer labs in less technologically advanced areas in the world. Check out my website michaelsiervo.com for more details.

Everyone Learns Differently: Style and Formats

Distance education can take many forms. The most common are:

- *Fully online*—Active instruction, testing, assignments, and discussion takes place online. I must admit that this took me some time to get used to but the quality of the courses and the support from the student community is surprisingly helpful
- *Simultaneous teaching*—Faculty teach online and in person at the same time; for example, a livestream of a lecture that students can attend in person or virtually. This format helps as the live lectures and conversations that come about during class can often lead to more meaningful dialogue. This in turn improves learning.
- *Blended or hybrid*—Between 25 and 50 per cent of instructions, assignments, and discussion takes place online. Students study course material outside of class and use classroom time to reinforce learning, ask questions, and interact with their instructor.

- **Face-to-face Web enabled**—Students "meet" virtually with their instructors (and other class members) via video chat or teleconferencing.
- **Emergency remote teaching:** Shifting of face-to-face, blended, or other courses to a fully online format in the event students or faculty are unable to come to campus.
- **MOOC (massive open online courses)**—Pre-recorded content/lectures available 24/7 with open-ended, self-paced learning. For me, this is becoming more and more popular as many students are more concerned with gaining knowledge rather than certificates. I personally complete courses as much as I can as the self-pace style is less stressful. Meaning I can learn without any added pressure.

Since COVID-19, many schools have started offering primarily online with delayed in-person start formats, where coursework will eventually be offered in person but has been delayed, and classes will be taken online until in-person instruction resumes. This may be different in different countries. In Canada, at the time of this writing some schools are not fully opened while in other areas of the world where vaccination is limited, schools have been shut down for months.

For years, people would mock someone who did an online MBA from the University of Phoenix. Now you can get a Harvard degree or take courses from Edx online and receive the same quality education from a beach in Palawan, Philippines. Education is out there however the same age-old issue still applies. Access to the education is dependant on the students ability to access the internet. You can get an online MBA but you need to be able to go online first.

One interesting statistic is that in 2020, 41 per cent of students indicated the quality of their online college-level learning experience was better than college-level classroom instruction, compared to 15 per cent who felt it was not as good. Overall, the disruptive nature of COVID-19 on an education system that hasn't changed much in decades has been more of a positive experience for the majority of students.

*Education is the great equalizer. It can pull people
out of poverty and change not only their world but
the world of those around them.—Michael Siervo*

I know I've spent a fair amount of time discussing education. It's something that is hugely important to me because I have seen how it can change lives. A pivot is all about making educated decisions on what is the best thing to do to move you in the right direction. It's really one of the industries that jumped out at me when thinking about those that have *had* to pivot. Knowledge and the transfer of knowledge can and will change the world.

Initially, the thought was that the education system would get crushed. However, statistics have shown that the pandemic has opened up opportunities to educate more people in a more efficient manner. Teachers are everywhere. Homemakers are sharing how to sew masks on YouTube. Tutors looking for side money are teaching Japanese students halfway around the world how to speak conversational English. Whether you are a student or a teacher, everyone can get in on this trend, no matter what your educational background

*The goal of education is the advancement
of knowledge and the dissemination of
truth.—John Fitzgerald Kennedy*

So whether it's the education system, grocery delivery, health care, and so on, the truth is that no industry is safe, as change is inevitable. It's simply a matter of how your business or organization will be impacted and to what degree. My guess is that you would rather be proactive than reactive.

Of course, not everyone is a business owner, but I would argue that many people would love to have the income that a successful business owner has. It can be done without having to leave your full time job. The concept of supplementary income is a topic that continues to come up as people look to survive post pandemic. This has caused another change in the economy, one that validates Gary Vaynerchuk's prediction about business in the modern era. One that has been popularized by efficiency master Tim Ferris. It's called the gig economy. With more people understanding the power of information and how one can access education at the click of a few buttons, the world all of a sudden opens up as we step into the gig economy.

How I pivoted

Alicia Siervo, President of Seniors in Action, a non-profit organization

There is one choice that significantly changed the direction of my life.

I have spent most of my adult life working in the Ontario Public Service (OPS) with passion and integrity while balancing work and family life. As a woman and a minority, nothing stopped me from having a successful career as a public servant in spite of the discrimination, politics, and many challenges in the face of diversity. I am so proud of my accomplishments and achievements as an individual, manager, and leader in a very complex, stressful, competitive, and fast-paced environment.

I had a very respected and responsible position as a payroll and benefits manager, with a good salary and benefits attached to it. It became my life and my obsession. I knew there was still room for advancement at the peak of my career, but I needed a change. Something was missing in my life.

I volunteered and was seconded to United Way, a non-profit charitable organization, for several months and loved it very much. It was an eye-opener. I immersed myself deeply in charity and volunteer work. It was an *aha* moment for me. This is what I wanted to do when I retired—be of service to others who are less fortunate and more vulnerable.

I took early retirement after 36 years of dedicated service to OPS and chose to make a difference. It was the single choice that not only changed the direction of my life but that of many others.

Retirement is great, but then I realized that as we age, it is easy to fall into routines that often lead us to brain-numbing activities. I retired from my career, but I did not retire from life. I found my way to volunteerism. It was my way to expand an overall healthy lifestyle. It allowed me to give back to the community and get involved in a good cause that adds meaning and a sense of purpose—all good things for my mental and physical well-being. With a vision of enriching the lives of our seniors, Seniors in Action (SIA) was born!

SIA is a non-profit organization established to answer the need in our community for a more diverse and inclusive seniors group, including those in social and geographic isolation. It is inspired and led by a group of seniors from all walks of life sharing the ideals of healthy living and standards. Since its inception in 2016, with over 100 registered and non-registered members, we have able to create opportunities for seniors to stay mentally and physically active (with walking, yoga, Zumba, line dancing, and field trips) and allowed them to participate in events that encourage greater inclusion and community engagement. For seniors, it provides mental activity, keeps weight in check, and cultivates a healthy heart and a sharp memory, all while giving them a renewed sense of purpose.

Then came the COVID-19 pandemic. It affected older people differently than the younger generations. Seniors are more likely to have dire outcomes from the virus, especially with their inability to be with family and friends and to go out and do the things they love to do with other people. The effects are compounded for any older person who does not have access to communication platforms like Skype and FaceTime or has limited access to phone calls. The absence of social contact creates isolation, loneliness, and depression.

There is also a fair amount of ageism, even if they don't say it out loud, that older people will die anyway—which is totally wrong. Age is just a number. So true! Aging does not prevent any of us from leading a fulfilling life. Seniors continue to contribute to our community, as we can all benefit from their wisdom, friendship, and experience.

The world has changed, and our lives have been affected by COVID-19 in many ways. It is stressful, and both physically and mentally exhausting. But in the fight against it, we have become more resilient than ever. With the COVID-19 restrictions, all our indoor activities and social activities were interrupted if not stopped. Change is not easy, but it is simple. We have accepted that things will change and we don't have a choice about it. But we do have a choice on how to react to change. We chose to manage it instead of the change managing us. As a leader, I chose to create change. I pivoted!

I never realized how much I enjoy walking. It is so refreshing! A breezy short walk with my son in the park sparked my idea of creating a seniors walking group. It was like a bolt of lightning struck me, and I could not sleep until I spoke to my SIA team. What's not to love about walking? The more I thought about it, the more it made sense to move from indoor to outdoor activities.

Walking is free and easy on the joints, especially for seniors. In addition to being an easy aerobic exercise, it is good for us in many other ways. It improves circulation, slows the rate of bone loss, lightens our mood, encourages weight loss, strengthens muscles, improves sleep, improves our breathing, slows down mental declines, lowers the risk of Alzheimer's disease, and allows us to enjoy a longer life.

Deciding to make a change was easy but getting our members on board was much more difficult because of the emotional process. We all have habits! It is easier to resist change than welcome routine. It is human nature.

It is so true that when patterns are broken, new worlds emerge. To convince my team that the new world I was trying to create could be better than before took a lot of planning, commitment, patience, and courage. As we waited for the new normal, we reinvented ourselves and found new activities together in our journey to health and wellness.

The words COVID-19 lockdown kept ringing in our ears. People were talking about it. We heard it on the radio and television, and read it in the newspaper. It was scary! But not everything was locked down.

We kept moving forward, opening new doors and doing new things. Like little kids, our curiosity kept taking us down new paths.

We created an SIA walking group, waking up early in the morning and exploring the beautiful parks in our community while practicing COVID-19 protocol, masking, and social distancing. We learned how to take photos and appreciate the little things around us. We became leaders in the walking group; we inspired and influenced other seniors and family members to learn and understand the benefits of walking.

We became tourists in our own neighbourhood, enjoying the beauty of God's creation. We walked and exercised in the park for fresh air. We sang and danced again as if there was no tomorrow. What a beautiful sight! We learned new skills and hobbies and read more books for self-improvement. We used our imagination and creativity for hopes and dreams that are not locked down.

The truth is that change can be a gift. It was for us—a wonderful gift that brought us joy every time we met in the park. I believe that it is the key that unlocks the doors to growth and excitement in any organization. It works in the corporate world, and it could work for us too.

Lack of access to smart technology, social isolation, and the inability to engage in physical exercise or participate in new routines are stresses seniors face when dealing with COVID-19, and some do not have access to resources to mitigate these stresses. Technology has emerged as an important factor for maintaining social connection as well as accessing mental health services.

A big part of my leadership role is to inspire my team to get out of their comfort zones—to assure them that even though they are on a new path, it is the right path for the right reason. I had many sleepless nights thinking about how I could support their needs in the fight against COVID-19. I reached out to our government and other community leaders for assistance and applied to the New Horizons for Seniors Program (NHSP) for funding. Our project was entitled Stay Connected with Technology.

With the funding support of the NHSP, we will be providing basic literacy computer classes with the use of iPads and smart devices.

Many seniors cannot access the computer or the Internet because of a lack of skills, equipment, instructional programs, and instructors; mobility problems; and language barriers. It is never too late or too early to learn something new. Attendees will learn how to access the Internet and stay connected with their community, family, and friends through Zoom as well as Facebook, Instagram, and other social media platforms.

We will have virtual classes, workshops, and information sessions on seniors' health, safety, fitness, and finances to protect ourselves in our day-to-day lives. In addition to our current program, we will offer wellness programs that stimulate the brain, provide education on elder abuse (including cybercrime and financial abuse), raise awareness for mental health and illnesses like dementia and Alzheimer's disease, and teach seniors how to care for themselves in light of their experiences related to COVID-19.

As the old proverb goes, "The journey of a thousand miles begins with a single step." Finding the right people and volunteers who are committed and who understand our change mission is the key to our success. We have been blessed to connect with the right people. Partnering with the Filipino Student Association of Scarborough (FSAS) to help us in teaching seniors within our community to become digital citizens is a good start. It will close the gap between the elderly and youth population.

COVID-19 brings the community together. Young and old working together can enhance the lives of seniors and bring generations together. By working together, young people and adults bring tremendous benefits to their communities while fostering respect and appreciation for one another.

Alicia Siervo
President, Seniors In Action
www.seniorsinaction.ca

MICHAEL SIERVO

How I pivoted

University of Toronto, Filipino Student Association of Scarborough, a non-profit student association

Bridging generation gaps and reaching outside our comfort zone

The Filipino Student Association of Scarborough (FSAS) serves the Filipino community at the University of Toronto Scarborough (UTSC) and within the Scarborough community. Our organization aims to create a safe and inviting space to bond with other students, discuss current issues that are important to Filipinos, and celebrate Filipino culture and its vibrant history.

Our organization has emerged and evolved over the years. There was a hiatus roughly starting in 2012, but luckily, the FSAS was founded again in the middle of 2017. We became an official club in 2018, becoming more recognized within the UTSC community. The majority of our initiatives were social events, which definitely helped with establishing ourselves as a campus club.

At the beginning of 2020, we hosted a Valentine fundraiser for families impacted by the Taal eruption. That was our last event for that school year before the pandemic hit. We had set up a movie night the following month in March, but unfortunately, our university had to cancel all events and gatherings amid the pandemic news. This was the start of the transition into the virtual world for our club and its executives.

The pandemic affected our funds and event turnout. We first thought that since events are held online, fees for event entrances and memberships weren't necessary. In addition, our club being a social and cultural club, the majority of our festivities and events happen in-person with fun games, activities, and icebreakers. These events had to be done virtually, and we enhanced our knowledge of various platforms in the process of organizing them.

It was difficult for us and for other departments to reach out to our UTSC community given this online environment. Despite this barrier, we believe this pandemic created a healthy challenge for us to utilize our resources and think of innovative ways to engage with our community. Examples of such include our Meet the Exec Mondays (MEMs) on Instagram and connecting with our community through other platforms, like Discord or Zoom.

When COVID-19 hit, we were saddened because we knew that this would compromise the in-person events we had planned for the term, and one of the main pillars of our club was the social gatherings. We thought that COVID-19 would not be around for too long, so we started planning ahead. But the news came in notifying us that the university would be in lockdown, transitioning to online learning. This prompted us to accept the online transition.

At first, it was somewhat of an annoyance and hassle to mitigate our plans, but we made the most of it. We did learn quite a few things while in lockdown, which built a stronger bond between us presidents and executive members.

Transitioning to the online world, we were able to embrace technology and learn from using available online platforms and resources to pivot in this new world. We also connected with our general members and other Filipino Student Associations (FSAs) in Canada through the use of social media and online events. By doing this, we maximized our engagement and involvement as a club to continue what we have established. We thought of innovative ways to engage with our community through the use of Discord and Zoom features and Instagram takeovers or social media campaigns.

During this time, we also stepped out of our comfort zone and participated in town halls with the MP of Scarborough Rouge Park. We wanted to amplify the voices of Filipino youth, as there are several barriers within the Canadian education system and a lack of mental health resources. From there, we met several Filipino leaders who reached out to provide valuable opportunities and services for our members.

Currently, we are working with Seniors in Action (SIA) to establish a new program called "Stay Connected with Technology." Our goal is to give students leadership opportunities by having them teach seniors basic technology and social media skills that will help them stay connected with family and friends. We also are passionate about bridging the gap between youth and senior populations, as this program is designed to facilitate friendships between the two. In an era where seeing only half of a person's face is the new normal, we believe that this program will promote connectedness in a unique way.

While our social events helped us gain traction and recognition as a campus club, we believe this pandemic has afforded us the time and opportunity to reflect on how to integrate more meaningful initiatives revolving around our culture and outreach. This year, we successfully organized two fundraisers, one that is currently in session and doing well (about $400 raised for farmers in the Philippines) and one that was aimed at providing PPE for health care workers in the Philippines who must purchase their own.

We have also implemented two social media campaigns, led by a co-president, aimed at educating our community about our culture and relevant issues: our Filipino Word Series and the series of posts made in light of the International Day for the Elimination of Racial Discrimination. Given the importance and success of these two initiatives, we decided to create a new position for next year, Outreach and Cultural Education Director, whose sole work will revolve around these initiatives. We also decided to dedicate a position solely for leading cultural events (Cultural Events Director).

The leadership qualities and organization skills we gained are permanent and will be carried along with us during these times. The online world is temporary, as the university is planning on a safe transition back to in-person learning. But this does not mean that the club would terminate all online functioning. We learned during this transition that using the technological platforms available would help us grow and flourish.

We, the presidents, are graduating this year, and we hope FSAS continues with its cultural and outreach initiatives. Hopefully, FSAS can host events like Filipino History 101, or teach Tagalog, Bisaya, Ilocano, or any other Filipino language. It is so important that we celebrate and keep the Filipino history and culture alive.

We worked with the International Student Centre to help facilitate a drop-in session to discuss anti-Asian racism, and we hope that FSAS can continue to collaborate with the university's departmental organizations for events like this. We have also reached out to the MP of Scarborough to raise awareness in our community about the rise of anti-Asian hate crimes and to push for more mental health initiatives for victims. As our club is becoming more recognized and established, we are able to reach a wider audience to bring awareness to Filipino culture and history, and to advocate against social injustices, among other issues and politics regarding the Filipino community.

Transitioning from normal life to living in a pandemic was surely a challenge for us all. Being one of the co-presidents at the time of the transition definitely felt overwhelming, since adjusting the club to be completely online was something we had never done before. Since one of FSAS's goals is to foster a welcoming environment for individuals who wish to express their passion and interest in Filipino culture, our main concern was how we were going to keep the club engaging for its members through online or virtual interactions.

Dealing with this challenge, and thus pivoting into this new world, required an open mind to try new things that would help strengthen the FSAS community despite the effects of the pandemic. Challenging ourselves to take on new approaches on the way the club would execute virtual events and maintain an online presence is what helped our club adjust to the new world. The 2020-2021 FSAS executive team did an amazing job adjusting to this new normal. From collaborating with other Filipino Student Associations across Ontario to fostering an online community via Discord and social media platforms, FSAS was able to grow as an organization in the midst of these challenging times. FSAS is a prime example that pivoting into this new reality is possible, and with COVID-19 bringing new challenges to us all, an open mind is key to bringing forth new solutions.

Board of Directors
University of Toronto, Filipino Students Association of Scarborough
Isabel Tuason
Mozelle Espiritu
Angelica Vilela
Joshua Belen

PART TWO

Old Doors Close, New Ones Open—Side-Hustling in the Gig Economy, Sales, and Winning the Mental Game

The dream is free. Hustle is sold separately.

CHAPTER 6
The Rise of the Gig Economy

DID YOU EVER HAVE THAT FRIEND WHO HAD A FULL-TIME JOB BUT in the evenings would invite you to see him perform at a bar? I have a friend like that. His name is Paul David, and to this day, I still find him one of the most interesting people I know. He would say, "After work tonight, come by the CopaCabana and catch my gig." He was always doing gigs every week.

I wondered where he got the energy to do it. I thought, *Wow, this guy really knows how to maximize his downtime.*

Now imagine a lot of people starting to do side hustles in their spare time. You don't need to imagine anymore, as it's happening right now. Welcome to the gig economy.

> *There is no downside to a side hustle. There are only benefits to building more than one source of income. A side hustle is the new job security.—Forbes*

What is the Gig Economy and why does it matter to you?

Over the last few years, the gig economy has been a buzz word in business. The gig economy is part of a shifting cultural and business environment that also includes the sharing economy, the gift economy, and the barter economy. The gig economy is essentially a free-market system in which temporary positions are common and organizations hire specific people for specific temporary projects or purposes. The term *gig* is a slang word for a job that lasts for a specific time. Musicians would say that they have a gig tonight, meaning they have a job or show tonight.

When you think about it, the building of houses and construction is a perfect example of a gig economy. Contractors share their specific talents and expertise in return for compensation. As a result of many contractors complementing each other's skill set, a beautiful high-end home overlooking the ocean is built in Malibu. Oh, how I totally wish I could be overlooking the ocean right now! I digress.

In today's world, the rise in gigs has come in the form of freelancers, contractors, consultants, coaches and you guessed it, even babysitters. The gig economy has always been here for years, but with the advent of COVID-19, the importance of this structure has impacted the perception of business models and would-be entrepreneurs. But just because this new economy has emerged more than ever in this uncertain world, why would anyone want to attempt to be a business owner? There's so much risk and uncertainty involved.

I remember my father scolding my brother and I as he tried his best to talk us out of becoming entrepreneurs. Perhaps it's a Filipino cultural thing, where there is a gravitation toward the safe jobs, such as a nurse, accountant, or government employee. Don't get me wrong— entrepreneurs are everywhere. But they are greatly outnumbered by the masses of folk not cut out for the wild ride of owning your own business. For most people, there is a peace of mind knowing that a steady paycheque is coming however for the entrepreneur having your livelihood in the hands of someone else is a risk in and of itself. Regardless, why would someone want to go into business on their own and why now?

First off, there are so many reasons for starting a business, such as you have a cool vision; you like the possibility of making lots of money or the freedom to work at your pace; you think you can build an empire; or you want to be the big Kahuna, Top Dog, Big Cheese, the shot caller, the Lady Boss. You want to stop answering to the Man. I totally get it. Who knows, maybe you want to own a business to impress others or stand out in your social circles. The reasons are endless. Sometimes the opposite sex finds it attractive that you own a business. I remember imagining how cool it would be to hand out my business cards to everyone I met even before I made a single penny.

Maybe you're tired of being underappreciated by a shitty boss in a company that doesn't light your fire. Perhaps you feel that you have a skill that can be monetized and commercialized but still have doubt. Maybe you want to become an entrepreneur because you need to come up with extra money to pay for all the diapers you have to buy for that fifth kid you didn't plan for. Whatever the reason, many people dream of being a business owner but never wake up and actually do it. The gig economy allows tentative people like you and I the environment to dip their toe into entrepreneurship while either having a full-time job or juggling other sources of income.

> *The biggest risk of all is listening to that stupid voice trying to tell you not to take one.—Michael Siervo*

On the other hand, many people have convinced themselves not to start a business even though deep down inside they wish they did. Some of the more common reasons are lack of resources, lack of knowledge, it's expensive, not enough time, not enough confidence in your product or service, and the big one: FEAR. This is, of course, until the boom of the Internet, the acceleration of the pandemic, and the emergence of the gig economy. More and more, people are venturing into business on their own. Whether it's out of passion or necessity, people's inner entrepreneurs are coming out in droves.

Old excuses don't apply here— no excuses, just pivot!

> *Once you get rid of your excuses, you have no choice but to be amazing.—Michael Siervo*

75

Let's break down why the old excuses we once told ourselves no longer apply in this new environment, and why the logical step is to pivot into something new, scary, and awesome.

Lack of Resources

Lack of resources used to be a huge issue. However, online businesses can be started with a simple website you can create using WordPress or a template. There are countless website templates you can essentially cut and paste to create a decent-looking online presence. Look, we're not talking about building the next Tesla. It doesn't take much to start a business these days. There's a company out of Israel called WIX. com that essentially is drag-and-drop website creation. No coding needed. Anyone can create a simple website in under an hour. You can create decent websites on Wordpress with little experience at all. It's not going to be the next Amazon but you can create an easy Shopify site in minutes.

The overall cost of doing business now can be lower than renting an apartment in downtown Manhattan. Heck, the excuse that you need a storefront no longer applies. E-commerce has opened the world of global markets. All you need is a computer and the willingness to learn.

Certain business types can launch with modest start-up costs of under $1,000. These could include direct-marketing sales, network marketing, consulting work, or even life-coaching. The reality is that the average cost isn't as large as one might expect. For instance, Canadastartups.org states that an average small-business owner in Canada spends about $5,000 to $10,000 to initially start a small business. You can essentially fund most of your business on a credit card (and get awesome reward points while you're at it) or with a personal loan from an angel investor such as your favourite Auntie Eva.

Governments around the world tend to encourage entrepreneurship, so grants, small loans, and micro-financing options are readily available if you take the time to look. The website www.

business.org has a list of the best 11 small-business loans of 2021. If you live in Canada, go check out websites such as loanscanada.ca, bdc. ca, or our always entrepreneur-friendly bank in Alberta, ATB (Alberta Treasury Bank). Money is there. You just have to look!

Lack of Knowledge

Lack of knowledge is simply an excuse not to try. I remember reading about this hippie kinda guy who started a software company out of a garage with his friend. With hard work and vision, he built it into one of the largest companies in history. The funny thing is that he never wrote code. They named the company after some common fruit and eventually revolutionized the way we interact with technology. Oddly enough, I can't imagine using another phone except for my iPhone.

Here's another one: Drug dealer turned rapper turned business mogul 50 Cent didn't know anything about the beverage business but made millions when his company Vitamin Water was acquired by Coca-Cola for $4.1 billion. From getting shot nine times while selling drugs on the street to selling vitamin water for millions of dollars— now if that's not the pivot of the century, I don't know what is.

In the past, fence-sitting wantrepreneurs would convince themselves that they were not business people or they didn't know anything about business. For years, I would talk to friends who had great ideas but would kill the idea before it would ever come to life because they felt they didn't have the right education. Steve Jobs and 50 Cent didn't have the knowledge, but they found people who did. You can too.

I remember reading a chapter in *Think and Grow Rich* about Henry Ford. Mr. Ford was being accused of being incompetent and that he was an ignorant man. When being questioned on the stand during a court trial about trivial things, he confidently responded to the lawyer questioning him with this line: "Let me remind you that I have a row of electric buttons in my office. All I have to do is press one of them to call the person who can answer any question on any subject I wish to know, relative to the business at hand. I take care of the business; they take care of the questions."

In the past, lack of knowledge and know-how would be a sensible excuse, as there was no point risking your life savings on a business if you had no clue what you were doing. Things have changed, though. Thankfully, as long as you have an Internet connection, the collective brainpower of the world is at your fingertips. Heck, remember I mentioned how Elon Musk saying that you don't need a college degree to be successful in business let alone even apply to Tesla. I know many poor professors and many rich high-school dropouts.

I admit that many of these younger people can't write for shit. I mean, their penmanship and cursive writing is worse than a doctor's. I'm sure their thumb speed and emoji game is on fire. Yet these kids get one thing right: You don't need to have a Harvard degree to start a business. You just need to be familiar with your favourite six-letter friend and destroyer of all Thanksgiving dinner debates: G-O-O-G-L-E.

Everything is available on the Internet. You don't need to be book smart. You just need to be, as my brother-in-law calls himself, "Google smart." You can literally google how to start a company, and there will be hundreds of posts on how to do it. There isn't anything in the world you can't learn on Google or through a YouTube video. The lack of knowledge is an excuse. Want to learn how to start a business? Google it.

Not everyone is like Elon Musk, who will risk everything on his vision to build Tesla and SpaceX simultaneously. He tightrope-walked the line of bankruptcy and failure many times with his all-in bets. Most logical human beings wouldn't have the stomach to put all their money into building a business, let alone rockets to Mars. The reality is that businesses, as mentioned before, can take a lot of resources and be expensive.

Opening up an office space or renting a building can be a huge financial commitment, and labour costs are high. As of 2021, in Calgary, Alberta, minimum wage is $15/hour and up to $16/hr in more remote areas such as Nunavut. The higher the input cost of products, the lower the profit margin. One of the forces behind the rise of short-term jobs that drive the gig economy is that the workforce is going mobile and work can be done remotely on digital platforms. Geography is no longer an excuse not to enhance your workforce.

Digitization is behind much of the gig economy, as old processes can be done more easily with new technologies and efficiencies. Software has replaced many simple tasks, such as accounting and schedule booking. So when it comes to the excuse of cost and resources, the digital world provides a lot of rebuttals.

Lack of Time

Many people will say that there isn't enough time to start a business, as they're busy raising a family or focusing on themselves or coming up with an excuse to binge-watch Netflix. (Sure ... convince yourself that you're watching Netflix for research. You're only lying to yourself.) Whatever your excuse is, keep in mind that you're not trying to create the next Microsoft. You simply want to earn more income given the spare time that you have. This pandemic has given us extra time! Let's pivot the energy toward things that can make money.

Everyone has skills and talents they can share. Why not make money in your spare time? In a later chapter, we will discuss some of the top business opportunities in this pandemic and beyond. For now, the premise is that you are simply trying to create a gig. A happy Uber driver once told me that he spent the last 18 years working at a large taxi firm as both a driver and a dispatcher. For the last three years, he has been an Uber driver. Change can hurt older industries, as is the case with the taxi industry.

He mentioned how he saw the writing on the wall and asked me the question, "When was the last time you called for a cab?" People are not ordering cabs. They use an Uber app and request an Uber driver. It's way more efficient for the client, and Uber ensures the driver gets paid immediately. In fact, in between rides, he does Uber Eats and drops off food.

This is a simple example of a pivot within a gig. This Uber driver works at his own pace, has more time with his family than ever before, and makes more than $40,000 a year in extra money. Don't sacrifice the important things in life, such as family and loved ones. Efficiency, technology, and new consumer demands are giving us more time if we simply find the right gig to fit our lifestyle. Find gigs that can be built around your family life rather than the other way around. We will discuss this in more detail in a later chapter.

Lack of time is a lack of priorities.—Tim Ferris

Lack of Confidence

I feel that this is probably the biggest reason people don't end up taking the plunge to pivot into entrepreneurship or in a new direction within their current business model. Some people simply believe that we will get back to normal and that the status quo will return. The real reason is that they don't have confidence in their product, skills, ideals, or strategy to make the leap. Most of all, they are afraid.

Fear is a difficult thing to overcome when money is on the line and your family's well-being is in question. Fear of venturing out of your comfort zone is paralyzing. It cripples people into staying still and eventually blaming external factors as to why they didn't pivot.

Fear is a lie!

I have always believed that FEAR stands for two things: (F)orget (E)verything (A)nd (R)un *or* (F)alse (E)vidence (A)ppearing (R)eal.

I believe in the latter. We often are afraid of things that don't even exist. We ask ourselves *what if the economy collapses, what if my suppliers close up shop, what if the plane crashes, what if, what if, what if.* We spend way too much time fearing our imagination rather than enjoying the moment of reality.

I am an old man and have known a
great many troubles, but most of them
never happened.—Mark Twain

Many of the things that we fear hasn't happened (such as a plane crashing), but better yet, they likely won't happened. Why stress over something that hasn't happened? Why fear the future when you're living in the present? The good thing about pivoting into a side hustle or launching a new product or service is that they tend to be lower-risk investments of mainly time and some resources that are done simultaneously with your current job. I'm specifically talking about the gig economy that many people have access to now.

It's not as scary as people think. It's just allocating time and effort to something that provides additional income or perhaps a new path for your existing business. I know of many successful salespeople who know that their companies may wind down in the near future due to technological advancements (think of the typewriter salesman). Rather than waiting for the day to come, they do side hustles in this gig economy that leverage their strength in sales. They slowly transition into a new venture once their current source of income dries up or forces them to make the change and leave. Whether they sell homemade baked goods, sell insurance policies, clean an office building after hours, or join a network marketing organization, they are pivoting into the opportunities that this gig economy provides.

A great example is my friend Erik Allan. He is an engineer by trade in the oil and gas industry. For the last few years, the oil and gas sector has been hit hard by low oil prices, decreasing global demand, market corrections, and now a global pandemic. The writing is on the wall that this industry is in massive need of a pivot.

Prior to seeing the magic tea leaves indicating a change in the economy, Erik started to look at other ventures. It wasn't necessarily to replace his job initially but because he wanted to do something that excites him. He followed his first passion, which was martial arts. He accidentally stumbled on a whole new martial arts community that was craving cool gear and accessories. From a small little passion project, Erik and his friend Kyle successfully carved out a niche in the world of apparel. They travelled to Asia with no clue on the textile industry and zero connections.

Watching their journey on YouTube is quite inspirational, as you see two foreigners exploring a market they know nothing about, in a country they have never been to, with limited resources to make it happen. Talk about having balls to step outside of your comfort zone to explore new opportunities! From there, Budo Brothers apparel was born. Now Kyle has left his job and transitioned full-time from a part-time gig to a full-time passion. Who knew that there was a market for badass martial arts gear that you could wear walking the streets?

Whether people dip their toe into the gig economy to put extra money in their pockets or to use it as a way to ease out of a job that doesn't fulfill them into one that gets them excited, the gig economy is open for business.

How I pivoted

Amanda Chen, Founder, The Salty Paloma

In March 2020, I was over the moon. I couldn't believe my life. I had to pinch myself. What began three years earlier as a small side-hustle product line of artisanal flavoured salts and sugars transformed into this elevated cocktail-class service hosted by some of the most talented women in Toronto.

Within the first week of March, we had already hit 50 students, which used to be the number of students we would have in a month. We were operating out of two boutique cocktail bars in the West End, booked solid every weekend for our open-level class, with private parties and corporate events booked up until the end of the year.

On March 14, the lockdown was announced, and I received two letters of termination from the bars I was working at to allow me to apply for EI. Then came the emails, one by one, of people cancelling their classes and asking for refunds. My heart sank as I watched the minuses grow, minute by minute. Whenever I would have a light week of cocktail classes, I would take an extra shift at one of the two bars I worked at. There was always a backup plan to keep my financial security in check. But what happens when all the backup plans vanish at once?

OK, before we get to the pivot, here's a little background on the cocktail classes and Salty Paloma. I was working full-time in digital marketing, with a specific focus in content strategy and social media. At the time, I was a freelancer at a digital agency and wanted to make something for myself. If you've ever worked at an agency, you'll know the feeling of perceived freedom in the ability to work with lots of clients in different industries, but the unfortunate reality is that the client will almost never sign off on your proposed idea.

So, in my desire to make digital content I actually would be proud of, I figured I would just create my own product to market. I had no experience with food or bartending, let alone business or operations, but I noticed that in Canada, we enjoy a good Caesar at brunch and seem to comment a lot on the rimmer. Yet there's really only one way to make a Caesar: Clamato juice and alcohol. And there are millions of margarita recipes, but no renowned brands of margarita salt. I thought: *I found my niche!*

I opened up Salty Paloma flavoured cocktail rimmers in January of 2018 with three flavours, and within a month, I got a small order from the Cocktail Emporium. I continued knocking at the doors of every boutique retailer in Toronto that had a little bar and cocktail section in their shop. From there, I started approaching restaurants and alcohol companies to see if there was anything we could partner on, and I started to make custom salt and sugar flavours that they would have exclusively for their marketing and promotions. I learned very quickly that making a custom flavour in bulk wasn't bringing in a lot of money for the effort, so I shifted my focus back to the end customer.

A friend of mine who is an esteemed self-made hustler told me about AirBnB experiences. She has a huge online presence and was invited to teach makeup classes. At this time, a lot of the experiences were photographers following tourists around for the perfect Instagram photos, an exclusive scenic tour, or a very authentic cooking class hosted by locals. I submitted an experience to teach cocktail classes, providing three recipes that featured a different salt to increase my product's exposure.

On Christmas Day of 2018, I had my first cocktail class of six complete strangers in my condo, and it was the most magical moment. Bringing people together, sharing stories, playing with cocktails— and many left with Salty salt jars. Merry fucking Christmas!

I started getting loads of tourists and even locals coming over for cocktail classes and realized there was a huge demand for this. But with zero experience, I needed to seriously upgrade my cocktail skills, so I quit my job and started working as a server assistant for $12/ hour and no tips, which was excruciatingly humbling as a 30-year-old woman. The competition was really soft, though, working with mainly beautiful young people under 25, mostly actors and models in training, who had no real sense of responsibility or even much of a desire to work in bars long-term.

Within no time, I found a beautiful spot in the West End that let me operate my cocktail classes while the bar was closed to provide a private experience, and then allowed my students to finish their last cocktail when the doors opened to generate more foot traffic. It was a win-win for everyone.

The next holiday season, I was booking so fast AirBnB had a glitch on their platform and made my experience unavailable. I was freaking out because I had some previous bookings from a while back and couldn't contact them. I guess it was time to start featuring the cocktail classes on my own website and driving people there. And as I let go of my attachment to AirBnB, Indigo came into the picture. They asked if I would like to be one of the first hosts for Thoughtful, an experience-based gifting program. I guess it all worked out in the end.

By March 2020, I had been working with alcohol brands to be featured at our open-level cocktail classes that would change every month. We even sold the cocktails at the bar so people who didn't take the class could try them. I was recruiting more and more talented women, and I had just started another partnership with a boutique hotel that was looking for local events to support. I was on the verge of buying a place for myself while the pandemic quietly loomed above me. I thought it wasn't my problem; it was just a thing other countries were experiencing. And then I was hit hard with reality. All bars were officially closed. Thank God I didn't put my money down on a venue.

Honestly, I thought to myself, *maybe this is a blessing. Maybe this is my chance to end Salty Paloma. It had a good run, I can walk out respectably. Maybe this is a sign.*

And then I received nonstop messages on social media asking me what I was going to do next. People were waiting to see what pivot I would make, as Amanda always has another way. Would I go virtual? I felt the pressure to do something, even though everything in my body was telling me to just let it all go.

I saw a bunch of bartenders offering cocktail classes, DJs hosting music sessions, dancers sharing their choreography, all for *free* on Instagram Live. And I was really upset about this. I was fucking angry. I know for a fact none of these people are making any money but are trying to stay relevant by offering free shit to people because we are all feeling sorry for everyone who lost their jobs or can't go out and do things. I just lost a shitload of money, and I had no prospect of money coming in. Doing something for free was the last thing I wanted to do.

Seven days later, I announced a free cocktail class on Instagram Live. I gave in to the bullshit.

As I promoted the event, I thought, *OK, is there any way I can make some quick cash out of this terrible situation I just created for myself?* I realized that all these bartenders on Instagram Live were showing how to make cocktails, but they had a full kit at home, which I knew only serious bartenders had. A regular person wouldn't have half of these things. So I created an ingredient list and drove around the city delivering supplies to anyone who wanted to attend. A lot of my friends joined in, and I dropped off some of my shaker sets for them to use as well.

That made me realize I also needed to find ways to shake and stir cocktails without fancy tools. So I brought out mason jars, water bottles, wooden spoons, and chopsticks. It wasn't as fancy, but if there's a will, there's a way.

I noticed that without bars or even liquor stores available to offer tastings or recommend one brand of alcohol over another, what were these brands going to do for marketing? Even billboards had no effect with everyone having to stay at home. We used to visit our favourite bartenders at our favourite local bars and trust that they would whip up something super-cool and hook us up with a new spirit they just started carrying. And more likely than not, we might pick up a bottle of whatever they recommended the next time we visited the LCBO (Liquor Control Board of Ontario). Without this in-person experience, the only real opportunity for marketing was digital.

It felt weird moving away from such a tactile, physical space, like working at bars, to thinking digitally. But it's like getting in a car after not driving for a while; you just need some time to get back into it. I decided to pitch to the marketing teams of massive alcohol brands this new program called the Stay at Home Cocktail Club—an url with all the social media channels I actually bought years ago when I wanted to expand Salty Paloma into a cocktail-kit delivery service. It's funny how the universe works.

As other restaurants in the city started to create ready-made cocktails as part of their takeout program, I deconstructed the cocktails so that there was more interactive play. People were bored at home and wanted to do things, feel more alive, learn something new. Like, for fuck's sake, people were baking bread! Of *course* this cocktail club was a great idea. And with the ability to deliver alcohol along with my mix, it was the perfect business opportunity for a lot of spirit companies looking for a digital channel on which to spend their marketing dollars.

I reached out to every brand I knew, proposed the cocktail club, and received lots of attention. But there was still some hesitancy, as it was a completely new program that had never been done before. Duh. The pandemic had never happened before, so naturally every other thing we do, whether you call it a pivot or whatever, has never happened before either. We can't possibly know if this is going to be successful or not. And this is when I realized a lot of businesses never really took a risk like this—one where the outcome was uncertain.

OK, so how do I help make the uncertain feel more certain? At least to marketing folk? I suggested making three cocktail recipes out of the ingredients I would provide in this cocktail kit, featuring one spirit brand, and even found a local baker to add in a little treat. (And to keep us from getting too drunk, lol. This was also a hospitality rule to promote responsible alcohol consumption.) And in the creation of these cocktail recipes, I would make three videos on Instagram, take loads of photos, and host a live cocktail class. A full package deal.

Out of the blue, Diageo, a massive spirit company that held loads of brands, came back to me. They wanted to begin with Don Julio, obviously, to celebrate Cinco de Mayo, and then for every week after, wanted me to feature a different Diageo brand on a two-month contract. Now here is the crazy thing: I had obviously never made a cocktail kit, or packaged it up, or made deliveries, or even filmed myself, and yet I sold this full package deal that locked me into two months of financial security. *Fuck, I'm in over my head.* I had no idea how to make this happen. I got what I asked for, but at what cost?

I started to obsess about the quality of my videos, thinking they weren't high-quality enough, knowing full well I was a one-woman show filming, editing, and posting this all by myself. With everywhere closed, I had to strategically plan delivery routes that included bathroom breaks back at my house. I spent a lot of time in the Dollar Store, one of the few stores that remained open, and labelled all the cocktail-kit ingredients with a sharpie on coloured construction paper. It was actually a very creative experience, minus the bladder scheduling.

But it was unsustainable. By the end of summer, when patios opened up, brands created cocktails in a can to promote drinking on the go, and people were having picnics at the park. I thought, *OK, I'm done now. I am exhausted.* Somehow I had managed to make myself even busier than I was already before the pandemic, and I couldn't keep this going.

I was doing all of this for the wrong reasons—just to keep Salty going. To look like I knew what I was doing. A form of brand maintenance and relevance. All of this was for everyone else. *But what about me? What do I want?* I refused to take on another spirit company and finally gave myself time to answer that question.

I enjoyed making videos at home, which prompted the idea of making more online content. Maybe I would start up a digital cocktail school with a bunch of online videos and courses. But something was missing. I guess you could say I fell out of love with making cocktails. Or maybe it was never the cocktailing that I loved. It was the hustle. The journey. And the maintenance part wasn't as attractive to me. Now that everything was set up, I wasn't as interested in keeping it going, expanding, managing, and operating it at a level that required more people than me to execute.

I started researching other types of remote or digital work and got very curious about business coaching. I spoke with over 50 friends and acquaintances who were freelancers, artists, self-made entrepreneurs, side-hustlers, and 9-5ers to figure out a one-on-one coaching program that I could offer with my experience. This came to me so quickly and so naturally, and I was invigorated again with the ability to help others.

But this time, it wasn't just any customer. It was a specific type of person. A person like me, who could be so much more magical if she knew how to get out of her own way, focus on the goal, and dive in fearlessly. I am proud to say that right now, I coach some of the most amazing women, who are both my friends and favourite clients.

With a focus on empowering others, I started talking to who is now the woman behind Salty Paloma, Evelyn Chick, an esteemed cocktail professional in the city who I am so proud to have. With her experience in the development and execution of cocktail programs and my pre-existing brand and customer base, we were a dream team to take the cocktail-kit program to incredible heights for the holiday season of 2020. We went from selling 100 cocktail kits a week to 100 cocktail kits a day, literally running out of all types of inventory, from salt jars to labels to cardboard boxes. We were insanely successful, and I was beyond grateful for this partnership.

Now, I had attempted to have partners with Salty, but nothing really worked out except with Evelyn. A lot of self-made hustlers out there might be afraid of getting a partner mainly because they don't think they can trust someone with their baby. And yet, loads of parents peacefully leave their kids alone, trusting teenage babysitters, and return home with most things still intact.

Some industry members might have thought of us as competitors because we were both empowered women working on our own cocktail programs and building our own personal brand. But I never saw it that way. Evelyn had all the skills I didn't have, and vice versa. But beyond skills, the key to a successful partnership is in outlining roles and responsibilities. We can't both be doing the same thing; that would just be redundant and usually amounts to most of the arguments you might hear between partners, both professionally and personally. When Evelyn said she wanted to launch cocktail kits for the holidays, I said, "Why not just do it for Salty? Why compete with each other when we don't have to?"

As we discussed the plans for the Salty x Evelyn Chick Projects holiday kits, I gave Evelyn the contacts to our brand partnerships and insights on which kits were more or less successful, and then gave her full autonomy over how she wanted to roll out the kits. All I did was what I was good at: digital marketing and content. Before we even announced the cocktail kits, I put them up on the website to make sure they were tested and ready to go for launch. And somehow, we had already received a bunch of sales. We didn't even have photos of the kits yet. I was bewildered that people would just purchase something online without seeing it, but I guess our loyal customers were waiting for Salty to bring back the kits from the summer. Now that's real trust in a brand. And trust us, Salty doesn't disappoint.

Leading up to the end of the year, I received the biggest custom salt order of my life: to make 20,000 units of salt for Grand Marnier. With the lockdown still in effect, I relied heavily on my parents to help find local suppliers. We made new partnerships with Chinese grocery stores and experienced a cardboard shortage in the realization that Amazon and pretty much every other online company (including ours) were over their heads in holiday deliveries. In six insane weeks, I made the equivalent to what a full-time salary would have been at the last agency I worked at to spend the whole year working overtime just to take two weeks off while still being remotely available and on-call. And somehow, I made the most amount of money I have ever made in my life and had the entire year of 2021 to live freely. And I thought back on everyone, including my parents, who looked at me like I was crazy when I said I wanted to start up a salt company. Who's laughing now?

With Evelyn taking care of the cocktail kits, I had more time to focus on my coaching and living remotely. I told myself I needed three things to allow myself to move to Mexico: enough money in the bank to live without a steady income, a second revenue stream or business venture, and the blessing of my parents. The first two were easy-ish to achieve; the Grand Marnier order put me in good standing, and the coaching was a dream. But getting the blessing of my parents was one of the most difficult tasks I ever challenged myself to do.

I have run away from my parents like most rebellious children do, realizing I would always have to return home and face the fact that they didn't accept me for who I am. I was on a mission to change that this time. It took until nearly the last day before I flew out for them to accept that I wouldn't be living out the expectations they had for me and to be OK with that. On the day I left, I suddenly realized how much I was going to miss my parents, especially my mother, Salty's MVP, the strongest human I know. Funny how things happen that way.

In January 2021, I sat down with Evelyn to talk about what to do next. The holiday was a shit show. No one could have guessed the cocktail kits would have been such a hit. But now what? January is usually the slowest time of year for bars and restaurants, mainly because people are tired from all the holiday parties and are poor as fuck after buying loads of gifts and treating themselves at Boxing Day sales. I shared my thoughts on turning the Stay at Home Cocktail Club into a monthly subscription program so that we could get a better idea of sales month-to-month. Although I might be fine with chaos and uncertainty, a business would generally be better run with more consistency.

As the lockdown continued on here in Toronto, with no real plans to change in the near future, I figured we might as well keep this going and really hone in on providing elevated virtual experiences with a special focus on cocktails. The cocktail subscription program would include a monthly meet-up to develop a community that we could leverage for more brand partnerships in the future. It was easy to set up, and in the first month of launch we already had 30 subscribers. Today, the virtual social hour is probably the only time you'll see me in the flesh, virtually, as I'm living remotely in Oaxaca as I write this story.

A lot has changed over the last few months. I have basically made myself obsolete with Salty Paloma and am in discussions to sell the business to Evelyn. I realize the commission structure we set for me to live humbly in Mexico is now a dead weight and compromising the ability to offer the best products and services Salty can offer, and that's the last thing I want to be. It's very hard for self-made entrepreneurs to let go of a business they created and called their baby, called a piece of them.

But Salty was never just me. It was always this thing outside of me, a message to empower female entrepreneurs that if you ever thought you couldn't make something happen, watching me retire at 32 off of a salt company will hopefully inspire you to get up and live out your dreams.

But let me be clear: I don't want to be the exception, the one who made it, the unbelievable success story that only Amanda Chen could achieve. Instead, I want us to stop looking for examples to follow but rather sources of inspiration to gain the courage to carve out our own path, a truly authentic one. As much as I created Salty and am so grateful for the fruits of my labour, when I self-identified with Salty, I lost my vitality, my light, my whole purpose of living—because Salty was all I was, and if it wasn't doing well, I wasn't doing well. Imagine the chains we put on ourselves when success is the only measurement of our self-worth! I can't live like that anymore.

Nowadays, I spend a lot of time reflecting on who I am, living humbly in small remote towns no one has heard of in the middle of Mexico, quietly taking long walks in parks, visiting as many coffee shops as I can, stopping to take photos of street art that catches my eye, meeting the most interesting people on my travels, and getting to know the real Amanda Chen—an artist, a creator, a writer, someone who lives her life with so much authenticity, truth, and courage, embracing all the beautiful uncertainty that this world has to offer.

Amanda Chen, Founder
Salty Paloma
www.saltypaloma.com

CHAPTER 7
Who Is in the Gig Economy?

*Give yourself permission to say YES to side
jobs, gigs, projects, and part-time work*

THE GIG ECONOMY IS GROWING FASTER AND FASTER EVERY DAY. Sometimes growth comes out of intention, and sometimes it comes out of necessity. According to the International Monetary Fund, the yearly unemployment rate from 2019 to 2020 has changed. I have many friends who have been let go from long-standing jobs—jobs they thought they would retire from. I know business owners who have seen their businesses flushed down the COVID-19 toilet along with their dreams and savings. In the United States, the unemployment rate jumped from 3.7 to 8.9 per cent. From where we are in Canada, the unemployment rate jumped from 5.7 per cent to a whopping 9.7 per cent. That's a lot of unemployed people. So the question is, who is in the gig economy and why?

This pandemic has caused drastic and accelerated change. As unemployment rates increase, the standard of living increases. There is a demand for some to "keep up with the Joneses" or simply stay afloat, as cash flow becomes more and more uncertain. I have a friend of mine who drives a fancy luxury car to maintain appearances for his executive job while driving Uber at night. The gig economy welcomes essentially anyone regardless of what your motive is. Companies, gig workers, and consumers all make up the gig economy. It isn't limited to one sector, but the more common ones are:

- IT
- software development

- project management
- accounting and finance
- education
- construction
- media and communications
- freelance writing
- arts and design
- transportation
- material moving

There really isn't a single profile or avatar of who is part of this gig economy which is great. That means that we can all participate and benefit from it. Construction workers and independent contractors have represented the gig economy under our noses for years. In 2017, 6.9 per cent of all US workers were independent contractors. According to the Bureau of Statistics, this number was 55 million people, representing 35 per cent of the labour force. Today, this is closer to 50 per cent.

As businesses attempt to pivot and adjust their sails to the changing winds, they look at reducing labour cost, improving expertise, and simply dipping into the massive global pool of talent. This means the gig economy is open to anyone. Years ago, if you had a skill, talent, or expertise, you would typically cater to local markets. Now you can sell your skills or talents to anyone in the world. The great thing is that there is a demand for it.

Let's even take a profession that is the epitome of catering to the local market, such as real estate. This is something I am very familiar with. You can take your skill set, which is the ability to "sell" a dream, anywhere in the world. Some of the top realtors have international offices. The globe is their massive real estate market. One of the top real estate sales people in the world is Ryan Serhant. Even before the pandemic he leaned into his strongest skillset which is "selling." In addition to selling real estate he pivotted and sold programs on how to be an amazing sales person. His sales courses are sold globally as his profession allowed him to pivot locally to internationally.

It is important to understand the gig economy, because anyone can benefit from it. If you are a small business that needs to survive and grow, you are no longer limited to talent within your city. If you think you don't need to outsource skills to other talent around the world, just try calling the call centre of one of the top banks in North America. I can almost guarantee that the person who answers is from the Philippines or somewhere abroad. Maybe you're a financial advisor at a large firm like Sun Life Financial and you call for tech support issues? Odds are, the person answering your call is from Ireland. Looking to discuss some affordable Web-development options? You can find someone in India for 25 per cent of the cost in your local market.

Now you may think that this globalization will destroy the local market. That's not necessarily true. It also means that you can share your skills with the world. You can earn extra income to complement your regular job simply by starting up a website or online store to sell whatever your heart desires. Perhaps you are a life coach who has built her practice mentoring people one on one. The emergence of Zoom and the adoption rate of people willing to jump in front of the camera allows you to coach someone in Manilla, Philippines, from your couch in Toronto, Canada. Trust me, I do it all the time. The extra money you earn from abroad or outside of your geography can be spent on local businesses.

The outsourcing goes both ways. We in North America can benefit from talent across the ocean and vice versa. While sitting in Toronto, Canada, I hired a Spanish teacher from Mexico. The reverse can also happen. I know of many friends who tutor English for executives in Hong Kong. Large companies have been navigating through the gig economy for years. No longer is this economy reserved for those select few who understand it; it's available for you *now*. It's easier to pivot and benefit from this concept than you think. You just need to get in the right mindset. Let me show you how.

Pivot and expand at a fraction of the cost

I first became intrigued by the concept of the gig economy thanks to author and podcaster Tim Ferris. I was intrigued not only by the side-hustle aspect of his life but also how he leveraged people around the world who participated in the gig economy. For years, entrepreneurs would struggle to expand their businesses due to labour cost, lack of skills, and no access to economies of scale. As mentioned in the previous chapter, there are millions of talented people around the world who have made a career partnering with entrepreneurs for a fraction of the cost. Since there is a lower cost of living in places like India, Latin America, or the Philippines, hiring staff who can work remotely can work wonders. It's a win-win as they make great money relative to their cost of living and you save on labour cost while hiring quality talent. Everyone wins when you find the right talent to help you elevate your business.

If you are a business owner, you might find yourself feeling overwhelmed or short on time. There isn't enough time in the day or money in the bank to hire more staff. Enter the virtual assistant! For the last two years, I have been venturing into the world of virtual assistants. I have hired more than 10 personally to handle tasks that are necessary but do not directly relate to a high payoff. These could be simple things like bookkeeping, customer service, prospecting, video editing, social media management, and even meeting scheduling.

A virtual assistant (VA) can help solve all those problems I mentioned above and more. You can delegate tasks to your VA, giving you more time to focus on other parts of your business. Outsourcing a job, no matter how big or small, allows clients to focus on what they do best and let a VA do the rest.

Virtual assistants offer a range of services. They provide administrative, creative, and technical support services for your business. Some of the most common tasks include:

- email and client management
- website design and maintenance

- content creation and graphic design
- social media management
- content writing and research
- project management
- calendar management
- administrative tasks
- blogging or ghostwriting
- SEO

but the list goes on and on!

VAs work remotely, often from home or an office space on the other side of the world (90 per cent of my virtual assistants are from the Philippines). I hire them for research and editing for my YouTube channel, blogs, and to proofread for spelling mistakes in the book you are reading right now. Since VAs are independent contractors or working through an agency, you can negotiate the terms and payment structure. You can pay by the hour, or a VA may offer a bundle of hours that can be used over the month.

VAs can also charge per project; for example, they will have a flat fee for writing a blog post or creating a website. Some will offer packages, such as a social media package or a website maintenance package, that will also be charged as a flat fee, but you will get a variety of services in one. The gig economy can benefit everyone. Whether you want to create a side hustle in this economy by teaching piano, narrating books, copywriting, doing voice overs or delivering food on your spare time, you can add extra income with little risk. On the other hand, if you simply feel overwhelmed by mundane stuff that takes away from your core income generating tasks, consider this pivot as a way to grow you business, cut costs, and get back more time doing thing you love.

How I pivoted

Troy Assoignon, International Brand Positioning Expert and Conversion Rate Specialist, Troy Assoignon International

Before the pandemic, we traveled to more than 21 countries. The market was ripe for the picking. We chose to work with almost anyone and everyone. My name was built off the results I would get for people. That's one thing I strived for early on in my career.

I focused on brand positioning and brand development for small- to medium-sized companies. We had identified the characteristics and the type of person we were looking for, yet we weren't hyper focused on our marketing, as we had a full roster. My first thought was, *I'll just focus on the contracts we currently have and spend the majority of my time getting them results.* That worked for a while—and took up almost my entire life.

Eight months later, I realized I hadn't put much effort into promoting myself or my business, and that the market was contracting a bit. A client I had worked with four years prior was about to hit his first $200k+ year. He reported that due to the pandemic, he had dropped down to $40k/year because the strategy we created pre-pandemic was focused on restaurants. Fortunately, we had a diversification plan.

We had two big contracts that consumed over 70 per cent of our time, and the other 30 per cent was left over for some smaller contracts. I didn't realize how burnt out I was, but I kept moving forward the best I could. After a few contracts were completed, I took a bit of time off and realized we did two things *really* well:

- We helped a company create pitch deck assets, and they had raised $4.5 million dollars with the assets we created.
- We helped a company that was scaling their ad spend campaigns to $30–$100k/per month (depending on the season) slash their CPA (Cost Per Acquisition) almost in half.

We went from working with smaller companies to purposefully creating relationships with bigger companies and people on the inside of bigger companies. Why? They had the cash flow to weather the storm.

As much as the pandemic was a drag for many, it really separated the wheat from the chaff and forced people to either level up their game and change the game or level out and stay the same. The time, effort, and energy spent working on bigger projects seemed to be less, and we got paid larger fees to work with existing business assets and infrastructure. This made me realize I wanted to focus specifically on creating pitch assets for capital raises and spend more time on larger-budget media buying campaigns. When we have a larger advertising budget, we can *really* make an impact.

If you're going through a crisis and trying to figure everything out alone, realize that there are people around you who want to help, but sometimes they just don't know you need help. Make a hot list of people you've helped over the years, reach out, and see if they have any resources or ways to help you.

Another thing I always teach people I work with is to figure out a way to generate monthly revenue. If you can get clients on a monthly retainer, you can be taken care of for a long time. Think of a service that needs to be completed over and over again, instead of something that is project by project.

Troy Assoignon, International Brand Positioning Expert
Troy Assoignon International

How I pivoted

Ken Doll, CFP, CLU, TEP, Certified Financial Planner at Objective Wealth Partners Inc.

Society is the culmination of events, developments, and changes. Our world is not perfect and is a work in progress. And while it may be debateable, generally we are moving in the direction of a more advanced, sophisticated, and hopefully more tolerant world.

Along the way, several things have happened to bring us to our current point in time. One of those events that has had a dramatic impact upon us this past year is the COVID-19 pandemic. Our lives, work, routines, and expectations have been stretched to a place that only a year ago was unimaginable.

While the world is constantly changing around us, I define *pivot* through my eyes as a major change in my personal life. So, let's have a look at how this past year has impacted my life.

The biggest impact has been professional. When COVID-19 hit, I was working for a large national investment firm, commuting to the office, and doing my work there on a daily basis. A year before COVID-19, I was dealing with three hours of daily commuting by public transit. This meant getting up at 6 a.m., leaving for work at 7 a.m., and getting home around 7 p.m. Because of where I lived, this was my daily reality.

Consequently, I moved downtown, where my commute to work became a short walk. Suddenly, I gained three hours in my day. This was great. And while I enjoyed living downtown and in close proximity to many social activities, I was barely able to enjoy my new downtown apartment, as I was always gone working or socializing. But that's how life was—at least before COVID-19.

When COVID-19 hit, the company I was working for was not a fan of having its employees work from home, but it did have us set up for working remotely when the need arose. Little did we know that the need would end up being over a year of working remotely. We were not even allowed to access the office for several months. Things were changing—and changing faster than anyone could imagine.

In recent years, I had occasionally thought about how nice it would be to be able to work from anywhere: camping, at the beach, or on a road trip. In reality, at the beginning of 2020, the technology, and more importantly employers, were just not there yet. And I figured it would be many years before remote work would be a realistic option. Be careful what you wish for, as a year later, here we are. While COVID-19 has been devastating for many and I do not want to take away from that, it also brought about positive change at an exponential pace.

COVID-19 opened up my world in some ways and closed it in others. Here I was now enjoying my apartment more, as I only ventured out on weekends to see my girlfriend, who also had her work and life changed by the events of COVID-19. Also, since I no longer needed to go into the office, I moved out to the burbs, where life was less complicated and more relaxing. I now woke up at 8 a.m. and worked all kinds of crazy hours as I struggled with self-discipline and many distractions at home. Being a night owl by nature, the most productive part of my day was the evening, when the distractions of emails, calls, and meetings subsided. COVID-19 changed my sleep and work patterns, and that's just for starters.

This change in working conditions also brought about changes in work attire, with less formal dress, less dry-cleaning, and no need to shine my shoes. Below the belt, my wardrobe changed to shorts and flip-flops—that is, until plantar fasciitis required a dedicated pair of indoor sneakers. Although I had been a fashion aficionado, my clothing purchases shifted from suits and dress shirts to khaki shorts and T-shirts. The transition was well underway.

What difference does a year make? Well, if it's last year, a huge difference. As I was working exclusively from home, Zoom meetings replaced face-to-face meetings. There was no more commuting, and I missed the camaraderie I had shared with my office colleagues. It was quite a change. Add changes in sleeping hours, working hours, and daily attire, and the result is a lot of change in a year.

And there were more changes to come. Fast-forward to February 2021. I saw a job opening for a financial planner from a firm in Toronto. What was different about this opportunity was that it would mean 100 per cent working for a company in Toronto, from Calgary, and also working 100 per cent from home, as my office would now be 2,100 miles away. This opportunity would have never been possible a year earlier. Amazing how remote work leapfrogged ahead twenty years in one year.

However, not all was good. Aside from my plantar fasciitis, many people were having a real struggle to pay bills, keep their businesses alive and profitable, homeschool their children, try and keep safe, wear masks, and constantly wash their hands. Most important, of course, was the tremendous health toll that COVID-19 was having on many people, especially the elderly. I am very fortunate that my life changed in manageable ways, and I was not out of work or struggling to keep a business viable. For this, I am very grateful. But as I thought often during this time, I had also worked hard to advance my career and put myself in this secure position.

So here we are, after a year of living in a pandemic. Our world and our daily lives have changed immeasurably as we navigate these unchartered waters. And we now eagerly await the post-pandemic world and its yet-to-be defined new normal.

Kenneth Doll
Certified Financial Planner

CHAPTER 8
The Entrepreneur Mindset

That which you focus on will dictate
your results.—Michael Siervo

IMAGINE DRILLING A HOLE IN A PIECE OF WOOD. YOU HAVE THE right drill bit, a drill with enough torque, protective wear to make sure you are safe, a piece of wood safely secured, and a small pen mark to focus where you will lean in and apply just the right amount of pressure from the drill to the board. Eventually, your goal, which is a hole in the wood, will be accomplished.

Now, imagine having all the right tools and drilling all over the place—or, worse, drilling a hole but not applying enough pressure (effort), or using a dull drill bit (wrong tool), or giving up millimetres before puncturing that hole because you thought there wasn't enough progress happening. So you jump to another spot on the board to do the same. In the end, you mess up the board with partially created holes or divots in random places. Even worse, you've wasted time in the process.

This is similar to what is needed to be a successful entrepreneur, omnipreneur, or side-hustler. The Oxford Dictionary defines an *entrepreneur* as "a person who organizes and operates a business or businesses, taking on greater than normal financial risks in order to do so." Essentially, it's a brave soul who is willing to help launch a new venture or enterprise and accept full responsibility for the outcome. The only way to win in this new reality as an entrepreneur is to have a laser focus on the goals you want to achieve. It is that dot you marked in the wood that is important, as you put all your effort into focusing on that dot. Eventually, you will get the goal you want. In our analogy it's a perfect hole. As an entrepreneur, it's a successful business.

Without a goal, you have nothing to aim for. Being laser-focused requires becoming dedicated (no matter what) to achieving that goal. Having all the right tools, targets, and plans is great, but things can only come together effectively with the right mindset. I hear many people become experts in negative self-talk, which eventually leads them to talk themselves out of venturing into a business or pushing to the next level in life.

Here are a few statements people tell themselves that eventually, their subconscious mind believes:

- I am not very good at anything.
- That's not my skill set.
- The economy dictates the success of my business.
- I'm not a good salesperson.
- I'm really bad with names.
- I don't have a good-enough story.
- I'm not a numbers person.
- People don't return my phone calls.
- It's so hard to find clients.
- I suck at prospecting.
- I don't do well on video or social media.
- I hate the sound of my voice.
- The economy has changed.
- My business is seasonal.
- I don't come from a family of entrepreneurs.
- That idea doesn't work in my industry.
- Monday is office day.
- I don't have mentors.

Unless you change these statements or get rid of them altogether, nothing will change in your life. You will just come up with more negative self-talk. As in the book *As A Man Thinketh*, the subconscious mind cannot tell what is real and fake, good or bad, true or false. It just manifests what you tell it.

The first step in creating a solid entrepreneurial mindset is simply to become self-aware. Be aware of the words you say to yourself and to others. This will impact your personal and professional brand, something we will discuss in later chapters. What are you telling yourself? Do the words support your vision, or do they sabotage it?

The more self-aware you are, the more you become what you are saying and thinking, the more success you will attract in all aspects of your life. The sad thing is that many of our thoughts throughout the day tend to be negative. Our brain is conditioned to seek safety and avoid harm. We don't realize that if we don't train our brain to think with positivity and courage, we have already lost the battle.

Fail Forward; Fail Often

Changing your mindset to one of a positive and successful entrepreneur takes time. However, once self-awareness and emotional intelligence kick in, it becomes natural. Instead of the instinctive negative comments or words we tell ourselves—such as *bad, wrong, failure*—focus on the word *learning*. If you have ever followed me on social media, I always talk about the word *failure*. To *FAIL* simply stands for:

(**F**)ound
(**A**)nother
(**I**)mportant
(**L**)esson

You will fail at times, but if you view this as a lesson, you are also learning and growing. These experiences of failure will protect you from making the same mistake twice—or worse, making the same mistake when stakes are high.

The way you frame things will dramatically change your future. If you suck at remembering names and continue to tell yourself you suck at remembering names, you are reinforcing your weakness. You are programming your mind to believe that you are that weakness and that weakness is you. It is hard enough as an entrepreneur to go against the conventional wisdom of playing it safe; it's even worse to have someone in your head continuing to feed you self-defeating thoughts.

However, you can't just say the opposite, such as *I am great at remembering names*. Your mind will call bullshit on that and revert back to bad habits. For me, I eventually live in the future and make bold claims, but I work my way up to that so my mind and body are not fighting against me. I would think something like, *I'm in the process of remembering all names*.

If you keep telling yourself *I hate sales*, instead tell yourself, *I'm amazing at helping people*. From there, you can ask probing sales questions in meetings because you believe you are amazing at helping people.

Make sure to focus on what you want and not on things you don't want. If you are telling yourself *I don't come from a business-minded family*, you can try saying *My family has taught me to manage risk*. If you say *I can't find any profitable clients*, try saying *I have highly profitable clients coming my way*.

The movie version of *The Secret* highlights a great example involving Mother Teresa. She always said she would attend a peace rally but never an anti-war rally. If you focus on anti-war, you get war! Avoid negative tones and words and focus on positive affirmations. If you focus on not being poor, you will be poor. Instead, focus on being wealthy and successful. What you resist persists!

Mindset is everything. What you think about will dictate the results you get in business and in life. Your thoughts completely control your destiny in every facet of your life. Napoleon Hill frequently talks about the subconscious mind. We refer to this as an integral factor in harnessing the Laws of Attraction.

How I pivoted

Danny Hagan, CEO of Magnolia Yard & Tree

I. Failed. Again.

As lockdowns were starting to be announced, all I could hear in my head was *I. Failed. Again.*

In 2018, I started up Magnolia Yard and Tree, wanting to revolutionize the landscape industry. Sounds ridiculous, doesn't it? I had quite a few years of experience working in this industry and identified a number of different problems. I also had a number of friends in the industry with their own companies. Those were the people who laughed the loudest when I said it. In 2017, I had looked into a few different opportunities, and I stumbled upon an article saying how landscaping is one of the least franchised industries in North America. I couldn't stop thinking about it.

I received quite a few laughs when I told people I wanted to revolutionize the landscape industry. People would often ask, "Isn't landscaping something you were supposed to do as a summer job in high school?"

My response was always that those kids don't exist anymore.

"Isn't it a summer job for college kids?"

Those kids don't exist anymore. I'm sure there are a few out there, but as a whole, the number of high school and college kids taking summer jobs or labor jobs is at an all-time low.

The fact that people didn't seem to take our industry seriously motivated me even more. Even to this day, it's interesting to see the expression on people's faces when I tell them what I do. Someone even referred to me as a "yard janitor" at a business event once, and the group he was with all laughed. Yes, they were a bit boozy, but I still think of that moment every time I send that guy an invoice for monthly services, and I add 30 per cent to his bill.

As everyone laughed, all I could think was that this industry basically has zero respect and even less of an online presence. So, step one became creating that online presence. In the previous company I'd worked at, one of the owners told me Instagram wasn't really a sales tool. This is a very common mindset amongst almost all of the landscape business owners I've met (face palm emoji). My idea was that if we took the industry online and had our SOPs so dialed in that we were unbelievably efficient, it would shorten our employee training time. With the proper equipment, the physical load is lessened for everyone.

Seems simple, right? Yet nobody was doing it. We could lower our overhead by taking multiple site visits prior to the sale out of the equation. Why isn't anyone else doing this?

Step two was to set up a site where people could basically order their landscape construction projects and landscape maintenance online through our site or social media. Seems basic, doesn't it?

Industry: "This is an unbelievably complex process and pricing depends on a million different scenarios, which is why it can't be done."

Danny: "Game On."

Like any other start-up, 2018 was tough for me. I worked my ass off and did what I could to get things off the ground. I started with maintenance, because I needed to build up that consistent monthly flow of revenue. The biggest problem I ran into was that I focused on marketing to premium homes because of the premium I thought I could charge. I realized this was not the case because, while the dollars were higher, our time on site was even greater due to how picky the clients were. To say 2018 was a good year is an overstatement; 2019 was basically the same, but with $8,000 less in revenue. What was I doing wrong? I considered giving up about ten times a day.

We did snow removal in the winter, and I was out on site, as we were short-staffed, the day that lockdowns were announced. It was a Sunday afternoon, and I heard it on the radio. It was terrifying. All our phones on site started ringing, as our wives were calling us, worried about the virus, employment, child care, and a million other things. At the time, I had 37 contracts with almost 300 properties in place for the upcoming season, and within 48 hours, I had zero. This was the moment I thought, *I. Failed. Again.*

I called up my buddy Scott who does concrete and said, "Man, we can't let our families down. When everyone else is sitting on their hands, let's double down and explode our companies."

His response was, "This is why we are friends."

Up to this point in my life, every other idea I'd had failed— thirteen different businesses, actually. My mindset was wrong. I thought everyone else had connections I didn't. I had surrounded myself with people who I thought had sound advice but had never actually owned a business or even taken a risk in their lives—or they were in a completely different industry. What was I thinking? Why was I just doing things like every other landscaping business? How could I revolutionize an industry like this?

I need to do things my way, I told myself. I had wasted the past two years busting my ass just to be in the same boat as everyone else, and I had zero to show for it.

That was the day I started over. This was my pivot. I fired the girl who was doing my website and went to town building my own Shopify website, which I had zero experience in doing. Let everyone else panic; I was going to essentially start a new business from my old one. The day the lockdowns started was the day I started the nine-month process toward the 328 per cent growth of my company. I knew 2020 was going to be my year, because I'd eliminated so many unnecessary meetings with clients. I actually worked even fewer hours than the years prior.

The path to growth involved a lot of sleepless nights. The battery on my phone was dying about six times a day because I was on it nonstop, working referral sources, teaming up with other small businesses in the industry, but most importantly pumping up my website for people who wanted to order their landscaping online.

I won't go into more detail on the path to growth and the processes I've gone through to revolutionize my trade and expand into other cities, since that would likely take another 300 pages. As of right now, I'm one of the only landscape companies from which people can order installation through our website, MyTrees.ca. People still think I'm crazy. I think they are crazy for not wanting to wake up to a bunch of sales that happened overnight from zero effort, but to each their own.

I guess what I'm trying to say is that if there is one thing this pandemic has taught me, it is to be different. I've been different my whole life, but at the same time, I tried to be like everyone else. That was one of the biggest mistakes I've ever made. The reason I failed before was because I wasn't listening to and trusting myself. I put value in everyone else's opinion over my own. I guess you could say that being left with zero options by COVID-19 meant I had nothing to lose. I finally just went for it. It's unfortunate that this is what it took, but I'm thankful for that. Because of the pandemic, 2020 were hard, but it turned into one of the greatest and most valuable learning experiences of my life.

Being different is an entrepreneur's greatest asset, yet so many of us aren't trying to be different. Why is that? Keep in mind that *thinking* you're different and *being* different are two different things. Don't confuse them.

Danny Hagan
CEO of Magnolia Yard & Tree
www.mytrees.ca

How I pivoted

Alex Beneficto, CEO and Founder of Beebop Doughnuts

Our first pivot happened even before we came up with Beebop. We really wanted to open up a fine-dining restaurant in Calgary, and like most aspiring chefs, we wanted to do a 12-course tasting menu with complimentary *amuse bouche* in between courses. It would be locally sourced, sustainable, and really expensive.

We showed our plan to an accountant, and he flat-out told us we'd go broke in three months. We were devastated. He said that in his experience, most restaurants fail—and even if we manage to survive the first year, it would be hard to remain profitable.

So we went home depressed and wanting to give up on our dream of starting a business. My fiancé and I talked, and we decided that we needed to open something different that was scalable and with a low overhead. Long story short, we landed on opening up a doughnut shop.

The second pivot would be how we operated the business. Beebop was supposed to be self-serve. We had our display cases custom-built so that they could be accessed on both the operator and the customer side. Our whole operation was based on the fact that customers would be able to help themselves to our products without us physically leaving our work area.

When COVID-19 hit Canada, we were still determined to keep the self-serve concept. We even bought boxes of gloves for the customers to use. But eventually, we had to serve the customers ourselves as the pandemic worsened.

The other pivot we made involved our events room, which was located on the second floor of Beebop. We were planning on having birthday parties, exhibits, and a lot more in that space. It wasn't a big space, but there was enough room for what we had in mind. Unfortunately, gatherings were restricted, and social distancing needed to be followed, which made a small room even smaller.

Parties that were booked cancelled, events were postponed, and all of a sudden we were left with an unused space. But right now, we already have something awesome planned for that space, hopefully before the year ends.

During all of these challenges, we never blamed COVID-19. We said if it was not a pandemic, it would be a different set of challenges. I had always thought that being an entrepreneur meant having an idea and money. Yes, money can start a business, but would it be a great enduring business? For me, I've realized—and I cannot emphasize this enough—that an entrepreneur must, above all things, be a problem-solver. We don't blame external factors that we have no control over and let them decide the fate of our business. We try to see not problems but opportunities to give more value to our customers, whether it be a service, product, or convenience. Every challenge makes us better, even if we don't get it right all the time.

I am not saying we have it all figured out, nor am I saying that we are a success or we're at the level we want to be. In fact, we are far from it. But we are proud to say that we faced the challenges head-on and will continue to do so until we reach or exceed our goals. I guess for me, to be able to successfully pivot, you have to pivot toward your customers and be willing to give them value and exceed their expectations.

Alex Benedicto, Founder
Beebop Doughnuts
www.beebopdoughnut.com

CHAPTER 9

"Me" Incorporated

I am always doing that which I cannot do, in order
that I may learn how to do it.—Pablo Picasso

THE KEY THING ABOUT PIVOTING IS THAT YOU ARE UNLOCKING A new side of you or a new perspective. Sure, the pandemic—or any crisis for that matter—is a great catalyst for change, but ultimately, if change is done successfully with long-term results, it starts with you. It's really about unlocking your potential to go all-in with this pivot. If not, you might as well slap a band-aid to the hole in the ship and just wait for it to sink. You need to get into the right mindset and understand that just as Jay-Z said, "I am a business, man".

For the first few chapters, my focus was on the history of business, the impact of the pandemic, the rise and fall of specific sectors, and potential opportunities this pandemic may present. Understanding how we got here is imperative to having insight as to where the world is moving forward. This is crucial, as it highlights the importance of what is needed to navigate the world that lies ahead. South Korean politician and diplomat Bak Ki Moon said, "There is no precedent in living memory for the challenge that COVID-19 now poses to communities and world leaders." He is in his late seventies and has seen a lot. We are in uncharted territory. Although history doesn't always repeat itself, it certainly rhymes.

Helen Keller once wrote, "Although the world is full of suffering, it is also full of overcoming it." She wrote that in a time when many felt that all was lost and that there was no hope. Today is no different. Many have lost a lot and continue to lose a lot. However, I believe that Helen Keller was right. We will overcome the suffering. In order to do this, ultimately, it comes down to mindset. This book is meant to not only give you tangible ideas that you can easily flip to but also inspire you and plant some key seeds so that your plans can be executed and sustained over time.

During this pandemic and throughout most of the world's challenges, we seek out motivational and inspirational quotes to uplift us. I, for one, have been a fan of them but have also cringed at the idea of them. Motivation and inspiration are temporary unless accompanied by the right mindset and a plan that can be executed over a substantial amount of time. For example, we all want to get in shape at the beginning of the year. However, come February, we have convinced ourselves that eating that bag of potato chips won't throw us off our workout plan. By June, we have completely given up.

The latter half of this book will highlight ideas, concepts, and techniques to help you thrive in this post pandemic world. Forget about the pandemic. Who knows? By the time this book is even published the pandemic may have passed already. That's not the point. Many of the concepts can still be used regardless of a pandemic. It's really all about how to pivot and grow into something better than you are today. You will want to utilize and perfect some of the ideas in the latter half of the book, just like the motivated guy who wants to get rid of his love handles at the beginning of the year. The question is whether you can sustain it. This is where mindset comes in.

There are many great books out there—such as *Think and Grow Rich* by Napoleon Hill, *Seven Habits of Highly Effective People* by Stephen Covey, or *As a Man Thinketh* by James Allen—that can help you get into the right mindset. Those books are timeless classics. Even modern-day books such as *Rich Dad Poor Dad* by Robert Kiyosaki helped change the way I viewed business, money, and cash flow. All of these can really help your mindset, and I highly recommend you read them. At the end of this book is a list of amazing books to help you on your journey.

However, for the purposes of this book, we will cover a very simple concept that will help prepare you for what lies ahead. Whether you are currently a business owner or are looking into the gig economy to generate more money (let's face it, who wouldn't like more money?), having the boss mindset is imperative. I call this the mindset of "Me" Incorporated. You simply have to go that extra step to thrive in this new reality.

It is never crowded at the top. Zig Ziegler said, "There are no traffic jams on the extra mile." Go the extra mile. Do more of what is asked of you. Your goal must be to get good, get even better, and then make yourself indispensable.

The Future Belongs to the Competent

Position yourself for tomorrow, as the future belongs to the competent. The future belongs to those who are good at what they do and are committed to getting better. Pat Riley once said, "If you're not committed to getting better at what you are doing, you are bound to get worse." Essentially, this means that anything less than a commitment to excellence at what you do is an unconscious acceptance of mediocrity.

In the past, you could get by with being average at your job. You could rise above if you were excellent at your job. In today's ultracompetitive environment, excellence is necessary if you want to keep your job for the long term. Stay committed to increasing competency. Your future depends on it.

Take Charge of Your Income

> You must take personal responsibility. You cannot change the circumstance, the season, or the wind, but you can change yourself. That is something you are in charge of.—Jim Rohn

People who take full responsibility for their lives and the decisions they make tend to be more successful and happier, have more self-control, and earn more than the average person. Studies have shown that the top 3 per cent in any industry have a unique attitude that makes them stand out. They view themselves as self-employed. They act as if they personally own the company they work for. They take a vested interest.

In addition, they have a true entrepreneurial mindset. The biggest mistake you can make is to think you work for anyone else but yourself. No matter who pays you, you are always self-employed. You are the CEO; you are a one-employee enterprise that is responsible for selling one thing—your personal services. You are the president, CEO, VP of marketing, and human resources department for your own personal services corporation and the boss of your life. You are completely responsible for everything that happens to both it and you.

Unhappy with how much you are making? Go to the mirror and talk to your boss. Negotiate how much you are worth, and then prove it. All of us are where we are in life, making what we make in life, doing what we are doing to survive in that life, and feeling how we feel in life because we decided this was true. Not happy with your career? Change it.

As the boss of your personal corporation, everything that affects your business impacts your personal life as well. They go hand in hand. How many times have you had a shitty day at work only to come home and argue with your spouse, take out your frustration on your family, or worse, take it out on yourself by abusing your body with alcohol or drugs? As the boss, you don't have the luxury of standing by and letting things happen, or your company will sink and fail.

I was playing golf one day, and one of the players in my foursome picked up random trash on the course and threw it in the garbage. My partner said, "You can always tell the owners and members of the golf club. Losers say, 'That's not my job.' Winners say, 'This is my company. Everything is my job.'"

In today's fast-paced business environment, every new concept, discovery, technique, or innovation is as relevant to your one-person corporation as it is to a multi-billion-dollar corporation. All the new articles and techniques on marketing or social dynamics that come from business thinkers can be applied to you. Those who commit to growing and finding efficiencies or continually looking for new ideas and insights will thrive rather than just survive.

Being the executive and president of the company of *you*, your goal must be to become a market leader. If you are not committed to being excellent, you are accepting mediocrity and potential extinction. If you are not getting better, you are getting worse. If you are not getting stronger, you are getting weaker. If you are not growing, you are dying. If you are not committed to having the mindset of being in the top 10 per cent of people in your field, you will surely end up far below. It is only a matter of time before complacency leads to irrelevance, which will then lead to the closure of your business. The pandemic doesn't care what stage you are in or what industry you operate in. You must have a forward-thinking mindset to adjust and pivot at every twist and turn. As boss of "Me" Incorporated, you must think strategically and ask whether your efforts towards a decision will set you up for future success. The future income of "Me" incorporated depends on it.

One example of being forward-thinking and taking charge of one's income is a small personal development and fashion organization called Spotlight Couronne Internationale. Five years ago, I met the two founders of this organization. Alvin Francia and Limuel Vilela were two high-energy individuals who were passionate about fashion and how it helped bring confidence to models. I knew nothing about them except that they posted a lot of travelling, personal style, and lifestyle pictures on social media. When I did more research, I learned that they both worked at WestJet, a Calgary-based airline. This explained the amazing travel photos that caught my attention, as it seemed like these two jetsetters were living the life.

One day, I received a meeting request from Limuel Vilela, CEO and Co-Founder of the company. Given that I admired what I saw from him on social media, I took the meeting to hear more about him and the story behind this organization. His background was impressive, from being an abandoned child living a doghouse in the Philippines to earning an education worthy of employment in Canada. His business partner, Alvin, was equally impressive, as they both grew beyond their humble immigrant beginnings to become one of the largest fashion-show organizations in Western Canada.

To get to that point, their story was riddled with pivots. The one that is relevant to taking control of one's income came when the pandemic hit. For five years, both Alvin and Limuel had organized the Calgary International Fashion and Arts Week. This annual show raised money and awareness for charities ranging from anti-bullying to cancer to most recently the Calgary Food Bank, while highlighting some of the best up-and-coming designers from around the world. Given the importance of putting on a good show, the recruitment of talented models was crucial. This meant lots of runway training and hours of personal development to instill confidence. With thousands of eyes watching and hundreds of photographs that would live on social media forever, models needed to have the confidence to slay the runway. This red-carpet event drew 400 to 500 guests every year for one night of glamour and fashion. The online shows received over 100,000 live views from all around the world.

As a passion project, the organization was never meant to be a sole source of income. Then the pandemic hit. The partners' primary source of income from WestJet was jeopardized as travel halted and layoffs ensued. Like thousands of people around the world, the two were laid off. Rather than simply accepting government subsidies while waiting for the economy to turn around, they pivoted and took control of their income. After reviewing the inventory of skills and resources they had available, they shifted gears into several new ventures.

With financial opportunities scarce in the fashion world, the two reached out to designers around the world to manufacture fashionable masks as soon as the pandemic hit. Leveraging their brand and following, not only did they provide income for these designers, but the sale of these masks doubled the income they were making during their full-time jobs at the airline. Further doubling down, they created a handmade accessories line that sold online.

With no official work in sight, the two took the time to enrol in formal education. They expanded their skill set into videography, business, and digital marketing. This allowed them to pivot what was once an annual fashion event into a full-time career in training for fashion modelling, pageant shows, and overall confidence. As a result, they expanded their studio to include photography, fitness, and runway training.

To this day, they are booked solid for twelve hours a day for weeks at a time, and they are seeking expansion into a larger studio as well as an international operation in Asia. When the prospects of employment income seemed bleak, they turned their passion into a revenue generator that surpassed the income they were making before the pandemic. What was initially a moment of stress and crisis turned into one of abundance and good fortune. To this day, I joke around with them as Alvin recalls how he mentioned to me 5 years ago that "We are not business people and know nothing about how to run a business." Funny how things have changed when the "Me" Incorporated mindset takes over. This is an example of leveraging whatever skills you have, enhancing those skills, expanding a side hustle, and multiplying your income. Many small pivots can add up to a massive career change in which opportunities surpass those which were present prior to facing adversity.

The 7 Rs to Pivoting Your Career

You don't need to own a business to pivot in business. Remember, you are the business, so pivoting in your career comes with the territory. I mentioned that you don't have to be an entrepreneur to have the "Me" Incorporated mindset. Everyone should have this mindset and take ownership of the income-generating machine. This machine is you!

As much as side hustles are attractive (and necessary), I have always been a supporter of the idea that you should leverage your ability to thrive in a career path that best suits your skill set and fulfillment level. Just because you have a goal of leaving your current day job to pursue a side hustle full time doesn't always mean it's wise. Modern management theory helps increase your probability of career success, which in turn can provide a strong foundation for your next pivots. The reality is, it's foolish to follow the romantic ideal of dropping everything and pursuing your dreams—going balls in without a parachute. That's nuts, and quite frankly, it's careless. When they put it in practice, most people find they don't have the temperament and grit to do it. Most people who venture into their own hustles *will* fail.

This is why I truly believe it's imperative to maximize your day job, find happiness in it, and use it as an eventual springboard to fund your side hustle. But before you can do that, it's important to assess how you can increase your career success before risking it all on an entrepreneurial dream. To increase your career success, you should familiarize yourself with what Brian Tracy calls the 7 Rs:

1. Rethinking
2. Re-evaluating
3. Reorganizing
4. Restructuring
5. Re-engineering
6. Reinventing
7. Refocusing

Rethinking

It's important to think and reflect on who you are and where you want to go. If you don't know where you are going, you might end up somewhere you don't want to be. Rethinking who you are as a person and what makes you happy is the start of determining if a change or pivot will take place. What fulfills your heart from a career perspective? This is crucial, especially when you are feeling lost, disoriented, discontented, or dissatisfied with your current situation.

I've referenced Simon Sinek's TED Talk on finding your *why*. As corny as it sounds, understanding what gets you up in the morning and what keeps you going is crucial. Given how life changes frequently, it's a good idea to rethink and replan the direction of your career. I have done this on an annual basis for the last decade. I ask myself, *Can I do this for another year?* Depending on what the answer is, I will know what direction I'm facing.

Re-evaluating

Similar to rethinking, you use this time to take a step back and look at your current situation in terms of the marketplace. Re-evaluating your situation from a career standpoint allows you to see if you are on the right track. After answering whether or not you could continue doing this for another year, you will need to re-evaluate that thought to determine whether it's based solely on emotion or backed by logic.

Often, when we feel stress or problems occur in our careers, much of it has to do with working in the wrong environment, wrong company, wrong team, or wrong surroundings—all factors that don't bring out the best in you. Your dissatisfaction may come from selling something you don't believe in or working for a company that doesn't share your values. You must put effort toward excellence. This can never be done when your heart's not in it.

This is when reality sets in and you must find the courage to admit that change is needed. Make sure that the work environment you spend the vast majority of your life in is in alignment with your values so that your talents, abilities, and desires are maximized. Another strategy that I have done is to give myself 10 straight days. If I wake up for 10 straight days and am not happy, fulfilled, excited, or motivated, I know I am due for a change. It doesn't mean you will quit your job right then and there, but it may indicate that it's time to re-evaluate your plan of action moving forward.

Reorganizing

Reorganizing allows you to examine what exactly you do on a daily basis and to work toward your goals. During this phase, it's important to assess whether your actions are logical, efficient, and aligned with who you are or whether you need to do things differently to get better results.

Once again, the concept of increasing competency plays a role, as new skills or techniques will allow you to perform with greater efficiency. By reorganizing, you can increase your output and results relative to your input of time, energy, and resources. I always lay out all my assets, skills, resources, talents, funds, and so on if I am going to make a career decision. I reorganize my time and my day. Perhaps I am unsatisfied because I'm inefficient with my day or I am not utilizing the right resources. Imagine trying to saw down a tree with a hammer. You can have all the determination in the world, but you don't have the right tool. Unless you are Thor, the God of Thunder, I doubt you can cut that tree down with a hammer.

Restructuring

Restructuring your activities is the phase in which you look at specific things and activities you do that contribute the most to your company of one and provide the maximum value to customers. Understand the Pareto Principle and focus more of your time, energy, and resources on the 20 per cent of your activities that contribute 80 per cent of value. We tend to mistake being busy for being productive. Focus on high-payoff activities instead of just being busy for the sake of being busy.

Successful people are simply those with successful habits.—Brian Tracy

Re-engineering

When re-engineering your personal business, you assess the processes you have in place from start to finish. What do you do the first thing in the morning that gets you to produce the most for your company and for your clients? For me, the first thing I do immediately when I wake up is meditate. No matter how much I may not feel like doing it, I know the impact it has on my mindset. It gives me the clarity to make wise decisions and the focus I need to win my day. For an athlete, perhaps it starts off with what they eat every day. That healthy fuel allows them to perform at an optimal level.

From there, you analyze the process and look for ways to improve yourself, reduce steps, consolidate activities that can be done together, or find opportunities to outsource tasks to more qualified and skilled people. Reengineering is an ongoing process of streamlining your day to maximize results. It involves focusing on how you spend the one asset you have that is not replenishable: time.

Reinventing

This phase is an amazing time to exercise creativity and put out certain energy to the universe. It is where imagination can go wild. Imagine how it would be if you had to start over. If your job or industry disappeared, what would you do? What if you had to relocate; how would you recreate your life? What if you entered a new industry; how would you brand yourself and stand out? What would you do differently if you were not scared? Where would you be in three to five years? What changes would you do in order to manifest the ultimate life? What would you need to sacrifice today to get everything you want tomorrow?

If you could reinvent your life, what would you do? The easiest way to answer many of these questions is to ask yourself what truly makes you happy and what you would need to do to feel that way for the rest of your life. When I transitioned and pivoted earlier in my career from Toronto to Calgary, I knew that I could completely reinvent myself. And so I did. I dressed differently. I explored restaurants I wouldn't have typically gone to. I went outside of my comfort zone to meet new people. I took that opportunity to completely reinvent myself into who I wanted to become.

This will happen many times in your career. When the initial fear of uncertainty is replaced by the excitement of reinventing yourself, the sky's the limit, and a new version of yourself is born.

MICHAEL SIERVO

Refocusing

> *Energy is never created or destroyed; it can only be*
> *changed from one form to another—Albert Einstein*

When we refocus, we really harness the laws of attraction. This ultimately is the key to your future and all that will make you happy. When you decide what you want, rethink your current situation, reengineer your processes, and reinvent yourself, you must refocus all your energy to that one goal and all the small steps you determined you need to do.

Over time, when you focus on all of these habits, activities, processes, and steps day in and day out, your life will change. I continually say, where focus goes, energy flows. What you focus on is so crucial. Perhaps your pivot is simply refocusing on what you love about your career or your life rather than what gets under your skin.

Most people are unsuccessful in life because they don't focus on the right things. They spend too much time on things that contribute little to their lives. They spend more time on things that add little value, such as complaining, sitting around, convincing themselves that being busy is productive, or worrying that they don't make enough money. Complaining won't fix any of those things.

Successful people have laser-sharp focus and are intentional in every action. Everything they do is toward the goal of improving their lives. They focus on the small things that make a big difference over time, and they do these things very well. This is the secret to every successful person.

Mastering your mind and your actions when going through the 7 Rs will reinforce discipline and habits that will transform you into the leader your one-person company deserves. Welcoming change despite discomfort and mastering the forces of change will ensure that you regain control of your life. You become the architect or author of your own life. Knowing that you have a system and plan in place to accept the positive changes that are necessary allows you to own any situation regardless of how unpredictable it may be. You are unfazeable. You have taken ownership and responsibility. You oversee your present and future situation. The future is yours. Design it with purpose and live the life you deserve.

How I pivoted

Andy Deonarine, CEO of CannSell and Managing Partner of Exodus Las Vegas

I'm no stranger to ups and downs as an entrepreneur. I have experienced changes in trends, the economy, and even the loss of lives through senseless violence at my beach club and restaurant in Mexico in 2017. Pivoting when confronted with the unexpected is not new to me.

However, the COVID-19 global pandemic has affected my businesses and those of my colleagues in ways nobody could have expected. The uncertainty, ever-changing projections, moving goalposts, and lack of ability to understand whether the end is near or not, combined with the long-term effects that shutdowns are having on consumer habits, have left many of us struggling to see the next move.

Currently, I am CEO of CannSell (www.cannsell.ca), a Managing Partner of Exodus Las Vegas (www.exoduslasvegas.com), and a consultant for global events. I have spent the last 20-plus years in industries targeting adults while navigating highly regulated environments in Canada, the USA, and the Caribbean. I fine-tuned these skills during a five-year stint at British American Tobacco, where I assisted with brand communication through ever-changing legislation around packaging and advertising. My experience has allowed me to become a trusted voice for regulatory-driven industries wishing to implement best-in-class communication practices. I have supported global teams from brands like Bud Light, Grey Goose, Moet, and Johnny Walker through large-scale events that force trial and drive sales through experiences that engage adults.

All of this experience was a natural transition into cannabis as the world's first G7 nation, Canada, legalized it for recreational and medical purposes on October 17, 2018. In my role at CannSell, I oversee the sole mandated training of all cannabis retail-store employees in the province of Ontario, Canada. We had planned to create world-class cannabis trade events and even built a mock retail store to take on the road to organizations and train groups in person.

These were going to be the differentiating factors in creating a brand beyond just an education web portal. However, both went out the window by the time we were able to close the acquisition in September 2020. The pandemic forced us to pivot and build a new strategy in an environment filled with uncertainty. We took the opportunity to optimize our online training program. We did a deep dive into the user experience, payment options, and overall content. We worked with our team and instructors to create live webinars for organizations to be certified over a full day. I do feel lucky.

They say timing is everything. If this pandemic had hit a couple of years prior, I do not know what situation my family and I would be in. To be honest, my daughter has been the most resilient in our household. She has not missed a beat even though she has spent the year in virtual school and with limited contact with her friends while stuck in our cubbyhole on the 32nd floor of downtown Toronto. By contrast, my wife and I have struggled to stay motivated and to keep active. Every day feels the same, but we push forward, focused on our businesses and trying to keep sane while we ride out this pandemic.

But when does it end? At times, we are left confused, discouraged, and wondering if staying in business is the right idea. They say strategy without action is only a daydream, but action without strategy is a nightmare. How do you create a strategy without knowing what the future holds? How do you initiate action when government policy and recommendations around COVID-19 restrictions change every few days? While one business of mine seems to be flourishing in this new environment, another hangs by a thread.

For over a decade, Exodus Las Vegas has been a premier service for those around the globe looking to experience Vegas's nightlife like a VIP. We work in partnership with the best venues in world-class hotels like the Wynn, Encore, Caesars Palace, and the MGM Grand. As you can imagine, with travel closed, social events cancelled, and the hospitality industry crushed by COVID-19, we had to essentially shut the business down.

Many of my close friends are also entrepreneurs. Some have found a way to flourish, whether that has been through a business that happened to be perfect for a pandemic or through taking chances and making changes to their strategy. Others have been left in limbo. While we are fortunate to be in Canada, where the government has provided help through subsidies, these will end soon. I am hopeful that we can go back to bringing thousands to Vegas in the summer.

Things have changed for us, no doubt. Our approach this season is more focused. Every penny is being scrutinized, and we rely on data more than ever to make our decisions. At the same time, we are aware of our responsibility to keep people safe and that the experiences we used to provide may be different when we emerge from the pandemic. I feel for everyone in the hospitality and events business globally. Many of us eat, sleep, and breathe this industry, and the rug was pulled out from under us overnight.

However, I am confident this industry will come roaring back. Once it is deemed safe, I believe people will want to celebrate, dance, and party alongside their friends, rubbing elbows and hugging each other like it is New Year's Eve for months on end.

Over the last year, I've had to be less rational and begin to move toward a more positive mindset to get me through this pandemic. We all know that better times are ahead. We are resilient, and I'm positive a bright future lies ahead if you can weather the storm and persevere.

Andy Deonerine
CEO of CannSell
Managing Partner of Exodus Las Vegas

CHAPTER 10

You Are the Brand!

I'm not a businessman. I'm a business, man.—Jay-Z

I REMEMBER SEEING A GREAT MEME ON INSTAGRAM OF THE FAMOUS rapper Jay-Z that said, "I'm not a businessman. I'm a business, man." Jay-Z went from selling drugs on the street to becoming a billionaire. He is the business.

Whether you love him or hate him, another great example is Donald Trump. He is the business. Some may know him as a real estate mogul, former president, government disruptor, and social media loose cannon. The reality is that Trump is his brand. Prior to being the former US president, the Trump name for years was notorious for extravagant things. His hotels were decadent and posh. He was known as an upscale character. The brand tells people what to expect from you.

Now, just as important as building a brand into one that is recognizable is to maintain congruence and be consistent with what you represent. Some would say that Trump has lost his way and effectively destroyed his brand. As the saying goes, "It takes years to build a brand and seconds to destroy it."

So what's in a brand, and why am I a brand?

Like it or not, people attach you to an expectation. How you dress, how you speak, what you post on social media, what causes you support, what profession you are in, and something as simple as what you drive—they all tell the audience something about you. This could be intentional or not, but people are judging you based on the information you put out.

In the past, people would hide behind the brand of their company and not their personal brand. This might have worked out in the past, but companies come and go. What is more powerful these days is the brand of the entrepreneur.

I remember watching an episode of Dragon's Den. The entrepreneur was pitching something (I can't even remember what it was). All the dragons had a smile on their face as the entrepreneur did his sales pitch. In the end, he got more than what he was asking for. It wasn't the business plan he was pitching to the dragons that won him the funding, it was his personality. Billionaire businessman Mark Cuban, owner of the NBA Dallas Mavericks, said something along the lines of, "I am not 100 per cent sure that you will succeed at this business, but I am 100 per cent sure you will give it your all." Mr. Wonderful, Kevin O'Leary, essentially reinforced this by saying that we want to invest in you because we believe in you as an entrepreneur.

With any sales pitch, investors will invest if they believe in the entrepreneur. They know that nothing is perfect and things will change, but the savvy entrepreneur will adapt and adjust regardless of what curveballs the world throws at him.

In today's world, the brand of the company isn't as important as the visionary entrepreneur steering the ship. Steve Jobs was brilliant at this. He convinced everyone of his vision of Apple and how it would change the world. He wasn't even a computer programmer, yet he founded one of the greatest companies of all time. In fact, this book is being written on a MacBook while my iPhone is playing binaural beats on my Apple AirPods.

Steve Jobs was a master at product launches and painting a world in which Apple would change our lives. Dell and IBM made great computers, Samsung and Google had better cameras on their phones, and Microsoft has an amazing tablet. However, people believed in Steve Jobs and his vision, not necessarily the product.

Another example that comes to mind and is more timely today is Elon Musk. He bordered on bankruptcy many times as he went all-in on his projects. His Tesla 3 was delayed for months. The company was burning through capital, and he had to choose between SpaceX or Tesla. If he kept both, there was a possibility that he would lose both. He became the lead designer for SpaceX and many other projects because he couldn't afford good ones at the time.

In the end, people kept pumping money into his companies. He always got funding, and he always delivered. Even when he didn't deliver, he delivered. When he claimed that the window of his cyber truck wouldn't break if you threw a brick at it, he threw a brick at it on stage. Lo and behold, it the window broke. In true Elon fashion, he took that failure and admitted the mistake as a learning experience.

As an entrepreneur and human being in this new post-pandemic world, you must be cognizant of your brand. Now more than ever, *you* are the brand. This all about the "Me" Incorporated mindset. Even if you don't have any business at the moment, focus on building your social profile so that if and when an idea comes up, it is aligned with what people expect. If not, you'll be playing catch-up trying to build a brand while potential customers go to the guy selling the same product, with the only difference being that he has a better digital presence on Google or social media.

If you are working with millennials, this is even more crucial as statistics tell us that millennials are analytical and do their research before doing business with someone. Here are a few quick stats to ponder on:

- 57 per cent of Canadian LinkedIn users are 25 to 34 years of age; 22 per cent of LinkedIn users are 35 to 54 (Statista, 2020).
- 41 per cent of millionaires have a profile on LinkedIn (Forbes, 2018).
- 55 per cent of consumers look online for reviews and recommendations (KPM, The Path to Purchase Journey, 2017).

Don't view social media as a tool for you to find business. Use it as a way for consumers to validate why people should do business with you.

Be like Mandela

I clearly remember the day when the great Nelson Mandela died. It was December 5, 2013. I was and still am deeply interested in the area of personal self-development and leadership, so when Mandela died, I was in shock. He was known as one of the world's greatest leaders. He led a country through some of the most difficult times in history. I wanted to post something on social media to pay homage to him, so I googled his name for a quote. The one that jumped out to me was: "There is no passion to be found in playing small—in settling for a life that is less than the one you are capable of living."

I have even heard Oscar-winner Denzel Washington use this quote in a commencement speech on YouTube. It's quite powerful. I scrolled for more quotes and found others, such as, "It always seems impossible until it's done." Or "It is not where you start but how high you aim that matters for success."

If you didn't know of Nelson Mandela, you could have easily mistaken these for the words of a motivational speaker. However, Mandela spoke from the perspective of a leader seeking freedom and equality during a time of racism. He focused on the freedom for people to live a better life. The lesson we can take from Mandela is that no matter what happened in his personal life and the flaws he carried as a human being, we know him for how he branded himself. We know him for what he represented. This is the importance of creating a personal brand. It is the core of self-definition, self-awareness, and accountability.

If you work for yourself, your personal brand will effectively resonate in your marketing material, bio, business card, logo, social media profile, online photos, etc. The great thing is that you are no-holds-barred and can go crazy on whatever you want to brand yourself as.

If you are an employee, your personal brand can leverage the existing brand of the company you work for. This usually means that the company has a larger brand than yours. If you don't like the brand of the company and are there for just a paycheque, you might want to find a company that you believe in, as if you are inadvertently leveraging your employer's brand anyways.

A great example of this was when I was building up my profile in the financial-services industry. I would only work for large reputable companies. Since I was a newbie to the industry, I needed credibility. For me, I leveraged a big brand to elevate my non-existent credibility. Throughout my career the brand I was always attached to was that I worked on big deals, with big companies that had big ideas. I am not saying to only work for big companies. Perhaps you want to brand yourself as someone who loves the energy of a start up company and truly embraces the entrepreneurial grind. If so, work for smaller, more nimble firms that allow you to grow and impact the direction of the company in a more meaningful way. Whatever your preference is, even as an employee, you need to brand yourself so that your peers and superiors know exactly what they can expect from you.

If you are in a leadership role, being cognizant of your brand is important. If people view you as a tyrant, they may only do what is asked of them out of fear and nothing more. If they truly respect you, you can get more out of them, voluntarily or involuntarily. This is the difference between being a leader and a manager.

So when we think about brands, we often automatically think of companies. If you follow Jay-Z's mindset, you are not a businessperson, you *are* the business. You are "Me" Incorporated. Knowing this allows you to make sure that all your actions are in alignment with what you believe. Having this mindset creates a clear image of yourself that will help you in every aspect of your life. As a result, your business will prosper, and so can other areas of your life.

Creating the Brand

Now that we know the importance of branding, how do you create a personal brand in this post-pandemic world? First, it's not as simple as hiring a graphic designer to create a logo for you to slap on all your social media posts. That's not a bad idea, but it's not everything about creating an effective and memorable brand that truly helps you stand out. Again, this new world has opened up the market and has made life more competitive than ever before. You're not only focusing on local markets but on customers who can easily buy the same thing from vendors all around the world.

There are several ways to formulate a brand. For me, I have essentially followed five basic fundamentals that helped me craft my personal brand:

1. *What is your WHY?*—your core purpose
2. *What is your HOW?*—how you will differentiate yourself from the rest
3. *What is your WHAT?*—what you do in terms of your character that stands out
4. *What is my WHO?*— the people you plan to service or associate yourself with
5. *What is your WHEN?*—When it comes down to choosing me or my competition, why should you believe my brand?

> *Your brand is what other people say about you*
> *when you're not in the room.*—*Jeff Bezos*

Branding is so crucial. For years, people would question why I would be active on social media, post on different forums, speak on different stages across the country, submit articles to different publications, or launch podcasts and YouTube channels. On the surface, it looks really self-serving, and likes and comments became a vanity metric. What many people didn't know is that I was following what Gary Vayerchuck had been preaching: no matter what, everyone needs to be cognizant of their brand.

Essentially, everyone needs to have a brand. Let me repeat: *everyone* needs to have a brand. If you don't establish your brand, society will establish one for you.

This idea of a brand is so crucial, even if you don't have a business, because one day you may need to use your brand to open up doors to opportunities. It is essentially the golden key to any pivot. If you are like the Kardashians, you can slap your name on anything, and it will be successful. The product isn't as important; it's the strength of the brand. Once you have a reputable brand, it's easier to get meetings with influencers, negotiate funding from potential investors, gain trust from an audience, and simply have an audible voice in this already noisy world.

Let's spend some time on expanding this brand of yours.

Why are you here?

We all believe that deep down inside, we have this unique special skill or talent to contribute. This makes us all different, but we all use the same language to describe ourselves. Just go on LinkedIn and check out profiles of real estate agents and insurance salespeople; the majority of them sound the same. Branding is about attraction, and it all starts with telling your audience your unique core purpose and why they should continue listening.

Your *why* or your core purpose is not a short-term idea. This is something you need to commit to, as it will follow you throughout any pivot you do now and in the future. It's not like an annual business plan with a deadline. This is a serious, long-term, potentially permanent thing that is attached to you by the hip. So let's spend some time looking into this.

First off, if you are going to create a brand, avoid using the same buzzwords that are sprinkled in every résumé that comes across someone's desk. We are all motivated, enthusiastic, passionate, driven, blah blah blah. Find words that resonate with your audience on a much deeper level. The best way to do this is to start with *why*.

Simon Sinek, bestselling author of the book *Start With Why*, nails it in his famous TED Talk. He busted open the gates to the whole world of finding core purpose, which has become a cultural phenomenon in both business and personal life. Simon Sinek preaches that "people don't buy what you do; they buy why you do it."

So if you've pivoted to selling homemade pastries made exactly like they bake them in this remote village in Italy by using Neapolitan ingredients as a way to preserve your culture, tell it in your story. Paint the picture of how you want everyone to experience the joy you had as a child biting into a coconut Italian cream cake or munching on Italian pignoli cookies at Christmas. Or perhaps you only use local ingredients from suppliers within a 50 kilometre radius because your farm-to-plate strategy is legit and you are a diehard local supporter.

Whatever your why is, tell a story and paint a picture that screams authenticity. We attract people to us when they believe what we believe. Most people talk about what they do and how they do it, but they miss the *why* they do it. That's a massive opportunity lost.

Make sure your Why is interesting

So many people are side-hustling homemade cupcakes on weekends or sewing homemade masks. Your side hustle to do photography is like everyone who learned to use filters on their iPhone or bought a DSLR camera and some lights. It's not unique, and it's uninspiring.

Don't take it personally. I'm not discrediting those side hustles; any side hustle is better than zero side hustles. However, if it comes to someone choosing your services versus someone else's, you need to find a way to stand out. Try printing unique designs on your cupcakes or infusing them with CBD if that's your thing. Maybe specialize your photography on boudoir pics, or be the expert at camera tricks using your iPhone. Whatever it is, now is the time to step outside of the comfort zone and stand out.

What makes you different?

In order to be irreplaceable, one must
always be different.—Coco Chanel

In a world where everyone is trying to make an extra buck to survive this pandemic, the competition for generic services increases. This means your voice can get easily lost in the crowd. So what makes you different?

This can be a frightening question to answer. We know deep down that you are different, but at the same time, most industries are competitive. In many cases, we are trying to do something similar to the next guy, just better. Be honest with yourself and don't believe in your own hype. Put yourself in the customers shoes and ask yourself "If this patron were to write a review about how a positive experience they had about your business, what would they write? What is makes my business stand out from other businesses selling the same product or service?"

Being different doesn't have to a massive shift to your business model. It could be the small things that patrons and customers notice. Things such as a special greeting when people walk through the door, an extra serving of bread when the competition charges, a video birthday greeting from the owner, or a beer mug set aside for a regular patron with his name on it, or a free pick up or drop off service to make your life more convenient. These little things reek of effort and care. These things make your business awesome and different.

Sho Sushi: Winning and Prevailing through Pivoting

The Japanese translation of *sho* is "to win, be victorious, to prevail." I think this word is important in any crisis. We all want to win during a difficult battle. Pivoting to be different is not only crucial for your brand but really risky, especially if you have established a solid name for yourself. How do you stand out in a crowded space then?

Let's take Japanese food for instance. I don't know many people who don't love Japanese food. How could you not? The flavour. The attention to detail. The experience. A perfectly sliced piece of unagi on a compact bed of rice accompanied by some high-end bluefin tuna is to die for.

However, sushi restaurants are a dime a dozen. They are literally everywhere. So how do you stand out and make people come in droves to try your food and soak up the experience? You make sure your product stands out while your brand is being reinforced.

Let's take Steve and Emily Thang, owners of Sho Sushi in Calgary. They have been a staple in the food scene for years, as they have served Japanese food from tourists and locals to some of the who's who in Calgary. Their clientele reaches celebrity friends to simple guys like me who love the place. In an ultra-high-competitive space, what did they do to thrive?

For one, Steve believed in providing not only amazing food but the best service around. In fact, he's the kind of guy who approaches each and every client in his soft-spoken manner and makes them feel like they are VIP guests. Steve remembers every detail and ask regulars questions about their family, work, and what's new in their life. Not only does Steve do this, but his wife is an even better host than he is. They make everyone feel like they are the most important person in the restaurant. I remember, every time I would visit, they would give me a sneak peak and a taste of a new items coming to their menu. You develop a loyalty and vested interest in their success as you had a say in that menu. They served food that patrons wanted.

Despite this, there were still 6 japanese restaurants within mins away from Sho Sushi. In order to rise above the competition, they had to stand out and be heard. Initially, they had three restaurants, which essentially served the same type of food, just in different locations. It wasn't enough to differentiate themselves from the other great sushi places in town. Competition was fierce and with the uncertainty in the economy looming, patrons were more discerning to part with their hard earned dollars. What did they do? They pivoted and changed two of their restaurants to serve a completely different market and thus create a new experience.

The first pivot was to bring in a completely different concept to Calgary. Instead of paying servers to take orders and bus the tables, Steve created Point Sushi, the first "bullet train" sushi concept. Essentially, patrons would order on this iPad. Within minutes, this lightning quick conveyer belt with a tray resembling a Japanese bullet train would zip by to deliver the food. This was super-cost-efficient. As the labour went down, almost zero mistakes were made, as the patrons placed their orders directly—and the experience was Instagram-worthy. Gotta be gramable these days to stand out!

The second pivot was the third restaurant. High-end discerning sushi-goers wanted something new. Here's where their restaurant Sakana Grill turned into Ponshu, one of Calgary's first high-end sushi Japanese-Izakaya-style restaurant. You won't see bento boxes or dynamite rolls here. Instead, try something you won't see that often, like yellowtail carpaccio or takoyaki poutine (octopus poutine). The place is slammed during openings or from Uber Eats orders.

Think their expansion stopped there during this pandemic? Nope. With extra space in the back of their original restaurant, Sho Sushi, they created Ajeto, which means "secret" in Japanese. This is Steve's version of a Japanese speakeasy. You wouldn't know this restaurant exists unless you went to the back of Sho Sushi and saw an old Coke vending machine. Pull open the machine, and you'll find the doorway to one of Calgary's coolest hidden gems.

Finally, among all these pivots is the main reason they have succeeded: attention to detail and a commitment to going all-in on service. He went even so far to bring in the same toilets with heated seats and multi-setting bidets that you would experience in upscale venues in Japan. If you're a regular, they want you coming back, as they offer fancy complimentary coffee or desserts that blow your mind. Steve's comment to me has always been, "Give away many stones and get a jade back in return." His brand is that he gives as much as he can (the stone) in order to get the loyal precious jade of a repeat client. If that client has to decide where to spend money, it will be at one of Steve's four restaurants. Regardless of the style of food he is serving, they maintain the same consistent service and detail with their brand. All of his restaurants are thriving and reservations are booked solid despite the pandemic. Talk about domination.

Whether it's the food business, consulting, massage therapy, or home building, the number one rule of branding is *be consistent*. It's OK to pivot, but you must remain consistent to what your clients expect of you. In a world of uncertainty, no one likes unnecessary surprises. Your consistency will make you different when everyone is running around trying to figure things out.

What's that You Said? I Can't Hear Your Voice!

It only takes one voice, at the right pitch, to
start an avalanche.—Dianna Hardy

OK, so you're building your brand or rebuilding your brand as you pivot. Your brand is being reinforced by how consistently you do what you do. You've worked so hard creating this unique story, so how do you shout it from the rooftops and let your voice be heard?

The answer lies in your brand character. It's all in how you act. Your voice is based on your overall behaviour. Your character governs pretty much everything you do and say. Many of the most successful people pivot and build new ventures with much fanfare. Even if it's a brand new venture, the loyal fans will buy the product. Why? Because they know what to expect from the entrepreneur and their brand.

We have created this vision of how we want people to see us, our business, and what we stand for. In our minds, the brand is clear. The challenge is whether it is clear in reality. Let's look at a few things to consider when it comes to aligning your brand with your character— aka your voice. For instance, consider the following:

- *How do you communicate?* There is nothing more important than communication when it comes to your interactions with people.
- *What is the vibe you put out?* Consider your grammar, choice of vocabulary, punctuation, phrasing, and tone in putting together a text, email, voice message, social media post, or anything that you ever write or say. Your verbiage is key. Let's be real: your target market will judge you based on how you articulate your value proposition. Be aware of the words and language you use in all your marketing material, websites, and anything written or said.
- *How does your social media look?* There's nothing worse than a guy who claims one thing and does another. He can appear kind, intelligent, and respectful at work only for people to be shocked to see vulgar, trashy comments on his social media. Your social media presence is the first thing people see these days to be cognizant of what your brand represents. Don't be a walking contradiction.
- *How much thought have you put into your social media and which platforms to use to maximize your energy?* I've mentioned LinkedIn several times. LinkedIn is a gold mine for anyone looking to connect with other business people. People are there for a specific reason—to build business contacts. Don't have a profile? Create one now. Facebook and Instagram (they are the same company) are so important. Consistency is key. If you have a professional page, consistently pump out content that shouts out your brand. We'll go into social media platforms later on in this book. Forget print media, as you don't get any meaningful analytics. Facebook has the best analytical tools available and can target any specific demographic with a few presses of a button. Don't waste that powerful tool.
- *How does your headshot look?* Invest in a good picture, dammit. I can't stand when people take the time to create

140

a wonderful social media profile only to top it off with a ridiculous amateur-looking profile picture that looks like they just cropped their face from a group wedding photo. If you want to brand yourself as trustworthy and professional, don't use a picture of you double-fisting two pitchers of beer at a frat-house kegger.

- *How do your title and description on LinkedIn and your email signature sell you?* Be creative but specific. One real estate developer put "Dream Builder | Creating the space where memories are made" instead of "professional real estate condo developers in downtown Toronto." The latter is so boring. Have some fun.
- *How is your touch and feel?* This isn't what you think. Imagine branding yourself as high-end but your proposal is printed on low-stock paper and looks like it was printed on a dot matrix printer with the ribbon almost done. (For you Gen Y and Gen Zs, you may not know what that means, but google *dot matrix printer*; it was archaic.) Make sure the look and feel of your business cards, client brochures, flyers, and proposals all represent the feel of your company.
- *How does your logo look?* Yes, this is important. Spend the extra money to get a nice logo created. If you don't know what to create, download Canva for free and research logo templates. Just make sure your logo represents you. Often this is what people will see before they even get a chance to read whatever is being handed out. Your logo should evoke the emotion, theme, and style that you want to represent. Keep it simple. Some of the most iconic logos are as simple as a swoosh, a fruit with a bite in it, three stripes, or a basketball player soaring from the free throw line. I didn't even have to show you these logos and you all knew I was referring to Nike, Apple, Adidas, and Air Jordan. Make it readable, simple, and memorable.

- *Have you customized the content and style of your website and every presentation you do?* If you have a fun and energetic website but your presentations are a snoozer that has everyone yawning after five minutes, you're in trouble.
- *Where do you work?* Your work space and environment tell a lot about your brand. If you are an artist or a creative, perhaps your office or studio is filled with colours in a bit of organized chaos. If you're a top-notch attorney, maybe you want an office that is sleek, sharp, clean, and to the point.
- *How do you look?* OK, this one might piss some people off, but it's so important. How you appear is the first thing people will have to judge you as they meet you. From how you dress, your appearance, and your body language, they all tell someone about your personal brand. One of my first mentors, Art Sanchez, would always tell me, "Mike, your suit looks like shit. Dress for the job that you want, not the job that you have." Impressions and appearances matter, so put some effort into your brand.

Why Should I Believe You?

Believing is seeing and seeing is believing.—Tom Hanks

You've decided to pivot in one way or another. You know you have to make some changes or enhance what's currently working. You've thought long and hard about your brand and what you represent and are aligning all your actions accordingly. Your target market is ready to see the new you. The problem is, how do you get them to trust you?

Seeing is believing. I believe that people are skeptical to begin with. Now more than ever, people will scrutinize you and question whether you are worth the money you are charging or if you can do what you say you are going to do.

People are simple. Let's put faith aside. Most people believe things that can be factually validated. This means you need to focus on appearance and accomplishments.

Social media has given every business license to show people what they do. Did something awesome today? Great! Post it on social media and use the right hashtags. Have a happy client? Awesome! Post a testimonial, or better yet, use what I call "the silent salesperson." Get a client to do a video testimonial pumping you up about how awesome you are and how you saved them thousands of dollars on car insurance.

Accomplished some milestones in the past? Amazing, let's relive it. Post old accomplishments to show new clients or remind old clients just how you've been able to do what you do. We even have a day once a week to remember the past. Use your Throwback Thursday hashtag #TBT and share the certificate you earned last year. Post pictures of the small village you helped (everyone loves a social entrepreneur), or show milestone sales that you hit last month. The humble brag is acceptable. You need to be your number-one fan so that other people will believe that it's OK to be a fan as well.

Show your accomplishments (degrees, awards, certificates, designations, and anything else that gives you the credibility to do what you do) and make sure your appearances match the brand you want to portray.

This section in branding could be spun off into a whole new book, as marketing and branding is such an integral part of business. We are just scratching the surface, but I want to implore you to really define what you want people to feel and associate you with before they decide what you *will* be associated with. Everyone has the choice to determine how they are perceived, so make it count when building your brand character.

Branding is the ART OF ALIGNING what you want people to think about your company with what people actually do think about your company. And vice-versa.—Jay Baer

How I pivoted

Adbul Basit Ahmed, CEO and Founder of Adesso Man

Change. It is something that we all resist and avoid. It can cause a lot of pain and hardship, as it requires letting go of the old, letting go of your ego, and allowing yourself to grow and evolve.

Wow, it's almost like I forgot how things used to be like. A lot has happened in the last year or so. Both personally and professionally. There has been this immense energetic shift in the world, and everyone is going through it at the same time. But it is also not that unusual, as it is not the first time in history that the world has changed so dramatically. I feel, however, overall, it has been transformational for us and pushed us to think differently as individuals and as a company.

Prior to COVID-19, we had just had a rebound year after being in a little bit of trouble after our stint in Edmonton. So we were feeling optimistic about going into 2020 and were thinking about growth, but at the same time still a bit cautious because we were well aware of how quickly things can change. When COVID-19 hit, we were in Q1, which is always slow for us as a business. We were trying to shift our focus to our online business, as we had heavily relied on our brick-and-mortar up until then. We had not found success online and had been investing heavily in marketing and really trying to create more awareness around our brand. We also had a big cultural shift internally and really focused on building a mission-focused brand that not only filled a niche in the market with our concept but impacted the community at large. We believed we had a much larger purpose than to be just a fashion brand.

It really hit me personally when the NBA season was cancelled and sports came to a standstill. You could feel the world was in shock and panicking, and we were too. There was a lot of uncertainty and fear that had developed, and we were very unsure of what we wanted to do. Our retail shops were forced to close, and our online business was nowhere close to being where we would have liked. We had bills to pay as a company, and our personal finances were going to take a hit. *So there was a lot going through our minds. How do we stay afloat financially? How can we continue to generate revenue? How do we help our community in this crisis? What is the most important thing right now?*

It was definitely stressful, and as an owner, you feel a ton of pressure and responsibility because you have your team relying on you to come up with solutions. It really did affect my mental health, especially when we were going into lockdown and I wasn't able to be around my team or have any way to express and release the stress I was feeling. We were quite fortunate that our government came through with the support that they did. It really helped us to keep things going and also develop a plan.

We did a few things right away:

1. As we are a consumer-focused company, we thought of what the immediate needs were. We developed products such as masks and hand sanitizers to support local manufacturing and also fill a demand in the market that would help our community and customers.

2. We also thought of all the ways we could improve our cash position, so we leaned out our operations and cut any non-critical functions, reduced our expenses (specifically payroll), and took advantage of all the government support that was available.

3. We thought of ways we could give back and support our community at large and donated a portion of our proceeds from our masks and sanitizers to help support the homeless in our city, as they were facing quite a challenge during COVID-19.

4. We came up with ideas and strategies of how we could stay top of mind with our customers. We continued to stay active on social media, invested in online marketing efforts to boost our online sales, and created helpful resources through blogs for our community, to help them through the tough times.

5. We leveraged our networks and partnerships to create collaborations and cross-promotions that could help us stay top of mind while also accessing a new customer base. We also just wanted to support our brands in the tough times, as we knew everyone was going through it.
6. We stayed positive and optimistic throughout. As a business, we knew the risk we took when we embarked on these ventures, and instead of complaining and feeling down, we went into problem-solving mode.

We also saw how the world was changing. As COVID-19 progressed, many other conversations that we had already been having internally started to come to light, such as social equality issues and our environmental impact as a business. We saw that there was no better time to establish ourselves as a mission-focused and community-driven brand that stood for something more than money and profits. We established our Adesso Listens initiative, which was developed to help raise awareness around social issues, support our community by building confidence in the most vulnerable members of our society, and raise funds for initiatives we cared about.

We had always felt that we wanted to move toward being a more purpose-driven company, and as we evolved in our business, COVID-19 really pushed us into this new phase. We remained transparent and authentic in our messaging and also relied on the goodwill we had created with our customers to support us through the rough times. Our amazing customers really showed support, and we saw an uptick in our online orders, which was a big reason for us surviving.

We have since been able to reopen our stores and boost our online presence, and even with COVID-19 restrictions in place, we ended 2020 on a high note. We learned a lot over the last year or so about ourselves, our brand, and our priorities. We have also seen how consumer behaviour and demand have changed, and we are looking to be flexible and adapt with the times. Our customers expect more from us, and it is our responsibility to become better at everything we do. We are focused on being consumer-driven and delivering a unique value proposition to our customers that creates value for them and the world at large. Our outlook is quite positive, and we feel that we have built up resilience as a team to tackle any future challenges.

My experience in the last year taught me to let go of my ego so that I could change and evolve into a new version of myself and help my company evolve in the same way. I had to learn to face my insecurities, self-doubt, and fear of failure to emerge as a more resilient and purpose-driven individual and leader. I had to let go of old patterns of thinking and develop a new set of priorities and purpose in my life. It has been life-altering for me. I feel that I have emerged with fresh mindsight around how to move forward in life and business.

My parting advice to entrepreneurs is to let go of your ego in your business. It is not about you or your success but rather about the people you serve and finding solutions to their problems. This requires foresight, humility, and agility. Create good intentions around your business and look to serve people in a way that will create real change in people's lives and your community. This is where you will find both success and fulfilment in your work.

Abdul Basit Ahmed
CEO and Founder, Adesso Man
www.adessoman.com

CHAPTER 11

Getting Social with Social Media

Social media is not just a spoke on the wheel of marketing. It's becoming the way entire bicycles are built.—Ryan Lilly

I REMEMBER READING GARY VAYNERCHUK'S BOOK *CRUSHING IT*. IT was mind-blowing and profound to me. From that point on, I tried my best to create a well-crafted brand that would represent me. I later read his book *Jab Jab Jab Right Hook*. It opened my eyes to the importance of social media and how a brand is only valuable if it's conveyed and communicated on the right media platform.

It's no secret that social media has dominated the way we live, make consumer decisions, view the world, and spend our spare time. The power of social media is undeniable. Throughout this book, I've shared ideas on the entrepreneurial mindset, the importance of branding, and how entrepreneurs have pivoted in this new digital world. It is social media that has allowed people to connect with their customers. Side-hustlers can sell their products and services through the power of social media. Now more than ever, social media has become an integral part of business.

When I first took my journey into branding myself, I was hesitant. For many, social media is a vanity vehicle, and I felt awkward going down that path. It is a way for many people to post their fake lives, showing fake experiences to impress people they don't even like.

*Too many people spend money they haven't
earned on things they don't need to impress
people they don't like.*—*Will Smith*

Will Smith nailed it in his quote above. Although it is easy to see how many people use social media to fill a void or to seek some sense of validation from their peers, this is not the premise of this chapter. I remember my older brother asking me why I was posting stuff on social media. When I responded by telling him I was trying to create a brand that would open doors for me, he didn't get it. He was still of the mindset that social media was a personal tool to share thoughts and family photos. To me, social media was a vehicle to reach out to as many people as possible in order to add value. Your pivot depends on adding value or it won't work. Social media is simply a tool to get your pivot across.

As a businessperson, I believe that it's not what you know or who you know, it's who knows what you know. Social media allows me to do this. It allows me to find new customers, clients, and opportunities. For years, the acronym *ABC* stood for *Always Be Closing*. Today, it means *Always Be Connecting*. If used properly, social media can help you pivot and connect with the right clients who are looking for exactly what you're selling. In fact, whether it's used to connect to your audience of potential clients or even used internally to efficiently share information within your organization, social media is necessary if you plan on pivoting successfully.

In this chapter, I want to spend some time looking at a few trends to consider when using social media to pivot. In all honesty, there is so much information on this topic that an entire book could be written on this subject alone. I'll do my best to share a few key gems of information to help you pivot correctly into the right platform for your business. These platforms are the most commonly used; however, I am sure by the time this book comes to print, there will be new platforms and apps on the rise. The goal isn't to share mind-bending ideas in social media but to remind you of how some tried-and-true strategies worked for pivoters and those seeking to connect with more people. Before we get into this, let's take a look at some important statistics to lay the groundwork.

Dataportal.com put out a report in July 2020 that examines changes in social media usage during the beginning of the COVID-19 lockdown period. Notably, there was a monumental increase in online and digital activities. With people staying at home, this was expected. Even before this pandemic, the importance of social media was becoming more and more apparent. In my opinion, this pandemic only accelerated what was going to happen anyway.

The report validates my suspicion, as the social media adoption rate surged by 13 per cent during this pandemic. Think about it. When was the last time you left your house without your cell phone? How long have you gone without going on any type of social media platform? Have you ever used YouTube to learn something during this pandemic?

You may not be active on Twitter or Instagram, but perhaps you are on Facebook. Perhaps you're a businessperson and don't have a Facebook or Instagram account, but I'm fairly confident that there is a high probability that you have a LinkedIn profile.

Consider the following statistics from the Datareport Global Review on social media:

- More than *half of the world* now uses social media.
- *4.66 billion people around the world* now use the Internet; of those users, *316 million new users* have come online within the last 12 months.
- There are a *5.22 billion unique mobile users.*

Within this report, one statistic jumped out and slapped me right in the face: 99 per cent of total social media users are accessing via mobile at some point. We can't escape it. If we have our mobile devices, there is a high probability that some sort of social media platform will draw our attention for moments of the day.

Only 8 per cent of the world's Internet users are not on social media, which suggests opportunities for future growth. And it's not only the fact that more and more people are on social media, it's the actual time spent per person that has increased. In Q3 2015, the daily time spent on social media by users between the age of 16 and 64 was one hour and 51 minutes. In Q3 2020, that number jumped up to two hours and 25 minutes.

Social media is so important that university and college courses are teaching social media in their curriculum. Below are some of the characteristics that make social media so unique:

- Social media is easily accessible. It's also the point of convergence where today's Internet-savvy audience comments and meets.
- It includes every generation and demographic.
- Social media opens possibilities of direct access to clients without any third-party intervention.
- Advertising through social media is pretty cost-friendly as compared to print, TV, or other traditional media.
- Social media also helps in search-engine optimization and increase in rankings of any company websites.

The characteristics above are crucial for any business in today's world. Communication level and engagement of clients go to different levels altogether when you are using this medium.

Knowing what we know, which social media platform makes the most sense to use during and beyond this pandemic?

That's a tough question to answer. Social media is like a rapidly moving train. If you jump on early, you're at the front of the train. If you jump on later, you're near the end. If you don't jump on at all, you'll never reach your destination. It's one of the fastest ways to grow your business. Some of the platforms that are relevant at the time of this writing may not even be around years from now. This is important to acknowledge, as putting your efforts into the wrong platform during a key pivot will waste your time, effort, and money.

To young kids or casual folks looking at social media as a fun pastime, this might not be as crucial, but for a businessperson or pivoter, it is important. You can always jump on the hot trend at the time and jump off when it fails to adapt to keep you interested. All of a sudden, I feel time-warped back to 2002, before Facebook was the top dog in the social media park. Every Asian in the world was on this platform called Friendster. It had 115 million users from all around the world. They officially closed in 2018 after a three-year hiatus.

Another example is the social media legend that was way ahead of its time: Vine. It set the bar high for how social media and video could simultaneously leverage each other. Sadly, after Twitter acquired it, business went down, as it couldn't compete with rival Snapchat.

My last example is MySpace. While it still exists somewhere on the Internet, it is nowhere near the pioneer of social media that it once was. In fact, this is an example of a pivot that went wrong. They pivoted away from "personal business" to more of a music-centric network for new artists. Facebook came along in 2006. At that time, MySpace was the most visited website in the world, but it lost 10 million unique users in just one month in 2011. Pivots aren't perfect, so deciding which social media platform to choose is important.

In this digital world, social media is the great equaliser. It gives anyone a voice and anyone an audience if you find the right platform of people willing to engage.—Michael Siervo

There is a plethora of platforms out there to connect with people from all walks of life. For those looking to pivot in their business or find a side hustle on social media, it is recommended by many social media experts like Gary Vaynerchuk to focus on just one (maybe two) to start off. Before we dig a bit deeper into which one or two to choose based on your pivot, there are countless books, podcasts, seminars, and courses out there that will do the subject justice as to how to crush it in each individual platform. I highly recommend that once you find the one that you like, go balls-deep and learn as much as you can. The algorithm on these platforms constantly changes, so you need to be on top of this or else your efforts will just lead to frustration.

With that said, if you're going to pivot into different social media platforms, let's take a look at who's dominating this space. View this information from the perspective of a marketer rather than a user.

According to our friends at statista.com/statistics, the most popular social networks worldwide as of January 2021, ranked by number of active users (in millions), are as follows.

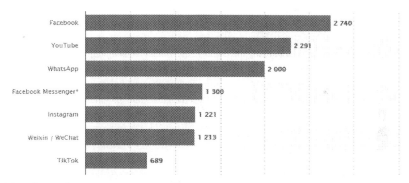

Number of active users in millions

Personally, I actively use the top five mentioned by www.statistica.com as a consumer, researcher, marketer, and nano-influencer. Now, I am not suggesting that you go all-in on Facebook because it has the most users. You need to dig deeper into who the people using those platforms are and if they are your target audience. I do believe that Facebook has to be among the top platforms to consider, even if you are only going to use the analytics provided by Facebook.

As a businessperson, I was surprised that LinkedIn was missing from this list. Perhaps I am biased, but in my opinion, if you are a businessperson and want to connect with other business people, LinkedIn is a must. Again, each platform has its own merits and functionality, so you need to be specific as to who your target market is, what you want to accomplish, what your time commitment is, and why anyone would seek you on that platform.

Here are the top platforms I would recommend. Keep in mind that I am recommending these based on simplicity, ease of use, and functionality. Other platforms will evolve and can dominate untapped areas, such as Clubhouse or TikTok. However, the platforms on this list are the tried and true that I consistently see as helpful for those who are pivoting or have already pivoted.

Facebook: The Godfather of Social Media

Facebook is just massive. I don't care that millennials say it's for old people; that is complete nonsense. You can't count out the most influential millennial in the world, Mark Zuckerberg, and say that this platform is irrelevant. At the moment, he's architecting the Metaverse which in my opinion will revolutionize the way humans interact. This is an example of how Facebook can potentially pivot and evolve as it has time and time again.

When young people moved away from Facebook and Facebook Messenger to WhatsApp, what did Zuckerberg do? He bought WhatsApp. Despite shifting demographics, no matter your industry, there's a space for you on Facebook. This platform is constantly evolving. Rather than simply a way to show off vacation pics of the family, it has become all-encompassing.

Side-hustlers can buy and sell via Facebook Marketplace. I don't remember the last time I used eBay or Kijiji. If you want to host a show, you don't need a TV deal to broadcast to your audience; just use Facebook Live, or better yet, use BeLive.TV. This is the easiest live-streaming platform for Facebook to grow your reach and boost sales. You can customize the entire experience to have a professional looking production.

Some of the leading industries on Facebook include financial services, technology, automotive, consumer goods, gaming, entertainment, and ecommerce. You can essentially find any target demographic on Facebook and boost attention with targeted ads. If you're just starting off and have a limited budget, start joining groups that relate to your product. Rather than flogging those groups with your business, take some time to engage and make your presence known. Respond and engage on posts within the group to establish awareness and trust.

One other approach is to start your own group and create your own community. My friend Lis Perez started a Facebook group called "The Extraordinary Life" because she wanted to connect with positive people who believed an extraordinary life went beyond material wealth. Within days, her group had over 140 members.

Her 14-day virtual retreat, which involved a daily presentation from a guest speaker (including yours truly), was seen all over the world. To this day, I still connect with new friends from Australia, England, South Africa, the Philippines, and the US. She literally had a dream about doing an event to empower people and *bang*! She manifested it into reality with little time, no money, and little promotion. The result was beyond what she expected, and I can imagine that this social experiment will evolve into a real-life 200-person event in Mexico next year. This is a great example of how Facebook was the vehicle to literally turn a dream into reality.

Another example is a highly sought after videographer team, Jose Lacera and his brother Edgardo from Now Way Jose Productions. During the pandemic, they wanted to create interesting and inspiring content that would look epic. Jose partnered with a super positive group called Astrano. They focused on mental wellness, meditation and cold therapy. The idea was to inspire people to do something that promoted mental strength and mindfulness while being able to implement it in their daily lives beyond the pandemic. The solution was to film a small group of adventurous people doing polar plunges in ice cold rivers in Alberta, Canada (Google "Wim Hof" as this stuff is amazing). They shared these videos on Facebook along with other platforms. What started off as a small group of polar dippers turned into a whole outdoor wellness festival that included outdoor yoga, breathing exercises, Russian banya experiences, DJ's, firepits and of course polar plunges. This group of millennials and Gen Y used old man Facebook to connect others and build one super positive community!

Facebook is a platform that is constantly evolving, so invest your time and effort in platforms that analyze your data and give you access to your audience while growing and evolving with your business.

YouTube: Seeing is Believing

Now, I'm going to date myself here, but when I was a young kid, if I wanted to learn something, I would either have to ask my parents or look it up in an encyclopedia. Yes, I know how it sounds. The encyclopedia sounds like the name of a dinosaur, because it's pretty much extinct. Now, if we want to learn something, we simply google it. We use the name of a company as a verb. If Google is the world's largest search engine, what do you think the second is? It's YouTube. Guess what? It's owned by Google.

I love YouTube as a social media platform. Many people are visual or auditory learners. YouTube hits both of those. If I ever want to listen to a podcast or music playlist, I simply search for it on YouTube. YouTube is impacting the Internet landscape as we know it. According to YouTube, as of 2021, there are 1.9 billion users (almost a third of the Internet). Over 91 countries have their own version of YouTube with local content.

When this pandemic happened, I had no clue what to cook. YouTube was my culinary instructor. Consider these statistics: 86 per cent of viewers used YouTube to learn new things in 2017, and 46 per cent of people felt more prepared for new tasks after watching a YouTube video. This platform can effectively make you smarter!

The great thing is that YouTube has allowed many people to pivot and create their own content or offerings with little money or resources. If you know how to cook, sew, sing, dance, or have any skill to teach the world, a simple YouTube channel can help you get your name out there. Heck, because I was tired of consuming negative content on social media, I decided to launch my own YouTube channel called "Ready, Set, RISE" to share positive stories about regular people doing amazing things. RISE stands for Real Individuals Sharing Excellence.

I knew nothing about being a YouTuber, but this platform made it so easy to create, post, and engage with viewers. As a result, this little project turned into a money-making endeavor as it opened up opportunities for me to create content for other people. (If you're reading this, please subscribe to my channel ... yes, a shameless plug, but trust me, it's worth following some of the stories.)

As a side hustle, YouTube lets you make money from the comfort of your own home. As of 2021, $2 billion has been paid to partners on YouTube content in the past five years. The growth rate of channels earning five figures on YouTube is 50 per cent year-on-year. If you're lucky, you're making six or seven figures on YouTube. However, even a five-figure earning is a great side hustle or livelihood for many people.

My friend Mikey Bustos made his career on YouTube creating video parodies of popular songs with a Filipino twist. Prior to becoming a Youtube sensation, he had dreams of becoming a R&B recording artist. He even placed seventh runner up in the TV show Canadian Idol. His career took multiple pivots from commercials, recording music, touring shows around the world to creating comedy sketches. It was YouTube that allowed the pivot that would create the success he enjoys today. His channel has over 4 million subscribers as of 2021 and has accumulated over 450 million views so far. According to nailbuzz.com, he is able to get an average of 150,000 views per day, which should generate a revenue of approximately $1,200/day ($440,000/year) from ads.

The cool thing is that most of his income doesn't come from his music videos. It comes from a very niche market about ants. His channel Ants Canada features everything you need to know about ants and how to build an ant farm. Talk about committing to a pivot, niching down and dominating your market. Mikey is awesome and his personality shines on YouTube as it does in person.

I recently started following another YouTuber named Sorelle Amore. She talks about her journey from being literally broke to becoming a millionaire. She took her love of travel, photography skills, and lovable personality and became a millionaire. Her YouTube channel branded her and created the following she needed. From there, she monetized her advice through social media courses.

In her first year, Sorelle made over $600,000 with her course. Search her on YouTube, as her pivot to becoming a millionaire is so raw and authentic. This is an amazing example of someone who constantly pivoted and found a platform that would highlight her skills, charm, and insight. Great job, Sorelle!

One thing I love about YouTube is that you can repurpose the content and share it on other platforms, such as Facebook and your website. Use YouTube to pivot and teach or demonstrate a skill or how to use your product. The power of demonstrating value cannot be denied, and YouTube is a perfect platform to demonstrate it to many people. So if you're going to go down this path, commit to making clear and consistent content, even if no one is watching. Eventually, you'll build momentum and attract the right audience.

Instagram: A Picture tells a Thousand Words

The attention span of humans is less than eight seconds. We are as easily distracted as a goldfish or a squirrel. Since this is the case, many people don't have the time to read or listen to a long podcast. For many, they want their quick hit of dopamine in a matter of seconds. This makes Instagram one of my favourite platforms.

For years, I didn't understand the value in looking at a bunch of pictures—until I got sucked into the awesomeness of Instagram. What was once meant to be a platform for people to post pictures of something they saw or experienced instantly has become a platform to inspire, educate, brand, endorse, and connect with like-minded people. From a branding perspective, you can essentially connect with influencers from all around the world. Globally, this photo-sharing app has 1.22 billion global users. In 2012, Facebook acquired Instagram for $1 billion, and its usage exploded.

The platform appeals primarily to users under the age of 35, with 71 per cent falling in this category. It's not to say that it's specific to that age group, as anyone can follow anyone else as long as the content resonates with you. Create great content, and you can resonate with a lot of people. In fact, the creation of the term *influencer* came from Instagram. Regular people could grow their following and essentially influence others to follow, purchase, react, or behave based on their influence. This became the birth of a whole new marketing channel that empowered regular people to monetize their time. Now you can create a professional profile and sell directly from Instagram rather than having to direct your customer to a website.

Currently, the US and India represent the two largest national demographics of Instagram users, with Brazil and Indonesia following behind. This means that the rest of the world is still catching up. I can only imagine that when the pandemic opens up and travel resumes, Instagram usage will increase even further. People want to share stories of where they went. So if you are a business such as a restaurant, Instagram is a must. Even making your food or environment Instagramable as a certain level will improve your brand.

LinkedIn: It's about linking up

The last platform that I believe every businessperson should at least have a simple profile on is LinkedIn. As of March 2020, LinkedIn had more than 740 million active users. If you are a businessperson, you may have used LinkedIn to market your brand, post industry thought leadership, or look for a dream job.

LinkedIn may not be as sexy as the previously mentioned platforms, but as of 2020, BusinessInsider.com voted LinkedIn the most trusted network in the world. The calibre of the audience on

LinkedIn is much higher, as it targets professionals, entrepreneurs, students, and anyone who wants to make business connections. According to the Pew Research Center, 37 per cent of LinkedIn users are ages 30 to 49, unlike platforms that target the younger demographic, like TikTok or Instagram. Furthermore, 49 per cent of LinkedIn users make more than $75,000 annually. In a study of 5,000 businesses, HubSpot found that traffic from LinkedIn generated the highest visitor-to-lead conversion rate at 2.74 per cent—almost 277 per cent higher than both Twitter and Facebook. For marketers and business owners looking to pivot toward making meaningful business connections to key decision-makers, LinkedIn is the way to go.

What I love about LinkedIn is that it is evolving its features, such as LinkedIn stories and my favourite, LinkedIn Learning. LinkedIn Learning is an amazing source for courses in such subjects as sales, photography, leadership, and technology. There are a vast number of resources taught by experts in that industry.

If you have the credentials and want to monetize your knowledge, consider creating paid courses on LinkedIn and allowing LinkedIn to drive the traffic. LinkedIn Learning is a great example of branding yourself as a subject-matter expert or authority while monetizing the platform. In the worst-case scenario, you can use LinkedIn Learning as an amazing way to learn new skills to help you grow. It's a win-win regardless of how you use the platform.

Overall, LinkedIn is one platform that has surprised me over the pandemic. The quality of content and connections is top-notch. It is the one platform where humble-bragging is welcomed. It's expected for users to talk about themselves and the value they bring rather than boasting about what they had for lunch.

Now, I know that there are so many other social media platforms that I left out. For the purposes of this section, I wanted to share what I have used and what I have seen from my colleagues who are pivoting to brand or converting followers to clients. Do your research and look at other social media platforms, as there may be one that caters more to your target demographic. With that said, I will mention that there are several newer platforms that I have strong confidence will be game-changers. By no means am I an expert in any of these platforms, but give them a try and see what works best for you.

ClickFunnels: One click away from conversion

Most people understand the concept of a sales funnel. It is essentially the steps along the sales journey that your prospects take in order to convert into becoming customers. I'm sure you've either been on YouTube or Instagram and a great ad comes on that hooks you in. You scroll through this landing page of information as your intrigue grows. The landing page sucks you in by offering a free eBook or a free webinar if you register now. The strategy is highly effective, as it's a low-cost way to get straight to the point without having to create a complex ecommerce website.

The sales funnel process has been around for a long time, but the concept of a ClickFunnel was created in 2014 by Russell Brunson. It is all about automating the sales process to control every stage of the buyer's journey. The funnel guides users through webpages (typically a landing page with awesome testimonials and pitches as you scroll down) and aims to sell your products and services along with upsells to other value adds.

Personal coaching, online fitness, and weight-loss programs are a great example of ClickFunnels: The primary goal of this type of marketing initiative is to increase the number of people who sign up for a weight-loss consultation. In addition to the program, there is usually the option to buy additional weight-loss products that can be beneficial when completing the program, too. The process would look like this:

- The prospective buyer comes across a compelling social media post, advertisement, or email with an irresistible offer (often a free program, eBook, or massive discount on a desired product). The prospect is compelled to click a link to explore further.

- This initial click would bring buyers to a landing page that offers you the opportunity to upsell a product. The page typically would bundle other products together to make the offer more appealing. This could be fitness gear or supplements to your online weight-loss program.

- To entice the user to buy, you would include a call-to-action to "Buy Now." The hope is that they click that call-to-action and continue to the next page, which introduces another product. Often there's a limited time offer. As the clock winds down, a sense of urgency builds to decide.

- If buyers decide they only want that first product and choose "no" for the second one, they continue to the page where they enter their information to sign up for a consultation and put their credit card info in.

- ClickFunnels essentially continue until users reach their end destination and are no longer interested in additional products or services. You can add multiple links to other pages as your client purchases more products along the way. From the ClickFunnels experts that I have spoken to, it's more effective to have one product per page; however, you can have multiple pages. The additional pages are a great way to increase your organic search-engine optimization (SEO).

With a majority of today's consumers beginning their buyer's journey online, full-funnel marketing is becoming the go-to approach to pinpoint which stage the consumer is in. Visualizing the buyer's journey in funnel structures will help you understand what approach you should take to gain repeat customers. Moving through Awareness-Interest-Desire-Action-Loyalty is the journey you want your funnel to take clients on.

If you want to dig deeper into this topic, check out books by ClickFunnel guru Russell Brunson. He has books such as *Dotcom*

Secrets and *Traffic Secrets*. If your pivot is to sell a product online and an e-commerce website doesn't seem feasible, try creating a landing page and then implement a ClickFunnel strategy. Invest in some convincing copy, set aside marketing budget for social media ads, create a clean funnel, and watch the sales come in!

TikTok: Not just for song and dance

I have to admit that when the Chinese app TikTok (*Douyin*) hit North America, my first response was, "Not another social media app!" I had my reservations, as all I saw was young people posting silly 15-second dance videos. As a busy guy, I really had no time to dive into this. However, as of June 2021, the app is available in over 150 countries and has over 1 billion users. It's been downloaded over 200 million times in the United States alone.

Although it isn't really my cup of tea (for now), if your brand's target audience includes anyone between the age of 13 and 60, you really need to consider getting on TikTok. The video-sharing app provides bite-sized content that is fun and engaging. According to App Ape, 32.5 per cent of the users on TikTok are ages 10 to 19, and 29.5 per cent are between the ages of 20 and 29.

The reason I mentioned that this isn't my cup of tea for now is that there is a high probability that by the time this book comes out, I'll be on it. TikTok. cannot be ignored given its deep penetration and access. An additional 60 per cent of TikTok's users are Gen Z-ers. Gen Z-ers are trendsetters. Next year, 74 million people in the US will be part of Gen Z, which will make it the largest generation of all.

A top trending song on TikTok is typically a top trending song on Spotify as well. This highlights the true influence of the platform. So, if your pivot involves being an artist, musician, speaker, or anyone who needs to become viral, you have to get on TikTok. If your song happens to go viral on TikTok, you'll be laughing all the way to the bank (not necessarily directly from TikTok, but from record sales and downloads of your song).

Can you pivot and make a living off TikTok? Yes, but it's not as easy as posting a video and expecting it to go viral. TikTok offers limited ad revenue to its creators, so you'll need to rely on sponsored posts, merchandise, and thousands of followers before you can quit your day job.

According to Forbes, the biggest TikTok influencers are Charli D'Amelio (101.5 million followers), Michael Le (42.4 million followers), and Josh Richards (23.4 million followers). All made at least $1 million in 2020. However, most of that money was earned through the sale of merchandise and sponsored content for big brands rather than ad revenue. In fact, TikTok only recently started to share ad revenue through its Creator's Fund, which content creators have criticized for being underfunded, as they claim it typically only provides a few dollars per day.

Again, this platform is in its infancy. However, given how the global acceptance is increasing, the low attention span of customers and the speed in which they want to consume it, my prediction is that it is a platform that warrants every business to think about this with strong consideration.

Can't forget this notable mention

Clubhouse: Eavesdropping with a purpose

Clubhouse made a splash in 2020 as this ultra-exclusive new social media app. You could only get access via an invite from someone who was already on Clubhouse. If you're not familiar with Clubhouse, it's an audio-based social media platform that is currently invite-only. You can essentially listen in on and participate in different conversations on different topics. Celebrities like Oprah, Kevin Hart, and others have been known to jump on. Grant Cardone and Gary Vaynerchuk are frequently on it. It's been even more of a rage for entrepreneurs ever since Elon Musk joined the audio-based platform.

The cool thing about this app is that you can be a fly on the wall to listen in on some great conversations and speeches from authority figures in any given industry. Imagine hearing Richard Branson give live advice on business. The knowledge and connections you can gain with other like-minded people is invaluable.

As of February 2021, the app has over 10 million downloads globally. What makes this so unique is the rawness of the platform. You can listen to people who "have the stage" and are keynote speakers. You can ask questions by putting up your hand for the administrator to give you the stage. Conversations are open and free-flowing, unlike structured, well-crafted posts.

I can see the value in this app, as there is a move to voice technology for many social apps, including voice-command capabilities on our phones, cars, Google Home, etc. YouTube and Instagram have visuals on lock for now. Pivoting into the realm of voice is the next step. If you are pivoting into creating your own stage or platform, Clubhouse is definitely something to look into.

In terms of using this platform to make money, it's still early. However, don't be surprised when the monetization becomes more obvious. I have not fully committed to using it. Given the unique qualities about it, it's hard not to at least keep an eye or shall I say ear to the ground, when it comes to it.

Five Essential Social Media Tips for the Business Pivot

I don't want to keep beating a dead horse, but you cannot ignore social media if you want to successfully pivot and grow your audience. Once you decide on which social media platform you want to focus your energy on, it's important to give yourself a fighting chance to succeed. I advise you to dig deeper into specific strategies on how to win in your chosen platform. Check out books like *One Million Followers* by Brendan Kane, *The Social Media Marketing Workbook* by Jason

McDonald, or *Hit Makers* by Derek Thompson. I'm not an expert on every platform, so find one and go all-in on it.

In the meantime, there are tips and strategies that are transferable regardless of what platform you choose. Below are my top five essential social media tips.

1. Map out your plan of attack

Just because it's free to open a social media account, don't get lazy. There are many tools available. However, it still takes time and effort, which represents a commitment and investment into your business. Hootsuite has a great checklist to help you set social media goals and objectives, research the competition, conduct a social media audit, and create a social media calendar. Use the 80-20 Rule: 80 per cent of your content should educate and entertain your audience; the remaining 20 per cent can promote your brand or pitch a product. Check out my website at michaelsiervo.com/pivot/resources for a few social media templates to get you organized.

Business objective	Social media goal	Metric(s)
Grow the brand	Awareness *(these metrics illuminate your current and potential audience)*	Followers, shares, etc.
Turn customers into advocates	Engagement *(these metrics show how audiences are interacting with your content)*	Comments, likes, @mentions, etc.
Drive leads and sales	Conversions *(these metrics demonstrate the effectiveness of your social engagement)*	Website clicks, email signups, etc.
Improve customer retention	Consumer *(these metrics reflect how active customers think and feel about your brand)*	Testimonials, social media sentiment, etc.

2. Commit to the right social media platforms for you

I went through a few of the platforms that I use and have seen either personal success or success from other business owners. Even so, there are many other platforms available for you to choose from.

You may assume that your Gen Z audience is not on Facebook, so you focus on TikTok. However, according to Facebook, a quarter of its users are ages 18 to 24. Don't make assumptions. Research all the features of each platform and make an educated decision.

In fact, you can start with one platform to really build momentum and then expand to others. The average Internet user has 8.4 social media accounts, so you have a fighting chance to reach them. For instance, you can use Instagram to build a following, Facebook to address common customer service issues, and YouTube for educational tutorial videos. If you plan on charging for your online course, look at platforms such as Kajabi or Udemy to put your course on autopilot. Do the analysis and find the right platform for you.

3. Get in the mind of your audience

Everyone is different. The beauty of social media is that most platforms have analytics and data that you can access. It's crucial to understand and know your audience. What do they like? What posts get the most engagement? What time is the best to post? Who is my demographic? Once you understand who you are resonating with, you can cater your message to them or adjust your message to attract a different audience.

4. Nurture relationships

When I first got into sales, I would tell my prospects, "I'm not here to close a sale. I'm here to open a relationship." This holds true in social media. One of the great benefits for small businesses is that it allows the entrepreneur to communicate directly with customers and engage with followers. Over time, you build trust, which can lead to more sales.

More than 44 per cent of Internet users use social media to research brands. People want to know who you are, why you do what you do, and what you stand for. Behind this digital reality, we are still human. We want to deal with humans who think, feel, and share the same values we do. Establish these relationships through posts and engage in organic content.

Like, follow, and share content that resonates with you from followers or content creators you want to connect with. Go one step further to mention and tag followers in your posts and stories. The odds are those people will follow you and reciprocate the gesture.

5. The trend is your friend

Social media is constantly changing. Pay attention to trends. This doesn't mean you have to react to everything that goes viral. Please don't do this, as there are things that go viral that really add zero value to your life. Remember "Damn Daniel" or "Left Shark" during Katy Perry's Super Bowl show? What a waste of brain cells.

Regardless, it's a good practice to pay attention to what's trending so that you understand what is resonating with society. If there is an important social issue that resonates with you, don't be scared to voice an opinion. People want to know that you stand for something rather than being a faceless corporation. Social listening is a crucial information-gathering strategy that helps you understand and connect with your audience and potential clients. Your brand is a voice. Don't be scared to use it.

How I pivoted

Alex Sundar, CEO of Alex Sundar Fit, online fitness coach

My name is Alex Sundar, and I am an online fitness coach. I help men and women lose body fat and gain muscle. My whole purpose is to cancel the noise of confusion and make the process super-simple for you. I don't just get people results; I make sure they keep those results for the rest of their lives.

First off, I just want to give love and a shout to Mike for having me be a part of this book. My intention for my share is to hopefully inspire you, and for you to take action on whatever goals you have. I want to show you that anything is possible with the right action steps.

But before we deep-dive into how I pivoted my business to be a massive success during COVID-19, you have to know and understand my story, where I came from, and why I do what I do. I am a 30-year-old man who was born and raised in Calgary, Alberta, Canada. I grew up in an ethnic family with two different cultures. My dad is from Fiji, and my mom is from the Philippines. This is important to know because my ethnic background and the way I was raised is the reason I am so driven today to make a massive impact on people through fitness and nutrition. It taught me many harsh and valuable lessons.

These lessons came from how I was raised. Many times, when I went to school and saw how other kids acted, I was shocked! I was taught to live a certain way due to my cultural values. I was always taught to follow and to not lead and have an opinion. Any time I would share something in vulnerability, which was some sort of dream or something I wanted to accomplish, it immediately got shut down by my parents. Because of that, I was a very shy and broken kid. I didn't know how to communicate with anyone, and I was shut off from the world. It was a very depressing time.

But I remember this moment when I was in grade 3 that shaped my vision today. I was in class, and I was talking to this kid named Cody. Now, I don't remember what we were talking about, but I do remember that I paused and looked around the room at the teacher and all the other kids. And in that moment, I saw society and how wrong it was. Kids were rude, loud, and disrespectful, and in turn I saw how adults were also like that.

I asked myself why there was so much pain and sadness in the world. And ever since then, I made it my personal mission to change that. I lived my life with a dream and a vision since that day, but I wouldn't tell anyone due to fear of being shit on by my family and friends. I wasn't allowed to dream or have a vision; I was only allowed to follow what my parents wanted.

This took me to grade 11, where I was in English class sitting next to one of my classmates. His name was Mark Bateman. He was a friendly guy who just asked me, "Hey man, how's your day?" Because of my conditioning, I didn't know what to say. I just sat quietly, all shook up that someone had talked to me in class.

I even remember that in the same class, a girl came up to hug me as a thank you, but affection was foreign to me. I was sweating buckets as I got the hug. Man, that was hard for me to go through, because I had this vision and this dream to impact and change lives. I said to myself, *what kind of pathetic fucker would be able to accomplish that by acting like this?*

So, I decided that I needed to take action and get super-uncomfortable. I decided that I needed to challenge myself and become a great public speaker, change my image, start to date, party, and experience as many things as possible. Because I had never experienced any sort of what I would call living.

And when I say everything, I mean *everything*—including experiencing drugs, going into debt, hard partying, and travelling. The reason for this was that I needed to understand how everyone felt when they were in those situations. How could I make an impact on someone's life if I had no idea what they had gone through? But I admit, it was a bit extreme.

As I was going through this experience, I became a personal trainer at the age of 19. Something I never thought I would ever do for this long was change people's lives through fitness and nutrition. I learned a lot of very hard lessons as I went through my journey as a personal trainer. I suffered for months trying to learn how to sell my first client and have the confidence to approach people on the floor. I worked at multiple different gyms in the city, and that's where I met and trained, as a client, your author of this book, Michael.

As I was going through this journey, I got very sick. I was diagnosed with two autoimmune disorders that crashed my energy and had a few major surgeries over the years where I was stuck in the hospital for an extended period of time. It actually got so bad that every few months, I would end up in the hospital as if it was a regular occurrence in my life. I missed out on a lot because of it: parties, dating, nutrition, powerlifting, bodybuilding, Olympic lifting, you name it. But because of that experience, I was able to transform lives, from people in a wheelchair who needed rehabilitation to professional football players to athletes at the Olympic level, and even to models and bodybuilders. I myself have done various sports, from martial arts to stepping on stage as a bodybuilder, CrossFit, Olympic lifting, and even powerlifting.

I am only 30, and I have pretty much done it and learned it all in the fitness industry. Through all of that, I had four other businesses as well. Unfortunately, all four of them failed, but I also consider them a massive success because I gained so many valuable lessons that I take away today in my very successful online fitness coaching business.

And that's where this transition happened. I went full-time online a few months before COVID-19. Now, I went online not to make money or build a successful online coaching business but to provide impact. I read this article on this lady who went on this horrible juicing cleanse from an online expert. This cleanse was so bad for her that she ended up in the hospital with permanent brain damage. I was not OK with that. I took it very personally, because I never took it on myself to impact thousands of lives through social media. I felt like it was my fault that it happened, and now I have made it my personal mission to make sure I can give as many people as possible the right information and teach them the right way to lose body fat, gain muscle, and live a fulfilling healthy life.

Like, can you imagine that? I teach people how to live to their fullest potential through fitness and nutrition. Because if you aren't working on your health and eating right, how can you function optimally? How can you serve your business, your job, your wife, and your family if you're not living your life to its fullest?

I am so blessed to know I have changed hundreds and thousands of lives in my 12 years of being a fitness coach. It's crazy for me to look at the last 12 years of my own personal journey and see how much I have changed—the vulnerability I am able to share, my increased confidence, and how I am just a savage ready to change lives. My friends, it all starts with us first. If I didn't take a step back from partying and working on my health and fitness to make sure I was running at 100 per cent, well, I wouldn't be writing this today. But now that you've heard a bit about my story, let's dive into how I pivoted my business during COVID-19.

So, my business was in a good spot before the pandemic happened. My clientele was consistent, I was making decent money, and I had an overall good balance. But I will be honest and say I just wasn't happy where I was at. It's funny that our businesses can be doing good but we can also not be thriving personally at the same time. So even though my business was doing all right, in reality, I was really bored. I wasn't challenged in any way to grow and expand my business. Part of that was because I was going through a big health issue at the time, I had just gotten out of a relationship, and overall I felt lost.

But then the pandemic happened, and everything changed. My income immediately went to zero, but instead of panicking like I am assuming most would, I took this as the biggest opportunity of my life. I told myself that if I couldn't succeed and grow my business and myself as a person, then I had no business being in the entrepreneurship space. I felt like this was the challenge I needed, so I got to work.

I immediately went on 75 hard, which is 75 days of a disciplined routine. This includes drinking one gallon of water a day, no alcohol, read 10 pages of a self help book, eat clean, workout twice a day and document your progress with a daily photo I invested all my money into my business by hiring business coaches Brian Mark and Cole Da Silva, who co-own PT Domination. I put my head down and worked on pivoting my business.

Now, I want you to understand that I only made these decisions because of my story. I went through some very harsh times personally, and it taught me one specific thing, and that is *grit*. You have a fucking choice every single day, every single bad scenario, regardless of lack of motivation, a family member dying, or heck, fucking COVID-19. You can either choose to show up or let the world smack you in the face.

I decided to give out the middle finger to the world and say out loud, "Let me show you who the fuck *Alex Sundar is and what he's about.*" And that's never giving up, showing up no matter what, and pushing myself to my physical and mental limits.

So I got to work, and I pretty much had to start my business from scratch. I had to start my new marketing plan from scratch as well. I feel like most people really underutilize a very powerful and free tool, and that is social media. One of the main tools I learned from my business coach was to use the power of organic social media to gain clients without the use of paid advertisements. I had to learn how to copywrite, how to grow organically, and how to make content overall that would attract my ideal client.

To be honest, it was fucking nerve-wracking and uncomfortable at first. I had no idea what I was doing. I hired a business coach, and I put all my trust into learning a system that would in turn grow my business into something that would be successful during the COVID-19 pandemic. But that's OK; I learned all these lessons when I was younger, so I got to work.

At first, it was just about posting and being consistent with it. I feel like most people wait to make the perfect piece first, which is the biggest mistake you can make. The reason for this is because you want to show people your journey as a business owner. The days of business-to-client transactions are over, and people are looking for person-to-person interaction. I get a lot more business nowadays from people watching my content transform over the last few months.

You need to focus on posting three different types of content to grow your social platform and maximize its usage. First is connection posts. You want to be vulnerable and let your audience know who you are and what your struggles are. The second is value. You want to show people you know what you are talking about. The last one, which is the most important one, is social proof. You want to show that your product works. Client testimonials are the number-one way to grow your business financially through social media.

Implement those three tips, and you will see your business grow and change dramatically. I'm talking about engagement. Who gives a shit about 100,000 followers? That's irrelevant. Focus on 1,000 engaged followers who love your product and you. Cause folks, we are in the business of making money, and you need clients, not followers.

I will also share my top two secret hacks on how I really gained traction and pivoted my business. Yes, those three different types of content posts are necessary, and doing them on TikTok, LinkedIn, Clubhouse, Instagram, and Facebook are all important. But one of the best tools people miss out on is going live on these platforms. Your audience needs to know, like, and trust you to buy your product off of you. So going live and dropping insane value is the best way to grow your business. I'd say that 90 per cent of my business revenue right now is from livestreams. It's insane what it does.

The last thing you need for your business is virtual assistants. In order to grow your social media presence, you need to be present for your business. That's hard when you're working out, running a business, and maybe you have a family on top of that. It's about saving time. Hiring virtual assistants to engage and expand your network on social media is a key secret ingredient. Heck, my social platform grows as I type this right now without me being on it. It's awesome. Social media is a long-term game. It's free advertising, and you would be dumb not to seriously take advantage of it.

I will be frank and say I would not have been successful without the amount of free time that COVID-19 provided and the impact of reinvesting in my business and getting a business coach. Sometimes when we are emotionally stressed, we need to hire coaches to point us in the right direction. It's exactly what I do for my clients when it comes to fat loss. I am here to direct you to know the right way to lose body fat and keep it off while drinking and eating your favorite foods and not having you feel like it's a diet. All of that is possible if you have the right mentorship in your life.

Instead of trying to figure everything out yourself, invest in someone, because in turn that investment will pay back 10 times what you put in. That is what happened to me. I invested in a business coach who showed me how to grow my business organically, and that investment came back way more than 10 times.

I have now built an online coaching business that is thriving and consistently growing every single month by using organic social media from Instagram, Facebook, TikTok, Clubhouse, and LinkedIn. I have gained skills to be not only confident on all platforms but also grow and scale my coaching business. I now have a team of three other coaches, a few virtual assistants, and more to come this year. It's exciting to know that I have been able to completely pivot my business by taking advantage of the current times and using that to impact thousands of lives in my new network.

I have recognized that the possibilities of what you want to accomplish are endless if you have a vision and are willing to work your ass off to get it. My business has scaled and grown over COVID-19. I have doubled the pricing for my coaching packages as well as increased the level of service to an exceptional level. If I can pivot, I know you can too. If you're reading this and you connected with my message, I would love to connect on Facebook, IG, TikTok or even Clubhouse. Find me all under @alex.sundar_.

And if you're looking to create the best version of yourself, it all starts with fitness and nutrition. I am one of the best in the business, and if you're serious about pivoting your business and life, reach out to me on social media, and we can have a conversation to see if you qualify for my coaching program and if I can help you. Everything starts with how your body feels, and if you can get that going, your mindset will follow with it.

Alex Sundar
CEO of Alex Sundar Fit
@Alex.sundar

CHAPTER 12

Sell or Die—Why You Need to Learn to Sell

I have never worked a day in my life without selling. If I believe in something, I sell it and I sell it hard.—Estee Lauder

FOR MY ENTIRE BUSINESS CAREER, I HAVE BEEN IN A SALES ROLE. Whether it was selling clothing in a retail store, providing merchant services to small- to medium-sized businesses, or creating institutionally credible solutions for high-net-worth clients, one thing I have learned to appreciate is the art of selling.

If you are reading this, there is a strong possibility that you already understand the importance of sales. For those of you who have gotten by up to this point by avoiding your fear of sales, now is the time to overcome your fear. Whether you are a local baker who makes the best pecan pies in town, a mechanic who specializes in turning gas-powered vehicles into electric ones, or simply an entrepreneur who wants to focus on your strength while outsourcing your weakness, the art of sales is imperative to surviving in this new world.

For many, the idea of sales conjures up the image of a used-car salesman dressed in a plaid wool jacket strolling up to sell you that lemon of a car on his lot. Or perhaps sales reminds you of a slick-haired businessman in a fancy suit trying to convince you to buy an expensive insurance policy that you don't need. It's guys like these that give the skill of selling a bad name.

Let me be clear: Selling is not sleazy. People are sleazy. They are the ones who can rip you off and leave you with buyer's remorse, not the actual activity of selling.

Why do I believe that selling is mandatory? Yes, you heard it: *mandatory*. Like, I mean life-and-death-type mandatory! Mastering selling, or at the very least feeling comfortable with it, is a necessity. It is an imperative core competency that you must have if you plan to pivot in anything in life. Life will hit you with ESPN turn points, where you need to make a key pivot or your plans will fail. Selling isn't just convincing your team that this course correction is needed. You also need to sell to the most important person in this equation—yourself!

*The first sale in every sales process is to
yourself. You can't sell what you don't believe
in. At that point you are just conning your
customers and yourself.*—Michael Siervo

Now, I'm not saying that you must be able to close massive high-ticket deals or make millions of dollars to change your life. Selling is essentially the skill of conveying your intentions so that someone else buys into them. A mother must be able to sell the idea of eating green veggies to her 5-year-old. A single guy at the bar needs to sell the idea to that hot girl he makes eye contact with that he is a worthy candidate to spend her time with. Employees must be able to sell the idea that they deserve that raise or promotion over other viable candidates.

Selling is key. With everyone penny-pinching and watching every dollar during this pandemic, why would anyone choose to let go of hard-earned money and give it to you versus that awesome gourmet cupcake company down the street?

You must convince people that you are the best choice for that particular need, or you must convince them that they need your product. It's not about manipulation. Selling is all about communication. I am a big supporter of focusing on your strengths and outsourcing your weaknesses. I know how to tune my car, but I'm not going to do it. I know how to cook (well, kinda), but I'd rather leave the fine dining to the red-seal chefs.

Even if you decide to outsource the selling tasks, you must be able to convince the salesperson that your product and your vision is worth putting her neck on the line. When I started mentoring younger salespeople, I would always tell them, "The first sale in any sales meeting is to yourself."

The discerning potential customer can smell bullshit a mile away and won't fall for fluff. Be straight up and sell like you're selling the cure to cancer. Believe in it, and your customer will believe in you.

If you still don't believe that everyone must learn how to sell, let me give you an example of the best Uber driver I've ever met. It was Christmas Eve, and my wife and I were heading to the airport to fly home to Toronto for the holidays. I ordered an Uber to take me to the airport. I've taken hundreds of Uber rides before, so I wasn't expecting anything new today. In fact, I was tired and just wanted to get to the airport.

As the Uber driver pulled up, I noticed something different. He was wearing an elf costume. *OK, interesting, but let's see where this goes.* I opened the door for us to get in and saw the most decorated Hyundai Sonata I had ever laid eyes on. I mean, I felt like I was a gift underneath a Christmas tree. It was decorated with Christmas lights, the cushions were in holiday décor, the air freshener smelled gingerbread and Michael Buble was singing carols in the background. This was amazing.

But wait: it gets better. He offered us each a bottle of water and an unopened bottle of eggnog. He even asked if we were meeting anyone at the airport. He opened this small treasure chest filled with gum, holiday candy, breath mints, dental floss, lint rollers, Tylenol for a holiday hangover, or feminine products in case it was that time of the month. This guy was ready for anything.

As tired as I was, I was curious to know this guy's story. I had to ask. He said Uber saved his life. 2 years ago, he was down in the dumps and got let go from his job. Uber was all he could do. Rather than accept this as a temporary gig, he went all-in and put his heart into this new role.

He continued to give us statistics on Uber, the history of the company, the average rides, his ranking, and the top five key interesting facts about Christmas to start a conversation during the holidays. This guy didn't just drive us to the airport. He sold us on his Uber experience and that he was the best Uber driver we had ever experienced.

He was right. As a result, I tipped him double the price of what the ride was worth. Customers are willing to pay whatever price you ask if they see value—even more so when they *feel* value. That drive sold us on the idea that we were the most important cargo he had ever carried to the airport. He sold himself that he was going to be the best Uber driver and sold his customers to believe the same thing to be true. His efforts paid off as he mentioned that he makes more money than his previous job and feels fulfillment doing what he does. That's going all into a small pivot and taking his brand and income into something much bigger.

Another example of a company that started off small and grew rapidly during this pandemic is Solomon Financial. The financial-services industry has been undergoing change. Financial advisors are a dime a dozen, and everyone seems to have an opinion on where and how to invest. Standing out can be a challenge in an ultracompetitive industry. Out of the change in business models, lack of compensation, and stigma around the financial advisory practice that were impacting the livelihood of several advisors, Solomon Financial was born. With a team-based approach, it took the traditional one-on-one approach and multiplied it several times to maximize the skill sets of each team member.

I remember sitting down with founder Dan Dyck as he explained this model. Some financial professionals are great at prospecting and marketing. Some prefer exploring their analytical side as they work behind a computer screen. Some are strong on tax and estate planning. And some are excellent at putting it all together to explain to Mr. and Mrs. Jones on their farm in central Alberta. As a result, each team member practices as a specialist while the client benefits from a larger service model.

Dan explained to me how the business was based on selling concepts and methodology in face-to-face seminars. So when the pandemic hit, their entire sales model was impacted. Large 40-to-50-people seminars were reduced to Zoom meetings. With every other advisory firm hosting Zoom calls, Dan doubled down and greatly increased the marketing budget. Using Facebook ads, video marketing, increased social media presence, and sales funnel strategies, the company was able to drum up some noise within its community.

What started off as a handful of financial advisors has now grown to a family-style culture of over 100 advisors across the country. Their pivot was to double down on their story and sell it like cowboy hats during a stampede. If you believe in what you are selling, you will go all-in and increase your efforts to get your message across to anyone who will listen.

Selling is mandatory. If you don't learn this skill now, you will die a slow economic death. If you are like me, you'll be asking *What's in it for me?* The concept of selling makes sense theoretically, but what are some of the real benefits and important things to consider when selling? Let's dig deeper into a several areas around selling.

Just Learn to Sell: Network Marketing

Aside from my first job flipping hamburgers at McDonald's, my entire career has been in the world of sales. In high school, I sold men's shoes in Scarborough Town Centre Mall in Toronto. I worked my way up and sold clothing at the GAP in university. Heck, even when I was a kid, I would sell lemonade to the neighbours and lollipops to other kids in the schoolyard. In university, I got myself involved in my first multi-level marketing (MLM) scheme selling high-end vacation memberships. At 20 years old, I was selling each membership at $5,000 a pop to people in my age group. I remember making over $20,000/month by the age of 21. I was crushing it as I learned some key skills in persuasion and sales.

Sadly, what I also learned was that not everyone took sales as seriously as I did and therefore lost money and time participating in an MLM strategy. I'm not going to knock the MLM system, but it's not for everyone. I do recommend that you join one if you want to learn sales. Find one with decent products that you don't mind consuming. Don't knock MLMs, as there are a lot of successful side-hustlers making massive income in this structure. Some of the real value is the sales skills you will learn, the thick skin you will build to handle rejection, and most of all, the camaraderie of the people in that cult.

Yes, I called it a *cult*. Now, this comment might be a bit controversial, but a cult isn't a bad thing; it just means *culture*. Wikipedia defines a *cult* as "a social group that is defined by its common interest in a particular personality, object, or goal." Of course, there are some whacky religious cults out there that will make people do stupid things. Many cults are bad, but for the purposes of this chapter, let's just use the word *cult* to describe *culture*.

What I do respect about the MLM culture is that they support each other, they recognize how difficult it is to succeed, they have processes, they seek mentorship, and they focus on a major aspect of your ability to pivot—the ability to *sell*. Sales was something that I always felt was crucial. Now more than ever, I believe this to not only be true, but a matter of survival.

How I pivoted

JP Villegas, Presidential Director of Nu Skin

We started 2020 with all optimism. We had travel plans lined up. We had such hopes for a great year that we entitled our yearly leadership bootcamp "VISION 2020."

Three months later, our vision for 2020 would be challenged by a global pandemic. When vision is unclear, we usually slow down. But when you're committed to a vision, you pivot and find ways to pull through despite the challenges.

The year 2020 was bittersweet for us. We were faced with many challenges and a lot of pressure. But this adversity also brought out the best in us. The path of the most resistance is the path with the most results.

I've been involved in Nu Skin Enterprises for more than 20 years, and much of what we do is empowering people to improve lives with rewarding business opportunities, innovative products, and an enriching uplifting culture. I've built my business over the years by coaching and mentoring potential partners in coffee shops and doing business presentations in our walk-in center. Much of our business and training has been done face to face.

So when I heard that a long lockdown would be implemented in our city, it brought about worry, fear, and anxiety, as this would affect the way we do business. I wasn't only worried for my family but the families of the dynamic team I worked with. I took my accountability to them, their dreams, and their families very seriously.

Since meeting with partners and customers was out of the question, we had to quickly shift gears to keep our business going and growing. It was at this time that I realized the years invested in mentoring leaders and our business system prepared us for such a time as this.

With the help of technology, we were able to pivot quite easily by shifting our movements to online platforms. This shift enabled us to transition online and pushed our creativity by tapping new frontiers of expansion. This catapulted our growth to numbers we had never experienced.

The year 2020 surely was nothing like we planned. It forced us to make changes to how we did everyday life. We had to accept that change is inevitable. We had to learn to shift. We had to learn to pivot. The Chinese word for *crisis* is composed of two characters: one represents *danger* and the other represents *opportunity*. There are still winners in any given situation. If you can recognize the danger but still focus on looking for opportunities, you will be able to overcome the setbacks and let them spur you to a great comeback. COVID-19 is a wake up call for all of us that at any time, we can lose our job, our business, even our lives.

This crisis really exposed many leaders. It helped us determine where we are and what areas of our lives we need to improve on. It also exposed our faith in God or our lack of trust in Him. If there's one thing that separates surviving and thriving during a global pandemic, it would have to be the word *intention*.

Being from the Philippines, resilience is the number-one trait most of us have. We endure natural disasters, typhoons, earthquakes, geopolitical issues and more. We quickly adapt to any challenge. We survive. But what would help a leader keep a business thriving during a crisis? It would be *grit*. It's that strong intention to do more than just the average to accomplish the extraordinary.

It's going to take a fight to silence the doubt in your mind and become disciplined to act on your dreams continuously and consistently. That's why I keep encouraging my partners to fight for their dreams, fight for their families, and fight for their unborn leaders and the families that are dependent on them. I truly believe that you will always get what you fight for. And the best way to fight is to fight on our knees with faith.

We are all faced with all kinds of uncertainty. The best way to overcome it is to feed our faith and starve our fear. You have to learn to *faith your fears* in order to face your fears. Faith is the key.

So I encourage everyone not to just master your business—master yourself. View every challenge as a character-building opportunity. Remember, the greater the challenge, the greater the molding of your character. The greater the molding of your character, the greater the influence you will have. I pray you will live a life of purpose and be an inspiration to many. God bless us all.

JP Villegas
Presidential Director of NuSkin
www.nuskin.com

The Sales Myth

As sales expert Grant Cardone once said, "Sell or be sold." He continues to say, "Everything in life is a sale, and everything you want is a commission." The thought of *commission* may make some people cringe, but the reality is that if you are a business owner, you work for commission. We just call it the bottom line, the profit margin, the moolah!

You can have the best product in the world, but if you can't sell against your competitors or successfully convince your prospects to consider you, you're going to die. Seriously, you are going to financially die, and your company will fold. Sales isn't the sleazy idea of manipulating and robbing someone, only for them to have buyer's regret later. Selling isn't a slimy used-car salesman convincing you to buy a lemon. Selling isn't sleazy. People are sleazy. Selling is necessary.

Five key reasons why selling is so important

1. Selling is the grease that makes life go around

As I mentioned before, selling is vital to survival. That lion in the jungle needs to sell the fact that he's one badass cat that you do not fuck with. He's not the biggest, smartest, or fastest, but dammit, he sold the entire jungle on the idea that he is not one to be messed with.

This is life. You need to sell yourself to everyone looking at you. Regardless of what the pivot may be, people need to believe you can do what you say you will do. We do it every day, consciously or unconsciously. The process of learning to sell is not just about selling a product to a customer; it's about going beyond your comfort zone and facing your worst fear. It's about manning up and selling your courage to yourself rather than buying the load of crap called fear.

Fear is the primary reason most brilliant ideas don't get off the ground. They stay on the planning table never to be marinated, cooked, served, enjoyed, and remembered. Fear is the reason most people are afraid to quit their jobs and start a business. Fear is the reason most people don't dare to dream big, and that's why they remain small. We need to sell ourselves first before we can ever sell to anyone else.

The fears we face become our limits.—Robin Sharma

This is why I emphasize that entrepreneurs accept selling as a part of the job and then commit to understanding the power and influence that this skill has. Selling is all about facing and overcoming your worst fear and growing beyond your comfort zone. It is all about acknowledging that you might fail and having the courage to do it anyway. Don't sell yourself short. You can do this.

2. Selling isn't about a product or service; it's about building trust

As entrepreneurs, it's no secret that one reason why we sell to our customers is to increase sales and profits. However, before we earn the opportunity to exchange our amazing widget for a few of our client's hard-earned dollars, we must establish trust. We also sell to our customers to establish rapport, build a relationship, and increase their loyalty and patronage. We are earning trust. In return, this trust builds a sense of comfort and familiarity that hopefully will generate repeat sales and referrals. Brand-building, brand loyalty, and every aspect of branding boils down to selling. And selling boils down to building trust.

Sales is not about selling anymore, but about
building trust and educating.—Siva Devaki

I know I talked about building a brand in a previous chapter. Branding is all about emotional selling with the strategic use of words, images, and actions. Statistics show that it is easier and less expensive to sell to a loyal customer than to a new customer.

Think about the top brands you support. Do you find yourself drinking Pepsi or Coke? Eating McDonald's over Burger King? Staying at a Marriott or a Holiday Inn? Driving a Mercedes or a Toyota? Or think about something as simple as going to your favourite breakfast place every morning with your wife? Whatever it is, we are creatures of habit, and once that brand has won us over, it's a tough habit to break.

According to a Nielsen Report in 2019, the global average of people willing to try a new brand or product is about 42 per cent. If you are an entrepreneur in the US, the average is 36 per cent. Think about this for a second: you have less than a 50 per cent chance that you will pry that loyal customer away from a competitor or vice versa. Selling your brand and the experience that comes with it helps build a moat around your clients and gives you a fighting chance for the 50 per cent who are open to try what you do. It's competitive out there, so sell like your life depends on it.

3. Selling is necessary for growth

So you've decided to pivot in this environment. This is a challenging time for anyone, let alone a business, to make any drastic moves. The reality is that you need to grow your business. Many businesses are pivoting because their traditional business models have equated to a drop in sales. So as much as it's great to think about the business expanding, for many, the growth is coming from a depressed level. They need to grow just to get to pre-pandemic levels.

So how do you grow? You need to sell. As entrepreneurs, we sell our competence, business ideas, and plans to investors, all in a bid to raise capital, future partnerships, or even some funds to keep us afloat. Lack of sales skill is the primary reason most brilliant ideas don't get funded. They have an amazing business plan and pitch deck but botch expressing why their home air purifier and sanitation system is necessary for keeping a family's air quality safe. Without the ability to sell this idea, the business is doomed before it can even start. The growth mindset comes when you try to solve a problem that people have or sell them on the idea that there is a problem that they didn't even know existed.

> *Don't find customers for your products, find*
> *products for your customers.*—Seth Godin

Even the process of raising capital via an IPO (Initial Public Offering) requires you sell the public on the competence of your management team and the market accessibility of your products. Raising capital, in the most simplistic terms, is selling. Even raising credit to run your operation requires you to sell the idea that your business is sustainable, viable and cashflowing positive. You sell your credibility to suppliers to get credit lines. If you don't know how to sell, you will not be able to get goods on credit from suppliers. Even if you do, the largest credit allowance will be given to the business owner who displays the ability to sell products faster and make returns.

4. Selling inspires people to act

A friend of mine once told me that *act* stands for "Action Changes Things." People don't usually act with vivacity and energy unless they are inspired. The greatest motivational speakers and orators are amazing salespeople. They sell people the idea of believing in themselves or sell a cause that might tug at customers' heartstrings.

As entrepreneurs who are pivoting in this new environment, we may not be pivoting alone. Our organization may consist of a team that has been with us since day one or is still holding on to the notion that we will get back to "the old way" of doing business. We sell our business goals, objectives, and long-term service benefits to our team, all in a bid to motivate them to go all-in.

Motivating employees to increase their productivity is selling. Getting them to act and go against their comfort level is not an easy thing to do; however, a pivot cannot be successfully done if those you rely on do not have the same buy-in that you do. Part-time efforts give you part-time results.

A leader must INSPIRE or this team
will EXPIRE.—*Orrin Woodward*

We sell our business mission, vision, and long-term goals to highly skilled professionals to win their confidence and buy-in. One of the major business challenges entrepreneurs face is transferring their passion to the team executing the plan. Your ability to sell your business mission to your top management is the determinant factor that will forge them into a team.

Apple's founder Steve Jobs was hands-down one of the best pitchmen in history. He revolutionized how an executive pitched a product during an unveiling. He knew how to touch the heartstrings of people in such a way that they bought into the Apple culture and vision. He painted a picture of what could be possible if you followed him. Former Pepsi CEO John Sculley was in a comfortable career making more money than most would imagine. Who or what could make him pivot away from the comforts of the world he knew? Steve Jobs did. A salesman through and through. Just read what he said to spark John to act and join Apple, according to Sculley's book *Odyssey: Pepsi to Apple*: "Do you want to spend the rest of your life selling sugared water or do you want a chance to change the world?"

If you can't sell your business mission and vision to your business team, your family, your support system, or anyone you need to be part of your journey, you will have a hard time getting them to act with full commitment.

5. Selling builds the confidence that you need to be a communicating pro

Love him or hate him, one of the best salespeople in the world is Donald Trump—yes, that large orange man with a comb-over that needs its own social insurance number. Heck, this real estate mogul, social disruptor, TV star, and business savant was such a good salesperson that he convinced the American people to vote him in as the 45th president of the United States.

> *I couldn't sell him on my experience or my*
> *accomplishments, so instead I sold him on my*
> *energy and enthusiasm.*—Donald Trump

It takes balls and confidence to do what he did. Mastering sales reinforces your communication skills, which eventually allows you to be a networking, marketing, and communication pro. No matter what your pivot is, business will always flow toward the great communicators. The biggest business contracts, monster deals, and acquisitions will always go to those who have the ability to communicate in the right language to the right people and in order to sell themselves.

Selling is communication. Communication fosters confidence. Confidence attracts success.

Pivoting is difficult and, in many cases, involves a lot of moving parts or people to help it happen successfully. The art of selling starts with you. You must sell to yourself that the pivot makes sense and is the right move. Then you must take that same energy and gusto and sell that to everyone who will be involved. Let it sink into your skull that building a successful business or pivoting in a new direction can never be possible without selling.

Ten Quick Tips to Improve your Sales Skills

Simplify it. The little things count.

I've spent my entire career in the sales industry. I remember my first mentor, Art Sanchez (man, he was such a hard ass, but I learned a lot), telling me that in order to be successful in life, you need to learn how to sell. And sell I did. I wasn't a natural sales person as I was shy and pensive. I lacked the confidence to speak up. Over time, I learned that I couldn't accomplish anything meaningful if I didn't put in the work to develop this skill. It was a gradual process but one that taught me many lessons on how to improve.

Success is the sum of small efforts, repeated
day-in and day-out.—Robert Collier

Below are some very simple techniques and tips on how to improve this vital skill. If I can do it, so can you:

1. ***Think with the end in mind. Set defined goals and expectations.*** Knowing what you want out of the pivot, the situation, the conversation, or any engagement where your sales skills will be in question is important. Set defined goals and sales targets. Action without a goal is like aimlessly sailing in the ocean. It's pointless.

2. ***Read books and take courses.*** Google and the Internet have made it possible to access anything at the touch of a button. This includes resources on sales. There are countless sales professionals who have solid courses to help you improve your skills. Look at guys like Dan Lok, Grant Cardone, or Jeffrey Gitomer to name a few. I've learned so much from reading their books and watching them on YouTube.

3. ***Don't fear public speaking.*** Many high-ticket sales come from having a face-to-face conversation with a prospect (or a Zoom meeting in this new world). I found that if I could speak in front of a large audience, I could speak even more confidently one on one. Take up the opportunity to do public speaking. Emcee an event, host a party, or join Toastmasters. Get out there and start owning the stage.

4. **Practice and role play.** This is one tip that many people don't do. Rehearse in a mirror or in front of someone. Practice! Don't listen to what NBA great Allen Iverson said about practice. Practice is key. Rehearse and role play over and over again until you've envisioned every case, objection, or scenario in your mind. When the moment comes for you to close the deal, it won't be uncharted territory. Act as if you've been there before.

5. **Find mentors.** The fastest way to earn anything is through mentorship. Beyond watching and copying what mentors do, we can talk to them to gain insight on their experience and success. Ask them what they would do in various situations or how would approach a sales meeting beforehand. Mentors have so much wisdom to share, as they were once nervous salespeople trying to pitch their goods.

6. **Think about what's in it for the client.** Empathy is such a key part of sales. Effective salespeople can put themselves in customers' shoes and understand their perspective. Bring this sense of empathy and understanding to every step of the sales process. Ask yourself, *What would make me buy this product?* Better yet, ask yourself, *Would I buy from myself if I was the salesperson?* Understand customers' needs and solve their problems. I used to always tell my team that "I'm not here to close a sale. I'm here to open a relationship."

7. **Master the art of questioning.** Questioning skill is a huge part of any successful sales process. Ask insightful and well-researched questions that don't come across as generic. Cater to clients and ask questions that make them think, things like "If you could change one thing about X, what would it be?" or "Knowing what you know now, what is one thing that is preventing you from moving forward?" Ask great questions,

then shut up and practice active listening. People are willing to open up their lives if you ask the right questions.

8. ***Know your shit and increase your confidence.*** The worst thing is when salespeople must pivot because they know the deal is shot, and then they try to sell something they know nothing about. It comes across as both desperate and amateurish. Know your value proposition inside and out. Trust that you have more knowledge about your business than anyone else. When you are the subject-matter expert, your confidence will show. When you are confident, there is a higher chance of a sale. People deal with people who they feel know what they are talking about.

9. ***Have a positive attitude.*** Mindset is key. Sales is a tough slog. You need to get used to rejection and countless objections as to why a customer won't do business with you. I joke around that my nose is flat because of all the doors slammed in my face. Regardless, keep a positive attitude. No one wants to do business with a Negative Nelly. Show enthusiasm and excitement for your product and for the opportunity to help solve a problem. Where focus goes, energy flows, so focus on being optimistic. You're one *no* closer to a *yes*!

10. ***Seek feedback.*** As you work on improving your skills, seek feedback from trusted colleagues and friends. Consider a different point of view so you can adapt better in the future. Have a mentor or colleague join you on a sales call to observe first-hand or rehearse and practice your pitch to a potential target audience. Feedback is one of the greatest ways to improve. You don't know how good or bad you are until you see it from someone else's point of view.

How I pivoted

Nathan Amor, Owner of F45 Inglewood and Legacy

Before the pandemic, I had been a successful investment wholesaler for 16 years. Life was great. I had been ranked #1 in the country four of the last five years. Deciding to shift my attention to a completely different industry was a massive pivot in itself. I'd always wanted to change lives through health and fitness and making a shift to become an F45 studio owner made logical sense to me.

It was around July 2019 when my team and I initially started working on the project of getting the F45 open. It was an exciting time. We were finally ready for our big opening day, scheduled on March 7, 2020. There was a buzz around town, as we'd had a lot of success bringing on new members even before the doors opened. Without a single person stepping on the mats, lifting a weight, or doing a push-up in our facility, we had already signed up about 110 foundation memberships. To put this into perspective, the average studio opens with about 75. We were ecstatic.

As you may know, opening a gym has a lot of upfront costs. The equipment, the buildout, and all the marketing to get the foundation members excited would definitely be an investment, but one we expected to generate revenue. The model was set, and we were ready to go.

As we started to open on March 7, the realization hit that the pandemic was impacting people's decisions about leaving the house and on how they would proceed with their social interactions. After only one week of operation, we recognized that many of our members were afraid to come in. We had no choice, so on March 13, we decided to close the doors of the F45 that we had just spent six months trying to get open.

At the time, we were confident that it was really only going to be a two-week shutdown in order to flatten the curve. We had no idea what COVID-19 was or what was about to hit our society and the world in general. As a result, we wanted to do our part to keep our members and our community safe. Abiding by provincial regulations and under the advice of health professionals, we closed before the government mandated that everything shut down.

After we closed our doors, we had no choice but to pivot. Our business was predicated on people coming into our gym. After we shut down, we made a quick pivot so that we did not lose the momentum we had built with our foundation members. We doubled down and increased our marketing budget. We spent about $20,000 on social media ads, which quickly opened the doors to online workouts.

We really had no idea what we needed to do. When you're in a desperate position, you just have to find the courage to do what it takes to stay afloat. We had to stay positive that it would work. We went from 110 founding members down to about 30 to 35 members who joined our online workouts.

About two months into the lockdown, we did another pivot. We decided to start renting out equipment, as people desperately needed a fitness outlet. Initially, we were hesitant to rent out equipment. These pieces of machinery were all brand new and had never been used. We decided to cater to the demand of our members and allow our members to rent the equipment so they could add intensity to their home workouts.

We weren't out of the woods yet. The pandemic continued to make life difficult for us. Moving online wasn't as seamless as one might think. I am a businessperson and not a personal trainer or online fitness guru. We were just a couple of financial services professionals trying to diversify our income streams, and now we had to really think outside of our comfort zone. We dipped into savings to continue to ride out the pandemic.

In June 2020, we breathed a sigh of relief as we were allowed to reopen. It was like someone injected fresh life back into us. There was so much pent-up demand that the studio started rocking. It felt really great. In a former life, I had been a DJ, so I was able to increase the energy by DJing some high-energy vibes.

As good as all of this sounds, though, the downside is that we've had to change our business model. People in this environment really feel a sense of community and belonging. We root for each other during each workout. This was dampened now that we could no longer do high fives, we could no longer share equipment, and we could no longer move around the room, which was a massive selling feature of the F45 fitness model. Now we had to operate with 3-meter spacing. There was no moving around the room. No shared equipment, and we max out with 14 people per class versus the original 36.

As much as the energy was back, we had to mentally shift gears to these new confinements. We understood the circumstances and were just thankful that the gym was even open. From a business-model perspective, though, this obviously has a major impact on the ability to have increased revenue streams. We knew the real value of the F45, but the new reality was that the quality of the product we were so proud to provide had to be watered down.

Nevertheless, even with all of the restrictions from June through December, we were able to grow the business by sheer determination. We maintained a positive energy so that members would continue to feel a community vibe. If we showed stress, members would be turned off. Who would want to go to a gym that has negative energy? For a few months, we became profitable. Then boom! We get slapped with another lockdown.

We had to go back to where we had been a few months earlier. We transitioned back online with all of our members. This time, we had a bigger base with more of a following. Our location still maintained the desired positivity that people needed. Even though it was online, members desperately needed a positive community to relate with.

We provided it. We had about 60 members follow us online. This time, we rented out equipment without hesitation. Our members had weights and resistance to increase the intensity of their home workouts. It was time to kick up our livestreams.

This elevated online experience continued from December until March 8, when we were allowed to reopen. This time, however, we were only allowed low-intensity workouts, plus members had to wear masks while working out. Talk about a watered-down version of the real thing! This took away 50 per cent of our workouts, because typically, we would do one day of strength training and one day of cardio. With the new restrictions, we were only able to run strength resistance training. And as you can imagine, it's very uncomfortable to wear a mask at any time, especially when working out.

Our programming had yet again been watered down. Nevertheless, we adapted. We pivoted. We changed. You can't lower your energy and enthusiasm, even though you feel like it. A gym is a place for positive vibes, so we stood by our brand. As a result, we've been able to bring most of the members back that we had from last summer. In fact, we've been growing. About 10 to 20 new members signed up over the last several weeks since we were allowed to reopen.

So as a business owner, I have learned several valuable lessons and insights. First of all, I was very happy that I did not quit my job to jump all-in on the F45. Throughout this pandemic, I still had a job that gave me stability and an income to support my family, as well as the funds to keep my business afloat. If you're going to start a new business, make sure you can do it financially. Sometimes going all-in sounds like the right decision, but having diversified income streams makes even more sense.

Secondly, make sure you have a team of professionals around you if you're going into an industry that's new to you. Lucky for us, our trainers are certified personal fitness trainers. They know what they are doing and did an amazing job with the move from the gym to online workouts. For a regular civilian like me, there was so much peace of mind knowing that I had smart people around me with the skills and expertise that I lacked.

The last lesson I would share with new business owners or ones in the middle of a pivot is to build something more than what people see on a business card. I learned, especially regarding the fitness community, that we were not just building a gym; we were building a community. Through all this, we have become very close with a lot of our members. When you build a loyal following and community, members tend to stick together through thick and thin. We needed each other during this pandemic. We supported them, and they supported us. We wanted to be there for them, and they wanted to be there for us. We all waited with excitement together for the reopening after each and every lockdown. We were in the same boat together.

This helps immensely with your mindset, especially during a time when the future is so uncertain. At least we knew with certainty that the bonds we were building were real and genuine. We are committed to creating an environment and vibe that we will continue to grow and develop as we come through the pandemic. We pivoted from simply selling a gym environment to creating real bonds and community in the process. This is something that will continue well beyond the F45 workouts.

Nathan Amor, Owner
F45 Inglewood and Legacy
www.f45training.ca/inglewoodcan

CHAPTER 13

Plan to Succeed

Success doesn't just happen. It's
planned for.—Anonymous

In previous chapters, we jumped into the DeLorean and travelled back in time to get a grasp of business before the pandemic. History has shown us that one constant through time has been *change*. From there, we used the pandemic to highlight the change we are experiencing today and saw how it simply accelerated several inevitable trends, mainly technology, and why everyone should have an entrepreneurial mindset. You may never open your own business, but when you view yourself as the business and the owner of your time, opportunities to move from *pandemic* to *profit* greatly increase. Now that the mindset is there, it's time to start putting it into action.

Ever since I've been in business, I have always been told by my mentors that "People don't plan to fail; they fail to plan." This resonated so much as I was maturing in both business and my personal life. Failure is all around us. Whether it's in a business venture, a personal relationship, or a sporting event, people don't expect the outcome to be a failure. Those who have a solid well-executed plan are usually the ones who win.

I also saw a quote somewhere that stated, "If the plan doesn't work, change the plan, but never the goal." This is also very true, as people tend to give up after the first hint of failure.

You have picked up this book because you have a goal you want to accomplish, whether making additional money, keeping your business from failing, staying above water when drowning in debt, or growing with the new digital opportunities this pandemic presents us. The reality is that you shouldn't be planning simply because of a pandemic. It's such a defensive mindset, and by the time you implement it, it can be too late. Instead, plan to win rather than plan not to lose. This could be a pre-pandemic plan rather than a post-pandemic plan.

Planning is *vital* in every aspect of your life if you want to succeed. There is no point in even setting a goal if you don't have a plan. You are simply setting yourself up for failure and disappointment—or, worse, just wasting your time. Time is one resource that you cannot replenish, so planning how you will spend your time is important.

Given how fast a pandemic or any future crisis can happen, preparing for the worst and expecting the best is the prudent approach. At the time of this writing, we are in full lockdown, and vaccines are slowly making their way to the masses. I am crossing my fingers that this pandemic ends; however, it will leave us with things to think about in the future. As a small-business owner myself, it is important for me to see the overall landscape that I am working in, and to identify trends and think about them. In North America, the American dream is alive and well. Entrepreneurship is taught in schools. Iconic entrepreneurs such as Richard Branson, Elon Musk, and Kanye West show that being a businessperson can be cool and impactful. As mentioned above, entrepreneurship is not all Instagram worthy pictures on social media. It's a grind and you must understand the environment you will be grinding away in. Below are some statistics I have collected for you to consider.

Statistics for small businesses to consider in 2022 and beyond

How many small businesses are there in the US?

Currently, there are over 30.7 million small businesses in the US, according to the Small Business Administration. The SBA defines small businesses as firms that have fewer than 500 employees. So this means that many highly valued start-ups in the US are within the definition of a small business.

The definition of a small business varies around the world. For instance, in Europe, a business is considered small if it has fewer than 50 employees. In Australia, a business with fewer than 15 employees is considered a small business.

Regardless, the odds are that if you are reading this, you would likely fall into one of these definitions of a small business. Planning is important if you want to succeed. More and more start-ups are popping, but that is a positive thing and one that give you hope.

How many jobs are created by small businesses?

As a small-business owner, there is a lot riding on your shoulders. No pressure, but much of the economy is driven by small businesses. People need you to make the right decisions, as 1.5 million jobs rely on small businesses annually. This accounts for 64 per cent of new jobs created in the US according to Fundera (2019).

The survival of small businesses is crucial, as there tends to be a systemic effect. When small businesses succeed, there are of course financial rewards to be reaped, which in turn can fund expansion and creation of more jobs. Another benefit is that the creative contributions and start-ups fostered by the small-business community breed new trends, technologies, and ideas that lead to new industries and opportunities. Whether these companies ever expand to be large corporations or remain a side hustle from your basement, you can never discount the importance of your success. Plan for success, as many rely on it. As yourself, are you up for the added responsibility?

Small- and medium-sized businesses are huge drivers of the economy

I mentioned earlier that small businesses are responsible for creating a large number of jobs. These employees earn a living, and in turn spend their hard-earned money on other items. This feeds other businesses, and the cycle of spending continues. The velocity of money is the grease that keeps the economic machine moving.

Not only do these employees trade their time for money, but they contribute to innovation across companies, firms, industries, and countries. How many inventions, software, or new technologies are needed for us to remain efficient in our daily life? These all started off as small businesses but have become important parts of our lives. The small little kiosk in the mall selling cell phone cases or the landscaper that comes to my home to remove the leaves from my eaves are all needed. I would be pretty pissed off if my brand new iPhone dropped without the protective rubber casing or if I had to climb up a ladder to clean those leaves.

Small businesses make our lives easier. It's all part of the ecosystem. And it's not just our local economy that benefits from small businesses. Accessing better global markets helps improve knowledge, networks, digitization, and any advancement in local markets as well. As they say, think globally and act locally. Ask yourself, is does my business or does this pivot add value to the lives of others?

What is the top reason for opening a small business?

I mentioned earlier that many people dream of opening a small business. Who wouldn't want to be the big boss with access to resources, jet-setting around the world and making lots of money? However, this isn't everything. A survey done by Guidant Financial in 2019 revealed that 55 per cent of respondents said the main motivation for being their own boss was the freedom and control to make their own decisions.

Another reason for starting your own hustle is to pursue your own passion. In fact, 39 per cent stated that this was their primary reason. Among other reasons were being unhappy with their current employment setting, lack of funding, insufficient retirement planning, unexpected life-changing expenses, and having a sense of control over their time. Pivoting in any business is difficult. People looking on the outside see success however behind the scenes are many long days, late nights and lean pockets starting off. Is your *why* enough to keep you going when people abandon your idea and things look bleak? Make sure your reason is rock solid and unshakable.

Who is more likely to start up a side hustle?

Statistics show that there is a new generation of entrepreneurs who are more likely to start a side hustle. Side hustles have been around for years. Mothers would bake goods to sell to neighbours or babysit other kids if they were homemakers. Fathers might take on part-time jobs on weekends to get a bit of pocket money. When looking at which generation is getting into the gig-economy and side-hustle mindset, it's the millennials and Gen Z-er's who are 188 per cent more likely to create a side business than baby boomers or traditionalists, according to a survey from SalesForce in 2019.

The reason these demographics decide to start a side hustle is primarily due to a burning desire to do something they are passionate about. In fact, 48 per cent of boomers, millennials, and Gen Z-ers feel the impetus to start a business because they want to bring an idea to market that they strongly believe in. Where cost was once a major deterrent in venturing into the world of entrepreneurship, the rise of online marketplaces like Facebook Market, Amazon, and Kijiji; the opportunity to outsource talent at a fraction of traditional costs for local skills; the acceptance of online buying habits; and the demand for more options and solutions make it even more attractive to address client needs from your home. Are you in this demographic? If not, can you access or partner with those who can inject energy, ideas and passion into a venture?

What is the biggest challenge small businesses face post-pandemic?

Starting a side hustle or new business brings challenges that one may not face when employed. According to CNBC, in 2019, 52 per cent of businesses surveyed felt that one major problem was the quality of labour available. Small-business owners claim that it is becoming harder and harder to find quality talent in local markets. This is exceptionally difficult for businesses with more than 50 employees. For smaller-sized businesses, the biggest challenge is financing or lack of financing. With razor-thin margins, entrepreneurs have to learn how to do more with less. Creative thinking and pivoting into new opportunities is a must in this new reality. Do you have resources available to get you by during lean years or do you have facilities or connections that will lend you money when times are tough? It takes money to make money, so make sure you know who has your money.

What are the top digital marketing channels among small-business owners?

Going digital is a given. It's no surprise that social media is the new way to consume content and information, and 64 per cent of small-business owners who were surveyed by the *Manifest* in 2019 say that social media is their main focus and marketing strategy. Nearly all small-business owners interviewed are doing some type of business advertising. The majority of this advertising is done through digital mediums rather than traditional channels. Most people skip through TV commercials, pay for YouTube Premium to eliminate the advertisements, or scroll through what's trending on Google rather than reading a newspaper cover to cover. Here is the breakdown of where advertising dollars are going:

- social media (64 per cent)
- online marketing (49 per cent)
- print marketing (36 per cent)
- television (22 per cent)

Some older audiences enjoy the touch and feel of a newspaper while reading and sipping their morning coffee. However, for the advertiser, digital as a medium of advertisement allows for a more targeted customer approach. Accessing analytic tools or reports allows businesses to adjust if need be to see whether an ad is working, or pay for Google Ads or Facebook Boosts to get their message out there. Up to 73 per cent of marketers believe that social media has been "somewhat effective" or "very effective" when it comes to creating awareness of their products. Ask yourself, do I feel comfortable promoting my business in new platforms and mediums? If not, can I hire someone who will be the face or voice of my business?

The reality is that the years after this pandemic will be difficult. The world has recalibrated in so many ways that businesses have to make difficult decisions as to whether to do what they have always done or adapt to new ways of thinking. Understanding these statistics and trends allows you to determine the type of pivot your business will need to make to survive. In the next chapter, we will explore a few examples of businesses that have pivoted successfully in this environment.

How I pivoted

Russell Peel, founder and owner of Muteki Strong Academy and MMA

Pivot ...
  No, not like that, Fuckstick!
  Do you want to get knocked the fuck out?
  In the pugilistic arts, one thing always remains a key to any fighter's success in battle: changing direction with your footwork to elude your opponent and create openings. This has been a fundamental technique used by the best world champions of our era. Learning to pivot will help you win not only in battle but in every aspect of life. When life throws you a shitstorm, you need to learn how to get out of the way. Last time I checked, being covered in shit (100 per cent other

people's shit) is not that fun. So you might want to pay attention to what I'm about to teach you.

My name is Russell Peel, and I have chosen a very unusual path in life. You see, I've never been normal, and I knew I was put on this magical rock flying through the universe to do something special. The blueprint was never given to me, so I had to go out and find it the hard way, one concussion and nut shot at a time. Finding the way to get there has taken me on an amazing journey, living overseas in Japan for 11 years and becoming a professional athlete in two different sports. All of that to find out that the journey has just begun and never ends.

I am a specialist in the pugilistic arts. It is all I've ever been interested in from early childhood. Efforts by my father to turn me into an academic at a young age failed. Science fairs were traded in for fist fights and detention halls. I had a fire inside me with no direction. Thank God for self-loathing, because every weak point I had got turned into a strong point, and I was able to graduate with honors with a degree in criminal justice. I was on my way to law school and becoming the Canadian version of the American Psycho. Money, BMWs, nose beers, and douchebaggery were all on the agenda. But first, I needed a break.

Then Japan happened …

Thank fucking God.

I returned to Canada in 2013 after 11 years in a very foreign land as an accomplished martial artist, with black belts in both Kyokushin Karate and Judo and professional fighting experience in K1 kickboxing. I had experience training with some of the best fighters in the world, and a pile of trophies and medals. I knew that I wasn't going to be your average Joe Punchclock and that passing on the knowledge and experience I had acquired was paramount to my future, soul, and purpose.

Martial arts changed my life and gave me the direction I needed to focus that fire that had always been in me. This was my path. Changing lives was my mission. Muteki Strong was born.

What is Muteki?

Muteki (*mu-te-ki*) or 無敵, translated from Japanese, means "invincible" or "unrivalled." You know those headbands or hachimaki that Japanese kamikaze pilots wore as they flew their planes into enemy ships? Yeah, that is what was written on them. It was also the very spirit samurai warriors believed in when they went into battle— to become so strong, knowledgeable, and experienced that there are no enemies. No one is on your level.

Personally, this very belief, mantra, spirit, or whatever you want to call it has helped me to become the best version of myself. The Muteki mindset has helped me unlock all kinds of accolades as both a competitor and a coach. I was able to train five world champions in powerlifting, including myself; a national champion in MMA; and a stable of promising fighters and lifters. I've taken average Joes and turned them into savages. It's no secret. It is all about putting in the hard work, pushing past your own personal limits, avoiding shortcuts, and trying to be a good person. Follow a simple set of rules and be consistent day in and day out. On a long enough timeline, you will be miles ahead of the competition and on your way to becoming Muteki.

March 15, 2020 ... COVID Cancelled

I had a very successful seven-year tenure at a big box gym in Calgary, working with thousands of clients and impacting just as many lives—then, overnight, decisions by COOs, CEOs, VPs, and a bunch of other bullshit acronyms left me *laid off* and without a job. A microscopic virus named COVID-19 single-handedly took down the fitness industry. A shitstorm like no other. I was COVID Cancelled.

Since 2013, I have put in 12-hour days, six or seven days a week. I hit a bunch of accolades, went on fancy trips, and established myself as one of the top trainers and coaches in town. You see, I got caught in that fitness trap where you make all the sales and you train all the clients but only get paid *half* of what you should be getting. It was the proverbial carrot at the end of the stick, chasing monthly sales and training-session goals, blind to the reality that you are just another number. I was basically being a cuck in my own porn channel, watching life fuck my dreams while I sat in the corner fapping to what I could potentially become—stagnant, unmotivated, and wasting my talent.

Getting laid off and COVID Cancelled proved to be the best fucking thing that ever happened to me. All of a sudden, I had all this free time to gather my thoughts, detach myself from the rat race, and focus on my passion and purpose. No more fitness pimps shaking me down for half the money for none of the work. COVID Clarity had lifted me from my Stockholm Syndrome and all of the glass walls I had built for myself. I was motivated, energised, and ready to destroy any obstacle put in front of me.

That's when I decided to pivot and made the *best* decision of my life. I decided to gamble and bet all the chips on myself. Muteki Strong Academy was official. Nothing was going to stop me from manifesting my goals and dreams. The Muteki Mindset had never been stronger.

What started as a vision nearly a decade ago has now become a reality 41 years in the making—from a nine-year-old meat nugget with his first weight set to a world champion and successful gym owner. The road in between, and all of the mistakes made along the way, made me strong enough to carry the stress and responsibilities of today. A year ago would have been too soon, and yesterday would have been too late. Knowing exactly when to pivot is your key to victory. Pivot, side-step, and deliver the KO. When that shitstorm comes in full force, get the fuck out of the way!

So, what can you take away from my story? Follow a simple set of rules to become *invincible* and be able to take on *anything life throws at you.*

The Muteki Strong nine commandments:

1. Find what you are passionate about and become a master in it.
2. Have a clear vision of who you want to be, now and in the future.

3. Push your physical and mental limits beyond what you think is possible.
4. When life gets stagnant, move the fuck on.
5. Learn a martial art, preferably not a bullshit one.
6. Surround yourself with like-minded people.
7. Always give back to the community.
8. Find a mentor and become one yourself.
9. Don't be a Fuckstick.

Osu!

Russell Peel, Owner
Muteki Strength Academy
www.mutekistrong.com

CHAPTER 14

Think Pivoting Is Necessary? Prove It!

Believing is seeing and seeing is
believing.—Tom Hanks

IN THE PREVIOUS CHAPTER, I SHARED A FEW TRENDS TO CONSIDER while pivoting in your existing business or starting a side hustle to supplement your current income. But how do we know that this crucial pivot can work? The *Harvard Business Review* released a few examples of businesses that have been able to pivot successfully in the midst of 2020. I've shared some amazing stories of small businesses that have pivoted, but let's check out a few large business examples. Seeing is believing, so let's explore other successful pivots during this pandemic.

The COVID-19 pandemic has essentially forced businesses to change or die. This pivot is often included in a business model that is necessary for short-term survival and long-term resilience and growth. From local restaurants to larger companies like Spotify or Amazon, no business has been left untouched. But just because we mentioned how crucial pivots have been, it's important to note that not all pivots have resulted in profitable business performance.

There are three conditions that must be met for your business's pivot to work. First, this pandemic has intensified long-term trends. A business must align its model with one or more of these. Second, the pivot must come as a lateral extension of the firm's existing capabilities and align with its strategic vision. Finally, the pivot must offer a way to generate a profit that is sustainable over time while still maintaining or improving the brand value in the eyes of the customer.

The Trend is your Friend

At the height of this pandemic, massive uncertainty occupied the brain space of corporate decision-makers and key influencers. As the stock market plummeted and subsequently rebounded a few months later, there still remained a sense of uncertainty and mistrust that the rebound was real. Much of the economy was propped up by stimulus. What happens when countries stop printing money and run out of wind to pump up the economy?

Many believed this pandemic was the turning point to a new way of thinking and that the old way was done. Face-to-face sales jobs would be replaced by video meetings, and even doctor visits were replaced by medical hotlines offered by municipalities, cities, and states. Stay-at-home demands meant the end of commuting and the beginning of remote work.

To a certain extent, this was and is true. Many businesses will not go back to the inefficient way of contributing to traffic jams heading into the downtown core. In fact, real estate outside of the city started to increase in demand as the attraction of staying in downtown Toronto paled in comparison to working remotely in picturesque cottage country. Many pundits claimed that certain industries were doomed to fail and would eventually fall into bankruptcy.

The truth is that many companies dealt with this crisis by preparing for the worst-case scenario, creating contingency plans, and staying nimble enough to know when and how to pivot. Successful pivots lead to short-term survival along with the realization that this might lead to long-term growth. A solid pivot creates value for both customer and firm.

I work for one of the largest wealth management firms in the world. We are the go-to pension provider millions of people around the world. Connecting with businesses and the people we serve was so vital to our business. When it became clear that our sales teams would no longer be able to make face-to-face sales calls, we were ready. Prior to the pandemic, the sales team at Sun Life Global Investment believed that increasing customer contact was paramount. There was a massive investment in Web-based meetings to cut travel time and make it more efficient for clients and sales professionals to connect. Webex, GoToMeeting, and a newer firm called Zoom became the options to try. Half of the sales team would pilot this Web-based initiative a year before the pandemic took place. Zoom won the battle and became the conferencing service of choice.

This was a prudent move, as Zoom became the standard conferencing service when the pandemic hit. The simple user-friendly interface along with the fact that guests did not have to download a specific software to use the service made it the obvious choice. As 2020 closed off, the pandemic still remained in force, effectively wiping out many businesses that didn't see the theoretical meteor hitting the earth. However, Zoom stock skyrocketed in value, and Sun Life Global Investment celebrated its most successful sales years in history. Talk about a timely profitable pivot accelerated by the pandemic! Despite the initial grumbling of the sales team (we loved face to face in person meetings at on the golf course or in a fancy restaurant. Who wouldn't?), the pivot make financial sense for the firm and make record paycheques for the sales team. Sometimes it has to rain before the rainbow shows us the pot of gold!

Another pivot came in the form of music. As more and more people were forced to lock down in their homes, the boredom factor increased. Spotify, the global leader in music streaming, was positioned perfectly as a positive mood-changer during lockdown. Customers trapped in their homes escaped the noise of kids running around, a nagging spouse, or the depressing silence caused by the reality of a lockdown. Listening to songs seamlessly streamed to a playback device without any need for physical distribution seemed like a slam dunk, right?

Theoretically, this should have been a lay-up for Spotify, but the Swedish company struggled to pivot away from a key issue. Before the pandemic, the company believed that advertising revenue would grow faster than the free user base, which would positively impact the profit margins. Unlike Apple Music, Spotify relied heavily on free users who would have to listen to periodic advertisements. When the pandemic hit, companies slashed their advertising dollars, and therefore Spotify's revenue stream shrunk significantly.

So, if your main revenue stream dries up, what do you do? Spotify made a creative pivot and decided to offer original content in the form of podcasts. Now, podcasts have been around for some time. Joe Rogan did an amazing job making them popular. Now, people stuck at home craved creative content. Artists and users began to upload more than 150,000 podcasts in just one month. Heck, I even started my own podcast, called "Ready, Set, RISE," on both Spotify and YouTube.

Spotify signed exclusive podcast agreements with celebrities, making it the standard for podcasts platforms. As a result, Spotify went from being reactive to being more of a game-changer and trendsetter. The gold standard was for your podcast to be available on Spotify.

Digital platforms make pivoting much easier for businesses that can go from brick-and-mortar to digital. The obvious victims of the pandemic are retail and restaurants. The lockdown punched them in the mouth like a Mike Tyson right hook. Many owners had to make the difficult decision on whether to lay on the canvas and concede the ten-count or find a way to get back up. Typically, restaurants make money by turning over tables. When the lockdown prevents people from even sitting at tables, what do you do? Takeout, delivery, and catering are the obvious pivots.

Many restaurants were able to pivot by offering prepaid purchases at a discount. This could be used for takeout or when the restaurants opened up. Patrons essentially bought meals at a 50 per cent discount. The instant cashflow injection helped keep the businesses afloat as they tried to ride out the wave.

Some restaurants offered a flat rate for a set number of meals per week for a limited menu item. This kept costs low, as they were able to better predict demand. The tighter menu consisted of recipes that essentially used the same ingredients in multiple dishes. Many creative restaurants offered precooked dishes with additions or alcohol pairings. Places in Canada allowed patrons to purchase a bottle of wine with food delivered to their door.

Restaurants also took the home experience to a new level by offering simple deconstructed dishes with a link to a video that walked patrons through the preparation. This incorporated an immersive experience and an educational component. Many people who never cooked in their lives could impress their spouses with culinary masterpieces, with their favourite restaurant as their wingman! Sales for many of these adventurous restaurants jumped, as patrons would purchase days or up to a week of meals. Since many people worked from home, they eliminated the decision fatigue of figuring out what's for dinner.

I recall seeing images of empty shelves at the height of the pandemic. Grocery stores had this creepy end-of-the-world feeling. The crisis broke the supply chain. When the demand from restaurants and specialty stores rose, it opened up the movement to support local, presenting an opportunity for small farmers. Many small-scale farms skipped the distribution channels and promoted directly to the end user.

If they were cutting out the middleman, farmers had to invest in infrastructure, information technology, marketing, and logistics to get food from farm to table. This strategy proved profitable over the long term, and the support local movement increased. Shopify, a Canadian e-commerce site and the largest company on the Toronto Stock Exchange, saw farm activity boom at distances of less that 15 miles between seller and buyer. This was an area that giants like Amazon traditionally did not service.

Even large companies like Unilever had to make pivots in this crisis. Demand for essential products increased, so what did Unilever do? It focused on packaged food, surface cleaner, and personal hygiene products over its traditional money-makers, like skin care products.

During this pandemic, consumer preferences have changed. Established brands benefit less from brand loyalty. Consumers are more open to experimenting in the comforts of their home. Companies that did not focus on a socially responsible perception struggled as consumers started to demand social entrepreneurship. Perhaps the good thing about this pandemic is that it brought to light the need for us to love the environment and choose companies with a more socially responsible lean. As a result, many companies have decided to pivot into this trend.

For instance, in the investment industry, many portfolio managers have filters in selecting companies. They prefer an ESG (environment social governance) investment style. This is good for both the company and the bottom line. ESG investing indicates that the leadership of a company is more forward thinking and has an eye on future trends that may impact their company, including human rights issues, labour, whether or not their drilling impacts indigenous peoples, or whether the compensation of executives is aligned to performance of the company. Whatever it is, investors are more discerning as to whether this is not only a good stock but a good company in general. Many investors shy away from alcohol or cigarette companies regardless of profit.

Even traditional dating services had to pivot due to social distancing. Tinder had to follow the cue of social media platforms like Bumble or Facebook and ask, *If you can't go for a coffee date, why not try a video date?* It's safer, cheaper, and easier to leave a date; instead of running to the washroom and sneaking out of the restaurant, just click, and the date is done!

Now, I know I spent a lot of time going through long-term trends, as businesses need to identify ways to align with them. It's important to keep an ear to the ground and see what is happening in your country, community, industry, and client base. From there, you must find ways to allow those trends to highlight your strengths.

The pivot must not undermine the intent of the company

The condition is that the pivot must be a lateral extension of the firm's existing capabilities and strategic intent. A great example can be seen in the travel and hospitality business. Airbnb moved quickly with its model to help hosts financially by connecting them with guests. Hosts can offer online events focused on food, therapy, yoga, virtual tours, and other activities to increase engagement. This pivot allowed Airbnb to move from a matchmaking service of host to guest to becoming a full-range lifestyle solution.

Since many people are now living online, the future for a company like Airbnb is to leverage the experience-based business model and help travellers discover new destinations onsite or in the surrounding area. Airbnb hosts can curate fun things to do around the city or arrange in-house events for guests to keep the experience memorable. The capabilities to pull this off are still within the company's wheelhouse without jeopardizing its long-term intentions.

The pivot must be sustainable

Finally, the third condition is that the pivot must offer a sustainable, profitable model that preserves and improves brand value in the eyes of consumers. While this crisis doesn't necessarily mean doom and gloom for entire companies, it does help weed out the weak from the strong. Is your current business model sustainable?

For instance, in the financial-services industry, there are several ways to receive compensation. Some of the more common are front-end, deferred sales charge, and fee for service. Without going into too much detail, each option allows the financial advisor to charge the client based on agreed-upon terms.

In the front-end model, an advisor can charge a client an upfront fee, which is deducted before the investments are made. For instance, an advisor can charge 2 per cent. If a client has $100,000 to invest, the total amount invested will be $98,000 after the advisor charges her fee. In a fee-for-service model, an advisor can charge for services rendered (such as creation of a financial plan, tax and estate planning, and so on). This is similar to how dentists or lawyers would charge for their work. Finally, there is deferred sales charge. This was once the most common form, as the client would not have to pay anything. However, the financial advisor would be paid 5 per cent commission from the fund company whose investment solutions were then sold to the client. The caveat to this structure is that the client would be locked in for seven years. If the client decided to withdraw the money prior to seven years, there would be penalties.

Much of that industry used the deferred sales charge because the client would not have to pay out of pocket and the advisor would make a hefty amount of commission. Theoretically, the high upfront commission was meant to incentivise the advisor to client to work together for the next few years as the client built their financial foundation. With new regulations and firms reducing or eliminating this practice as a whole, many financial advisors have had to pivot and find other ways to be compensated. Businesspeople need to determine whether their revenue models are sustainable or under attack from new regulations, competition, industry changes, or client preferences. Is the pivot sustainable and are you compensated appropriately for your time?

With all of this in mind, the examples mentioned above highlight how these changes separate those who fail to pivot and those who embrace the new reality of shorter value chains, people working remotely in their pajamas, social distancing, increased comfort with video communication, transparency of how businesses get paid, consumer preferences, and new technologies that bring the world closer together. Humans are adaptation machines. Without the willingness and knowledge to pivot, the competition will evolve faster than you thus rendering you weaker or worse of, extinct.

How I pivoted

Filomena May, Senior Wealth Advisor with Filo Financial Solutions of Raymond James Ltd.

My journey in the investment world during COVID

Near the end of 2019, I felt this anticipation about 2020. I kept saying, "Big sh*t is happening!" Anxiously waiting, I felt it was going to be a year I would never forget. Well, I predicted that accurately!

The year was off to a great start as I had my debut on BNN in Toronto—an item on my bucket list and a highlight in my career. I was also in the thick of my busy season. I was ready to put my house of 20 years on the market and move into the house I had dreamt of having one day.

Then March hit. The markets being halted three times is something I had never seen in my career of almost two decades. I had experienced the 2008 crash, but this was on a different level. Within about a week of the markets tumbling, our country shut down, which ultimately left me shutting down the branch my team operated from and working from home instead.

Fast forward to over a year later, we were in the same predicament. It felt like Groundhog Day: I would get up, head downstairs in my PJs, and 12 hours later, I would find myself in the same spot. I was on pins and needles. Aside from keeping myself calm with all the uncertainty around the pandemic, I had to manage both the emotions of my two teenagers as a single mother and the emotions of my clients as I figuratively held their hand through the roller-coaster ride, coming through to some pleasant surprises in the markets.

I was fortunate that I already had most of my practice in electronic format and had the setup and ability to work from home. However, when I moved to my new home, the phone company was restricted from coming into my home to set up the fibre-optic Internet. Trying to run a business and having to tether off my phone was not a pleasant experience, but I was determined to push through the roadblocks.

The most disturbing part to deal with was having to let go of half my team, as I painfully came to the realization that they did not align with my practice. I'd been in expansion mode prior to the pandemic and was working on attracting more advisors and clients to my branch. This was the beginning of the "big shift" for me. It felt like the bottom fell out from under me, and I kept saying and repeating, "This will make me stronger and have me come back better than ever." Within a few months, half my team was gone, and I was paying for empty office space downtown.

I did not allow that to stop me, though. I set out my intention of finding my dream team and using this time of aloneness wisely. I remembered how fearful I was starting up my own company a week before the 2008 crash, thinking that my career was over, but I had been pleasantly surprised to find that the following year turned out to be the best of my career. I used that moment as a reminder that I was a queen of manifestation and hustle when I put my mind to it. Failure was not an option in my mind.

I interviewed to find my dream team; mentored university students at the University of Calgary (virtually, of course); developed a new website and social media; and began to study for more exams. Prior to the pandemic, my goal was to obtain my US license and expand into cross-border advising. I also chose to study the markets and research with more purpose and intent. I knew things were going to shift quickly. I needed to stay abreast of it with an unbiased approach, not taking in all of the media noise.

I hired a new assistant who didn't even last three months. Just as I was starting to feel defeated, not one but two people came knocking on my door. That is when I realized that if I wanted to take my business to the next level, this was the time to invest more dollars into my company and hire for different strengths in areas I was not strong in so I could be of greater service to the clients who rely on me and put their financial futures in my hands. I wanted to examine my practice with a fine-tooth comb and looked at the cracks that could be filled.

It also occurred that I was not the best HR person, so I created a position to encompass that role in addition to cross-training and training additional people as we grew. I never wanted to be in a position of vulnerability again. Sometimes, to make money, you need to spend money, and that was the risk I had to take. I hired a second person to work very closely with me and my future goal to work *on* the business rather than *in* the business. My aspiration and passion is to impact and empower people on a larger scale, as more people are gaining awareness of the value of expert advice to help build their personal and professional financial goals.

For the first time in a long time, I feel at ease about my team, regardless of the unexpected events that have come with COVID-19. Having symptoms at one point (luckily a negative test) made me realize I am not invincible and that I needed to make my practice more concrete should the unexpected happen. I had to prepare for the worst. I thought I was solid, but I needed to further walk my talk.

Coming out of this and having more staff and the added expense, I still ended up profiting by over 20 per cent and again hit the best year of my career. What I learned is that you need to spend money to make money, and to not get stuck waiting for the perfect moment. You need to adapt quickly and methodically in times of change. Last but not least, you need to surround yourself with people you consider to be your tribe and who push you, on the days when you struggle and feel defeated, to see what you've built, and who help you keep going despite what your emotions tell you. Perseverance wins the race!

Filomena May, President &
Senior Wealth Advisor
Filo Financial at Raymond James Ltd.
www.filofinancial.ca

CHAPTER 15
Pandemic Pivot Strategies

*Strategy without tactics is the slowest route to
victory. Tactics without strategy is the noise
before defeat.*—Sun Tzu, The Art of War

JUST AS IN BOXING, THERE ARE SEVERAL KEYS TO SURVIVING A
gruelling battle. You must have grit and determination, an action plan,
and the willingness to pivot should things change. In any business
environment. and more so in this current pandemic, the survival of
your business depends on your ability to pivot and be nimble.

At the peak of the pandemic, the US Chamber of Commerce
reported that one in five small businesses surveyed closed, either
temporarily (19 per cent) or permanently (1 per cent). Where I live in
Calgary, Alberta, Canada, the Canadian Federation of Independent
Businesses states that approximately 22 per cent of businesses had to
close down, while 80 per cent of businesses surveyed have made, are
making, or are planning to make changes in response to the pandemic.
Many have used this as a wake-up call to take precautionary measures,
whether it's for this pandemic or another crisis in the future. Whatever
it is, businesses must be able to adapt in order to better function or
remain at least partially open when this new reality fully opens up.
Below are a few simple pivot strategies and examples to consider.

Six Simple Pivot Strategies

1. Go digital and get online for e-commerce (or ease-commerce)

This is an obvious one, as we all got locked down into our homes wondering whether we had enough toilet paper. With uncertainty afoot, our behaviour pattern leaned toward going online. As a business, if you already have an online presence, you have an advantage. Some refused to advance digitally and are now scrambling to keep up.

Don't fear, though. Even if your business is a local brick-and-mortar store with a generic template website you got from GoDaddy or a high-school-project-quality website, there are several ways to maximize it or quickly upgrade.

The first is to build an online store. Customers either have limited access to your place of business or perhaps have become so used to ordering online that they continue this habit even after the lockdowns end. There are ways to leverage this trend. If you don't already have an online ordering service available on your website, there are several third-party vendors you can use.

Shopify, Wayfair, or even other major platforms make it easy to sell your products online. The Asian giant Alibaba launched a new set of e-commerce tools to help American businesses who are struggling during this pandemic to get digital.

Facebook Marketplace and other smaller online marketplaces like Etsy are popular with crafters and other more niche sellers looking for alternatives to or in addition to Amazon or eBay. In Alberta, a small company called Nimbly Market has allowed small businesses to sell on their digital mall and will even create a simple digital store for them.

Use delivery services such as Uber Eats, Skip the Dishes, or DoorDash if you are a restaurant. While you should expect to have some of your revenue skimmed off the top, it's better than closing your doors for good.

If this new e-commerce side of your business is awkward, take smaller steps instead of thinking you have to become a global distributor. Think locally and service businesses in a smaller radius. Be creative and reasonable with your service model.

Here are a few things you can try:

- **Offer free local delivery within a reasonable radius.** Don't promise you can service 45 minutes away, though, and expect to deliver a steaming hot pizza.
- **Enable touchless transactions, such as curbside pickup.** Add this functionality on your newly designed website.
- **Support the go-local movement by highlighting locally sourced products that are relevant to your business.** These locally sourced products will showcase materials or ingredients that are of interest to your community, whether it's a small batch of food or beverages from a local producer or farmer, or brands that support your local community.
- **Leverage social media.** Invest in Facebook ads or boost your content to showcase your goods. If you have little to zero social media presence, you're going to get lost in the crowd. Sure, you can rely on referrals or cater to a specific group. However, to scale to a level that can endure a crisis, you need to broaden your audience. Social media is the easiest and most efficient way to do it. The challenge is to make yourself stand out in a very loud digital world. There are strategies in this book that can help.

One Japanese restaurant in my hometown set up a virtual tip jar to help support laid-off waitstaff, bartenders, or employees who do not typically get tips. Everyone loves a feel-good story, especially during difficult times. As humans, many will want to lend a helping hand.

2. Use your team as a source for ideas and solutions

Trust is a necessary element of any successful business. Your livelihood and the success of your business is dependent on the people who work for you and how well they perform their duties. Your employees are more than just your staff; they are a huge resource for business ideas. In many cases, they are on the front line, and they see what is happening *in* your business while you are working *on* your business. If you have developed a trusted relationship, they are the eyes and ears of your business, while you are the heart and mind.

Be upfront about the challenges you are facing and potential plans moving forward. Your team may not understand the full economic status of the business but is fully aware of the economic environment their employer is in. It's important to discuss safety precautions, immediate changes, and social-distancing procedures moving forward, along with any plans to pivot into new processes or models. Ask your team for feedback on ideas such as:

- Are there any strategies the firm should implement?
- What products should we add, remove, or improve?
- Are there any new business opportunities that we can capitalize on?
- Does the team have any hidden auxiliary expertise or talents, such as art, marketing, musicianship, performing arts, or anything else that may help to differentiate or pivot the business?
- Can we consider job rotation to maximize the talents of our team or change up the duties? Different roles can include local delivery, customer service, or sales, while changes in duties can include expanding the hours or working flexible hours.

3. Identify current needs by listening to your customers

The reality is that your customers are the lifeblood of your business. They pay the bills that keep the machine moving. Now more than ever, it is vital for business owners to strengthen and deepen loyalty with existing customers. It's also important to actively listen and adapt to what they need. Customers want to have a vested interest in the business they love. In many of the top restaurants I have frequented, I have been asked to give feedback on new menus or product launches.

Here are a few things you can do:

- **Try customer surveys.** These are amazing tools to simply empower customers. Use online surveys through email, social media, or services like Mailchimp or SurveyMonkey. Your customers can give you invaluable insights about your business and products, which you may not have been able to notice yourself. Again, your customers are your honest eyes and ears.

- **Numbers don't lie, so look at the data.** Understand where your business is coming from, where your sales are being generated, and how you are marketing to your target demographic. Create an ideal avatar by understanding the profile of your best customer. Look at what worked and what didn't. Take a step back and be honest with yourself.

- **Ask for support on social media so that you can gain social proofing.** Seek out customer reviews, photos, and stories you can share on your social media to grow trust, audience, and engagement. Years ago, companies would hire celebrities to endorse their products. Nowadays, consumers want to hear testimonials from real people. Leverage influencers to get your products out there.

- **Understand trends and be forward-thinking.** Offer new services or products that can leverage new and upcoming demand. Keep an open mind on new niche products gone viral or newly passed laws that require your services (such as legal or construction help). Google, YouTube, and even your mobile phone tell you what's trending. Keep an ear to the ground and ride a trend you think will benefit your pivot.

4. Collaboration and partnership are key

Not only are you and your neighboring small businesses in this together, but you probably have other business partners (existing or potential) who may benefit mutually through innovative sharing of primary or secondary skills and resources.

Find ways to use your supply chain or partners to fulfill shortages of hard-to-find items or services in your area. There must be things in your community that you can partner with your neighbours to buy in bulk. For instance, smaller restaurants can do bulk orders of ingredients that they both may need for their recipes but need to purchase in bulk. Your recipes are different, so don't be so worried that someone is using the same ingredients. It's economies of scale, so learn to partner. We're all in this together.

Consider negotiating with local delivery, courier, or even taxi companies to help you offer or meet a demand for home deliveries. There are many people who are part of this gig economy and need extra money in their pockets. If they can add some extra deliveries to their regular route, it helps the side hustler as well as the local business. Create a delivery service out of nothing and generate money for two hustlers looking to thrive.

Ask your larger partners, like tech companies, if they could help you navigate the new normal by acting as consultants for your business or assisting with marketing or even customer data analysis. Some organizations who can't help financially may still be able to offer free advice or even mentoring sessions. One thing I have learned is that this pandemic has either brought out the best or the worst in people. Thankfully, I have seen the former rather than the latter. Ego tends to step aside when we are all in the same boat. Even the big boys want to see their small colleagues survive.

Return the favour by promoting them. Everyone loves a feel-good story of generosity that people can resonate with. Many of these larger businesses are looking for ways to position themselves as such.

Discerning customers who are holding on to their hard-earned money want to do business with companies that are likeable.

Collaborate with other small-business owners to develop value-added bundles, co-op marketing, or cross-promotion plans. For my smoothie franchise, it was difficult to pivot. We bundled protein shakes and wraps at a discounted price for the surrounding gyms. The traffic helped, as everyone was trying to stay mentally and physically healthy while saving a buck. Gyms would cross-promote the need for a healthy diet, and we would promote the need to stay in shape.

If you are a restaurant needing to add more space, especially for outside dining, talk to the owners of locked-down neighboring shops or parking lots to see if their areas could be used for customer seating. As long as you are abiding by local rules and regulations, you can social distance effectively using other people's real estate—with their permission, of course. In areas in Vancouver and Toronto, I saw streets completely shut down to create patios for local restaurants. Can't eat inside? Take it outside and breathe some fresh air.

5. Diversify, adapt, and add business models

Sometimes, pivoting may necessitate doing something with your business you had never previously considered. Take Mindas Brewery in Calgary, Alberta, Canada. When sanitizers were running low, they turned their facility into something you would never think of. With the skills to create and bottle alcoholic beverages, they decided to pivot into the sanitation business. Talk about something I'm sure wasn't in their five-year business plan.

There are so many other examples, as broadening your services or products comes in many different forms. While foot traffic to your establishment may be down or even restricted by local ordinances due to COVID-19, there may be other ways to utilize your space and staff for generating revenue—like Ken (you'll meet him in a bit), adding another offering that leveraged his existing business to generate a new income stream and expand his business model.

Social distancing has impacted other businesses that rely on foot traffic. Whether this pandemic prolongs the social distancing or establishes new practices in how space is used in businesses, wise entrepreneurs must find ways to maximize the space they have available.

Here are a few cool examples.

- **Turn your restaurant into a market.** In Atlanta, a handful of restaurants have converted into makeshift markets by repackaging their bulk items like rice and flour, dry goods, and even paper towels and toilet paper, which can be ordered online or from new "menus" for touchless, car-side delivery. I have spoken to some entrepreneurs in Edmonton, Alberta, who have turned their parking lots into night markets where late-night shoppers can go and have the same Asian market experience you would enjoy in Bangkok or the Philippines.

- **Teach live online classes or produce videos on the skills your business prides,** whether it's cooking lessons, kickboxing workouts, hair-styling and beauty tips, or even virtual professional services, from accounting to counseling. At first, the thought of sitting in front of a computer listening to lectures or classes online made me cringe. The reality is that it's not as bad as people think. After more than a year in this pandemic, people's behaviours and comfort levels have changed, so take advantage of the adoption of video conferencing by sharing your skills and talents without your clients ever leaving their homes. By making it convenient, you're actually freeing up time (or perhaps providing an escape from other time-consuming activities that they dread to do, like tending to hyperenergetic toddlers who need Mommy to jump at their beck and call!).

- **Expand your operating hours for dining or shopping or provide 24/7 customer service by phone or online.** This is a competitive way to build loyalty and serve more customers while space is limited. Since many people are staying home these days, our routines have changed so much that we can be up later. The extra two hours I have saved in the morning due to not preparing, dressing up, ironing my shirt, and commuting downtown allow me to stay up a bit later than normal. That late-night order of kung pao chicken seems even more delicious when it's convenient.

- **Become a convenient place for your community to accept deliveries.** You can partner with Amazon to become an Amazon Hub, housing Amazon lockers for self-service pickup or utilizing your own kiosk and staff.

6. Take advantage of this time to evolve.

Another great story is Kenneth Kuca, owner of Scalptech Inc. His business provides micro scalp pigmentation procedures (SMP) and certified training for aspiring tattoo artists. He is among the best in the world at tattooing receding hairlines onto bald men's heads in convincing 5 o'clock shadows. He essentially tattoos confidence for balding men. People from all over the world fly in to get this procedure done.

However, even as world-renowned as he is, the pandemic didn't allow travel, visitation, or educational classes to take place. Training was done face to face, so student practicums couldn't be done. This wiped out a large chunk of his revenue.

Rather than wait for the pandemic to end, Ken took this downtime to generate another form of income. Proper tooling and equipment such as needles are important as this new innovative procedure must be done properly or you can be left with an unnatural look. Just google "SMP Fail" and you'll know what I mean. The right tools made a world of a difference regarding the quality of work done and the level of confidence on a bald guys head. At the very least, a tattoo artist would go through many needles during a procedure, causing the costs to increase.

Ken took this opportunity to study and develop a more reliable needle specifically for this procedure. As a result, he established the standard needle used by all his students moving forward and many other micro scalp pigmentation artists. From being a technician, he pivoted into being a product developer. Talk about creating passive income streams!

Taking this time to evolve may also mean evolving into something completely different. Many businesses are now faced with the choice to either close or change. Sadly, I have to admit that I had to close a business. It just wasn't profitable. That's the reality, and I can't sugar-coat it.

For many, this pandemic sucks. However we can't continue to blame external factors outside of our control. I wasn't the only one facing this dilemma. Many of these changes may turn out to be more than temporary. However, the agility with which you're able to respond to this crisis, as unexpected as it was, can arm you with the skills and strategies to remain resilient for whatever comes next. What small business has an emergency pandemic contingency plan? I doubt many did. Regardless, I bet many are now skilled to handle anything, if they were fortunate to survive. Consider these strategies even beyond the pandemic as constant evolution is vital. Learn to connect and use the talent, skill and expertise within your own circle of influence to help you. You'd be surprised how beneficial a pivot can be when you know where to look, who to leverage, what opportunities present themselves and how to execute on the plan.

How I pivoted

Victor Lough, CFA CFP, Financial Advisor and President, Agile Wealth Management

The world is both more connected than it has ever been and significantly disconnected. I remember watching the issues with COVID-19 in China, and it seemed like a completely different world. I

MICHAEL SIERVO

have been fortunate to travel through China on a couple of occasions, and it is an amazing and beautiful country. The scenes playing out at the end of January 2020 were also incredible, though: building a hospital in a week; fog machines rolling down empty streets as people were sequestered in their homes; some people appearing to be forcefully abducted for treatment or hauled off to their homes for violating curfews. It was both unsettling and incredible. Things were distant then. We could see the impacts of the coronavirus, but it did not feel real, and it did not hit home at that time.

A couple of months later, it was on our shores. My business as an investment advisor was directly impacted in a few ways. First and foremost, my daily operations were impacted, as I had to work from home. Second, we were all impacted economically when the stock market declined about 35 per cent from the February peak to the lows of March 2020. We had no idea that this would be relatively short-lived at that point, and there were some startling events for market watchers. I did take some precautions when I first started seeing the virus and its impacts, but there was more than one day in that time frame where the precautions were not helping either, as safe havens were down along with everything else (not to the same extent, of course, but that is of little solace in difficult times).

I was still very fortunate, though. Not only was I able to continue working with very little interruption, but my business was growing. I was getting business referred, and people were looking to move to me from other institutions. This was excellent but caused me a bit of a problem. While I could set things up for me to work remotely, the dealer I was operating through at that time was not up to speed. At this point, they were still requiring wet signatures! I had joked in pre-pandemic times that you could buy a home for a million dollars with an electronic signature, but a change of address would require a wet signature.

At a time when meetings were nearly impossible and frowned upon, this posed a dilemma. I decided that the best way to deal with this was to print the documents, drop them off for people to complete and execute, and then pick them up again. This was a stopgap measure. It was not perfect, but it allowed me to get some things completed.

I had several documents that were straight-up not returned—or people would get through half or a percentage and decide it was too onerous. They were right! On one occasion, I dropped off approximately 180 pages for a couple strewn with dozens of "sign here" tabs. It was borderline unworkable. Something had to change.

Throughout this time, I began to investigate other options. I had to get an online electronic signature option, as this was simply costing me business. Just as important, it was making things too difficult for clients and would-be clients to do business with me. I searched and weighed my options. There were other companies, and many of them had options for electronic signatures. For me, that was a significant hurdle solved.

In all honesty, that alone was not enough to sway me fully, though. Perhaps naively, I felt that this virus and the associated societal impacts were going to be short-lived.

When I saw the economic impacts in China, I became immediately concerned about the supply chain and effects on some of the companies whose shares I held for clients. I was selling into the markets as we saw increased gains into the first half of February. I had taken a similar course of action in 2008–09 and knew that I would see some difficulty in persuading people to re-enter the market when things were bleak and the outlook was not as positive. I knew it was time to pivot.

The first big pivot addressed my administrative nightmare. I was working through a major dealership in Canada at the time, and as a corporation of a significant size, it was slow to respond to the pandemic. While others had been using electronic signatures and processes for years, our process still required wet signatures on paper.

The solution to this was for me to gain control over that investment process and find a way to move from my antiquated paper transactions to going fully digital. I was already licensed as a portfolio manager and had most of my accounts as discretionary management. But when the firm I am with today offered up the opportunity for me to have my own pooled mandate, it was the absolute tipping point in my mind.

This meant that I could invest entirely as I saw fit and gave me full control over that process. On top of that, there was no more need for signatures. Welcome e-signatures! With that out of the way, I could focus on money management.

My journey to portfolio management and investment management had more simple beginnings. In 2009, on my way to work, I was listening to Howard Stern, and the conversation was about Bernie Madoff. Howard could not believe that people had invested with advisors who had then put their money with Madoff (who was running a massive Ponzi scheme), and they lost everything! To paraphrase, Howard said something like "people invested with someone and they took their money and invested with this other guy who stole everything?! What in the world is going on?!"

That hit home with me. That is how my business operated. I would have people invest with me and then invest those funds elsewhere and assume that the large institutions were doing their due diligence. To be fair, they were, or at least 99 per cent of the time they were. But I didn't want to be viewed that way.

I started my move to portfolio management shortly after, and here we are about 12 years later. Now I have full discretion and can manage my client portfolios in their best interest without any restrictions. If I am going to pivot, not only is it good for me as an entrepreneur, but my clients will benefit as well.

How I pivoted

Jordan Guildford, Founder and CEO, Gems for Gems, a registered charity

Proactive. Collaborative. High Impact. Revolutionary. Refreshing. These are words that have been used to describe our charity from day one. Celebrities have joined Gems for Gems as ambassadors. Men and women have come together to end the cycle of domestic abuse proactively. Gems for Gems has broken the mold and created a new outlook for the future of charities through its lean organizational structure; the way it utilizes and empowers the community; and its completely unique, solely forward-focused approach. Although those attributes enabled our organization to flourish, it also gave us an inaccurate sense of safety regarding what was to come regarding the unprecedented COVID-19 obstacles.

The Gems for Gems star was shining bright and headed for heights we had never even imagined could be possible. Our impact-led and solution-focused charity had already touched thousands, and 2020 was the year of international exposure, bringing our services to thousands more. Then, out of nowhere, COVID-19 hit.

The Gems for Gems mission is to end the cycle of domestic abuse by providing empowerment and economic recovery to survivors. We have been fortunate to have unquestionable support from multiple sources, but particularly from the community. Initially, the first lockdown brought with it a chance to breathe and get in front of the incredible momentum we had garnered through the past couple of years. It gave us an opportunity to strategize.

As a month passed, and then two, the weight and implications of what this might mean if it were indeed to last for the remainder of the year began to sit heavily. The events that led to our ever-expanding reach, like the Brett Wilson Garden Party and the Stampede Charity Barbecues, were now being canceled. Our monthly board of directors meetings started to get more and more somber as all our fundraising events were cancelled due to the lockdown.

The reality was that Gems for Gems, being the proactive charity it is, was not considered an "emergency response" organization. Our scholarships and other initiatives are designed to help women who are ready to take their life to the next level once they are no longer in "survival mode." This meant the government and private donors were now doing what they felt was the right thing to do by providing their support to shelters that could be there for survivors immediately. This was an enormous problem for the sustainability of our organization.

Gems for Gems always prided itself on being innovative and resilient, and this was an opportunity to show up in a space where most charities do not. Where were people spending their money? How could we work with what trends were already happening to benefit our bottom line? Then it came to us: online shopping. Articles about the exorbitant amount of spending on Amazon were hitting the news weekly. So we created our own clothing line.

The sales for this line soared. We utilized the Ghandi quote, "Be the change you want to see in the world" by putting the words *Be the Change* on every item. The public bought with pride and confidence, as we also decided all proceeds generated by this clothing line would be dedicated to the scholarship program. This decision brought in funding and provided competitive marketing at the same time.

As the year progressed, we focused on collaborating with those who were deemed emergency response organizations through meaningful and sustainable partnerships. Our team dug deeper than ever. Our ambassadors posted more and used new podcasts to bring exposure to Gems for Gems. Our celebrity ambassadors hosted an online event that brought international attention, which we thought could not happen in 2020. In short, our team, the community, and our leadership having open minds and humble hearts opened doors and increased our impact exponentially.

There were difficult times in 2020, but staying creative, calm, and focused on our mission got us through and has opened many new doors. Charities are like any other business in the sense that there will always be competition, a need for innovation, good times, and bad times. We continue to lean into the attributes we have and concentrate on being an impact-focused organization worthy of your contribution.

Jordan Guildford, Founder and CEO
Gems For Gems (Registered Charity)
www.gemsforgems.com

CHAPTER 16

This Won't Be Your Last Crisis

IN THIS BOOK, WE'VE TALKED ABOUT THE COVID-19 PANDEMIC IN detail. We highlighted specific stories of how businesses have pivoted in this environment. The reality is that this won't be your last crisis.

> *Within crisis are the seeds of*
> *opportunity.—Marilyn Monroe*

These are scary times for many, but the truth is that you have the choice to transform the current crisis, anxiety, fear, and doubt into growth, progress, and success. It's all in your attitude and perspective.

I remember working in downtown Toronto and being evacuated from our office tower. It was 9/11, and I was experiencing the idea of terrorism for the first time. I didn't know what to think. I spoke to many of my colleagues in business, and the initial response was one of fear, anxiety, and uncertainty. It's no different than it is now, and it is no different than the next pandemic or crisis that will hit you. Knowing that you will go through adversity again, it only makes sense to use many of the strategies mentioned in this book along with the stories as inspiration that better days are ahead.

This chapter focuses on nine simple strategies that will help you keep focus on opportunities rather than the crisis itself. Be creative, communicate frequently, have an open mind, and continue to approach the situation with a positive attitude when reading these strategies. It will help you navigate the days, weeks, months, and years ahead so that no crisis will ever throw you off course for too long.

Nine things you need to focus on during a crisis

1. Focus on others: This isn't only about you

During times of crisis, it's so easy to go into self-preservation mode. Of course you must think of yourself. Everyone knows the example that when a plane is going through turbulence and the oxygen masks drop down, you need to put it on yourself first and then help others. However, once you realize you're not dying, you need to quickly shift gears and start focusing on others.

Uncertainty can drive people into themselves. If you can't manage to get your bearings straight at the get-go, it's easy to feel isolated and helpless. We can ask ourselves, *Why is this happening to me? It's not happening to anyone else. No one will understand.*

Well, let's stop being melodramatic. Whatever is happening to you has likely happened to someone else. Trust that you are not alone. In this situation, one of the best strategies is to go in the opposite direction. Rather than focusing on yourself, expand your connections with others and focus on helping them transition their negatives into positives. The more you are able to spread helpful energy and focus on others, the less you need to worry about your own situation.

I'm not saying to neglect your responsibilities. But when you help others, the odds are others will help you. Become a source of stability and confidence to everyone around you.

2. Focus on your opportunities: Forget the losses

I remember losing close to seven figures during a combination of a collapse in oil prices, a plummeting real estate market, a deep recession, and now a global pandemic. I got my teeth kicked in. It was brutal. I kept replaying the foolish decisions I had made over and over again and how I could have avoided them. Even worse, I reminisced about the life and wealth I lost. It was utterly depressing.

Whether it's an economic disaster or maybe a marital breakdown, the things you had and the life you may have taken for granted could disappear. Some people may never recover and get over what they lost. They keep replaying the old life.

It reminds me of one of my favourite Netflix shows, *Schitt's Creek*. You have to watch it, as it highlights how an ultrawealthy family loses everything and ends up living in a shitty little town called Schitt's Creek. It's brilliantly written and entertaining, but what's equally appealing is how this family adapts, moves on from their previous life, and makes a comeback after six seasons.

It's so easy to fall into the hole of living in the past. It's an easy game to get stuck in. The best strategy is to start an entirely new game. Find new ideas. Use new tools. Create new energy. Develop new resources. Find new happiness. The world is constantly changing. It will not wait for you. As the world moves on, opportunities will present themselves if your mind is open enough to see them.

3. Focus on connections: Relationships are your biggest commodity

When a crisis or pandemic hits you, it's so easy to go into deficit mode. You hoard your assets. You count the pennies in your bank. You focus on your commodities. You put your energy in the things that you have, your inventory, the services you sell, and the business you still have (or what's left of it). During uncertain times, people become scared about the sustainability of their "things'"—the stuff they sell and the jobs they have.

However, material things can quickly vanish. Someone once told me that if you gathered all the richest men in the world and took their money, the odds are that within a few years, they would regain it back and then some. The reason is their connections. Your network is your net worth. Rather than focusing on your commodities and things, focus on your network.

Deepen the power and possibility within your relationships. This includes your family, friends, employees, advisors, team members, suppliers, banks, clients, customers, prospects, and even that resourceful friend you had in university. In fact, I would advise that you should be doing this religiously now. Dig the well when you are *not* thirsty—meaning, it's easier to ask for help from someone you have developed a relationship with rather than asking someone for help out of the blue. Every time you strengthen your network, your net worth will increase.

4. Focus on value: Forget about closing the sale

It's easy to go into desperation mode and focus on selling whatever you can when times get tough. I remember when I was in the insurance business, we used to say, "Insurance is a needs-based business." The agent *needs* that business badly. It was all about closing the sale.

But the fact is, most people don't want to be sold. They don't like being sold something, especially when times are tough. *Get the f*ck out of my face or stop calling my house during dinnertime.* People don't want to be bothered by sleazy salespeople.

What people really want during times of uncertainty is value. They want to feel that whatever they are spending their money on, they are getting something more than they expected. Create value, and you will create opportunity. This includes solutions that provide peace of mind, assure certainty, eliminate threats, promote ease of doing business, reinforce strength, and spark creativity for new opportunities. When you focus on solving for more dimensions of risk and adding true value, business will follow.

5. Focus on progress: Forget perfection

I remember watching this guy on Instagram. He showed pictures of how he looked a few months into quarantine. He was huge. The big beer belly, flabby arms, and man boobs were on full display. He decided to just exercise every day and be active. He would post his daily progress.

After two months, he commented on how addicted he was to seeing progress; it kept going. He showed off his transformation video, all done from his home. He lifted bags of rice, did push-ups, ran up and down the stairs, bench-pressed his kids, etc. No gym. No excuses! His final picture was shredded. I mean, beach-body shredded.

My point is, most people would look at him and ask, "Why? Why bother doing what you're doing? I can't see the difference." I say forget about negative comments and focus on progress. Are you getting better than you were yesterday?

Things may not be how they once were. New challenges, new obstacles, and new difficulties can either defeat you and give you an excuse to give up or reveal just how strong you truly are. The body can get stronger with exercise and resistance. Continued work against resistance will make the body stronger as well as the mind.

As David Goggins would say, you must callous the mind and become mentally strong. This strengthening of the mind will strengthen your character and your confidence along with it. Treat whatever you are going through as an opportunity where you can become the greatest version of yourself as you progress every day.

For me, I follow the same five things I *have* to do: exercise the mind, body, connections, wallet, and soul every day. Whether it's meditation, 100 push-ups and sit-ups, 20 phone calls to contacts, reading for 20 minutes, or doing something to increase my bank account balance, I accomplish this every day. I don't look at perfection; I look at progress. A marathon is completed one step at a time.

6. Focus on gratitude: You are enough

Let's face it. If you're reading this, you are going through shit or perhaps just went through it. Either way, any crisis, whether big or small, is tough to deal with. However, everyone has to make that decision to say enough is enough. It's hard, but an attitude of gratitude is so important.

I once read a quote that said if you focus on the things you don't have, you will never have enough. If you focus on the things you do have, you will always have enough. You need to decide whether to complain and bitch or be grateful and appreciate what you have.

In a time of crisis, the negative vibes and feelings can easily overwhelm us. This mindset can spew into other areas of our lives. The energy we put forth will come back. It will attract negative people and others who want to partake in the bitch-fest. Having an attitude of gratitude is hard. However, it creates a platform for the best way to approach the day.

Every morning, I meditate before I leave my room. It's 15 minutes of pure gratitude that I am alive and that I even have an opportunity to give the day a chance to get better.

> *Don't ever allow failures or misfortunes of the*
> *past deprive you the chance for success and*
> *opportunities in the future.—Michael Siervo*

Sure, you may have lost a lot of material resources, such as tools, systems, technologies, and information. It's easy to focus on what you lost. The deficiency mindset amplifies this, and it can be paralyzing.

Instead, focus on everything you are grateful for—the air you breathe, the family you have, the fact that you may be able-bodied, the safety of the country you live in, the food on your table, the contacts you still have, the knowledge of specific industries, the fact that you have all your teeth and a smile looks good on you—whatever it is, there is always a reason to be thankful. Being grateful for what we have and leveraging every remaining resource will highlight just how much we still have and how it's enough no matter what. Focus on this, and the opportunities will present themselves.

7. Focus on your reaction: Ignore the cause of the stress

I have always lived by the motto, "Life is 10 per cent what happens to you and 90 per cent how you react to it." My friends and I would watch a movie; some would hate it, and some would love it. We all saw the exact same movie, but each of us came out with our own experience.

Every experience you face really comes down to how you respond to it—simple response and stimuli, like what we learned in grade 5 science class. When things are rocking and rolling, the good times seem to be endless. People actually think they are controlling the feelings they are experiencing. When shit hits the fan and we fall flat on our face, we believe that also was in our control. It is the lack or loss of control that makes us feel defeated and depressed. We lose confidence in ourselves and doubt slowly starts to win the 24/7 war in our minds.

When you look at the most successful people in the world, they understand that things happen. There are things and events that a single person cannot control (such as a global pandemic), and there are things that we can control (such as our mindset). I am not saying to be blind to the reality that bad things happened. You can say "There are no weeds on my lawn" over and over again and pretend they don't exist. Or you can say "Yes, there are weeds on my lawn. They look hideous. Time to remove them." The most successful people acknowledge the event and adversity, take time to soak up the suckiness, and then shift their mindset toward greater control over their response.

I have been a huge fan of stoic philosophy, which is a great way to control our response. It teaches you concepts such as *memento mori* and *amor fati*. *Memento mori* reminds us that we will all die. So is this the hill, the fight, or the complaint. Will this moment be as important when I'm on my deathbed? *Amor fati* reminds us of the love of fate. This happened for a reason; how can I find love or benefit from what just happened?

Anytime there is fear, uncertainty, stress, discomfort, or doubt, we must focus our attention and energy on how we creatively respond to the situation. If it's negative, expect a negative outcome. If it's positive, it may take time, but good things are coming your way. It's your choice. Heck, if the movie sucked, maybe the popcorn and cocktails made it all worth it. Focus on your perspective and reaction.

8. Focus on your potential: Your previous self is gone

OK, so you lost half of your assets in a divorce and find yourself fat and alone. That sucks. Trust me, I can empathize. Many people define who they are based on external factors—their circle of friends, titles, net worth, jobs, etc. Take billionaire Elon Musk or Oscar-winner Denzel Washington for example. We place labels on ourselves.

Just ask anyone to introduce themselves, and they might say, "I'm an accountant" or "I'm a lawyer." No, you're not. You're a human being who happens to be practicing accounting or law at this moment. When these people lose their accounting job or get fired as a lawyer, they suddenly don't know who they are. Their entire persona and character were based on the title. When you lose your billions, you don't introduce yourself as "former billionaire" so-and-so.

Once that title or external factor is gone, people don't know who they are, so they keep trying to hold on to that and be what they used to be. They try to do the things they once did. Accept that you are not that person anymore. Cling to the hope that you are becoming a better person.

When I lost hundreds of thousands of dollars, the fancy cars, and the fat bank account, it certainly hurt. But I'm not that guy anymore. I accept that things have changed, but I'm happier now than I was a few years ago. The reason is that I am armed not with failure but with knowledge, lessons, and experience.

I suggest that from now on, you work on the inside rather than outside forces. Self-improvement and growth is an inside game. It involves a clear understanding of your dreams, goals, ideals, values, core principles, character, and all the things that make you awesome. These do not need to change regardless of the shitty situation you find yourself in. Instead, take advantage of the external circumstances and put those values to the test. Allow yourself to appreciate the past and look forward to the potential the future holds.

9. Focus on the now: The future isn't certain

For years, this has been a challenging topic. I would spend so much time visualizing the future. I would and still visualize manifesting my future reality in very vivid thoughts. I believe this is important, as it guides all the actions that will take you to your future life.

However, I believe there is a fine balance in how that energy needs to be spent. The concept of *future* is abstract. It doesn't exist except as an idea. Every man-made thing we see, touch, and feel has been created twice. As Napoleon Hill says, "Everything is created twice, first in the mind and then in reality."

As much as we must focus and have clear visions of the future, the only future that really exists is the one you continually create for yourself each and every day. Every thought you have leads to an emotion, which leads to every action you do.

Your future accomplishments and results are based on the contributions you make day in and day out. It's this compounding effect that adds up over time. Whether it's accumulating money, getting fit, or building a badass social media profile, it all comes with the actions you take today.

So as you go through a crisis, it's a good time to ignore the experts who never saw the present situation coming and, heck, ignore some of the know-it-alls that did see it coming. Instead, focus on what you can do over the course of each and every 24 hours that this life has blessed you with, as the next 24 hours isn't guaranteed. Only you can guarantee your effort. And you are the only expert you need about the life you are living. So make every moment count. Your future depends on it.

Do the little things that lead to greater things that your future self will be proud of.—Michael Siervo

MICHAEL SIERVO

How I pivoted

Nick Gemmel, CEO of the Pipe Dream Solution

I lost my job around the time that COVID-19 hit. Not because of the fucking virus, but because I was still not dealing with the end of my marriage almost two years earlier. Whether it's a pandemic, a personal crisis, a health scare, or a recession, something in life will knock you on your ass.

You see, I had been living on the road in the trades and the oil and gas industry since 1998, and I lost myself in the process. COVID-19 for me was a definite hit and a blessing at the same time—just as the end of my marriage was. However, when you are going through adversity, at the time it doesn't always feel like a blessing.

I have been an inspector in the oilfield industry since 2012. I was working farther and farther away from my family, and as I have already mentioned, losing myself as time went on. The pandemic was my opportunity to step back and truly look at my life and really dive into how I had gotten where I had gotten, and where I wanted to go.

With no income for months and months, it would have been easy to run from the pain and lose myself in substance abuse or worse. Thankfully, I did not run. Instead, I used this opportunity to dive deep—deeper than I had ever gone in my life.

The prior year, I had gone to rehab to deal with my depression from the breakup. I dove into the world of mindfulness, cognitive behavioral therapy, and the power of setting meaningful goals for my life. I had lost my job again for not giving 100 per cent, continuing to make mistakes, and being confrontational whenever someone opposed me. Without the tools I learned in rehab, I would not be at all equipped to deal with and come out of the other side of this setback.

Just when things started to get back on track financially, COVID-19 hit. What the fuck was I to do?

To keep my mind sane, I looked for help in the realm of coaching. I found myself in a coaching group called Men of Iron. Before losing my job, I had been challenged by my coach to start my own coaching group with tradesmen and oilfield professionals. Blue-collar men in my industry typically don't open up and allow themselves to be vulnerable. If this pandemic taught me anything, it's that now is the time to admit vulnerability.

Not only was this great for me to heal, but it was critical to my financial success. I found men just like me who were going through tough times and needed someone to confide in. I took the lessons from my heartache and was now getting paid to coach other men in similar situations. Unlike the past, where I would run and hide from my failures, I couldn't let these men down. I had to man up for them and for myself.

You see, in this coaching group, these men were going through their own struggles. Some were going through divorce, some were financially beaten down in their companies already prior to COVID-19, and some were lying about where they were in their marriages, their health, and their mindset. Many were in a dark place.

By navigating these men through their struggles, I was able to push through my own alongside them. Rather than taking out my frustration on my kids and those who loved me enough to stick around during my divorce, financial woes, and COVID-19, I was able to refocus negative energy and convert it into something positive.

After getting knocked down by a personal crisis, taking a financial beating from the economic conditions in the oil patch, and facing health concerns in a global pandemic, I found hope in helping others instead of myself. My pivot came from focusing on my own pain to helping others heal from theirs. As a result, I have now grown my coaching program significantly. I launched online training programs, created social media groups, explored different social media platforms that worked, joined engagement groups, and networked as if my life depended on it.

Despite COVID, I am planning the launch of a new company that is in the early planning stages. When historically I would have focused on the crisis, I began to see opportunity. A great example was the housing shortage in Kelowna, British Columbia. Prior to COVID, I wouldn't have the confidence to even try to solve this problem. Now I am in the process of exploring the opportunity to develop my own multi-family real estate development. This proves that tough times make tough people. Getting through trying times is not only about *mindset*, it's about taking *fucking action* on that mindset.

How many people have blamed COVID-19 for their results in the past year?

They put on a bunch of weight because of COVID-19.

They ruined relationships because of COVID-19.

They walked away from their businesses because of COVID-19.

At the age of 42, when I had every opportunity to use COVID as an excuse, I refused to take the easy way out. Instead, I grew my businesses, nurtured new and old relationships, got my ass in the best shape of my life, and contributed to my first book!

My coaching clients have bettered their fitness, have more fulfillment in their lives, have strengthened their personal relationships, and have improved their finances from surviving to thriving. As a coach I am so proud, as some of these men have started businesses during COVID-19. Like, are you kidding me? When businesses are failing, these guys are venturing into entrepreneurship and taking control of their lives.

To me, COVID isn't an excuse. It's a wake-up call.

If I was able to pivot into this new area of business, so can you. But it can happen only if you act and stop lying to yourself that what you are doing is working. That's when real transformation happens. When we look inside and make decisions based on our values and develop a life's mission, life starts to make sense.

The reality is that many of our lives were not working before COVID-19. COVID didn't create most of my problems; I created them. If that's the case, I can create my own solutions. I married who I married. I became disconnected from everyone. I did not save money or invest properly to generate passive income. I chose to work away from home in the oilfield. I chose to find destructive distractions to numb the pain I caused.

COVID-19 is not the problem. Sometimes the problem isn't the problem. Sometimes *we* are the problem, and our poor decisions are our own pandemic.

We all have the chance to look inside and make meaningful and lasting changes. But first, we need to get really clear on where we are and where we want to go, then find the courage to take the steps toward getting there. For me, those steps were rehab, mentorship, and coaching others. Nothing can get in your way if you have a plan and the determination to execute on it without an ego.

COVID-19 will go away, but will the bad habits, behaviours, and actions you do/have daily change?

Therefore my coaching group, the Pipe Dream Solution, works with tradesmen to hold each other accountable so that we break those poor habits. You don't need to take on my 90-day apprentice program, as you might not be the right fit. However, I encourage you to stop blaming COVID or other external forces and start owning the chaos that you created. Use the mess that you created as fuel to make the biggest comeback of your life. In the end, you'll realize that you are just like iron. You are stronger than you think!

Nick Gemmel, CEO
Pipedream Solutions

How I pivoted

Mark Hubbard, CEO of JeepDaddy Inc. and Custom Apparel Pros

Pivoting into a life of adventure and fulfillment.

My name is Mark Hubbard, and I've been fortunate enough to know Mike for right around 14 years now. Mike, being the consummate entrepreneur, actually inspired me to start a business of my own.

About three and a half years ago, I created a brand called JeepDaddy and started off with a small apparel website (www.jeepdaddy.com). It wasn't long before I realized this brand was not going to be lucrative enough on its own by simply selling branded apparel. Fortunately, I had the foresight to work with a developer who was able to template what I'd already built.

The new website allows me to quickly spin up apparel web pages for other brands, which gives them a dedicated page on our site and access to made-to-order apparel. We handle the apparel procurement process end-to-end, so our customers no longer need to worry about anything. Additionally, they no longer need to purchase in bulk, because each order is made individually at a large production facility in Detroit, Michigan.

The one thing our customers really love is that they no longer need to worry about inventory or financial transactions whatsoever. This allows them to focus their attention entirely on what really makes their brand money and not on making five dollars here and there on miscellaneous apparel transactions. They have found that our service saves them time and eliminates frustration.

Given the success we were having with the JeepDaddy website, we ended up creating a second website (www.customapparelpros.com) that has a much larger audience and allows us to provide the same apparel service to brands that are outside the Jeep and off-road industry, such as car clubs and construction companies.

Before the pandemic hit, we were already making some strong headway. However, at the onset of COVID-19, our order volume dropped quite substantially, and the production facility was actually mandated to close temporarily. When that happened, I was definitely stressed about the future of my business!

Fortunately, the facility was not closed for very long at all, and given the reduction of orders during that time, we were actually able to communicate individually with each of the customers who had placed orders to let them know we would be back in operation fairly soon. We did not lose a single order!

The year 2020 was an incredible one for me. I was already set up to be able to work remotely, so my girlfriend and I started on an incredible adventure, which has taken us all over the western US chasing our dreams and inspiring others to do the same along the way. We have been Jeeping our way from state to state and trail to trail for a little over a year now and consider ourselves truly blessed to live such a free lifestyle.

We go by JeepnGypsies on social media, so please be sure to check us out if you are interested in seeing what we're up to. We have tons in store for 2021. We have recently signed on with a sports entertainment company that is looking to turn our crazy life into a TV docuseries! The show will be professionally produced, highly cinematic, and aired ad- and commercial-free on YouTube, with the first season likely coming out in August 2022. It's sincerely incredible how things just seem to fall into place when you are chasing your dreams and passions.

For me, the pivot I experienced led me to appreciate the little things in life, even more than I had in the past. Whether we are 8 or 80, none of us is promised tomorrow. We need to embrace each and every day to ensure we truly appreciate what is right in front of us. We can no longer say things like, "We'll go there someday" or "When I save x amount of money, we can …" We must make our plans to do whatever we want right away and love every minute.

As a business, we have learned to be extremely agile and try to not overplan. Being able to take things in stride is critical. When a pivot moment arises, we quickly evaluate what changes could or should be made, stack rank them, and then execute. Agility and follow-through are the keys to our success and, even more importantly, our mental health.

I sincerely hope these few paragraphs have inspired you to get out there and live your life to the fullest. If you ever want to know more or to get in touch, please don't hesitate to contact me personally. Cheers and all the best.

Mark Hubbard, CEO
JeepDaddy Inc. and Custom Apparel Pros
www.jeepdaddy.com

CHAPTER 17

Conclusion
Life Is About Endless Beginnings

Every new beginning comes from some other
beginning's end.—Seneca, stoic philosopher

THERE I WAS, SITTING IN MEXICO, STARING UP AT THIS MAN WHO was beaming with joy as I gave him a $10 tip for serving us nachos and water to ease a hangover from the night before. After a bender from partying and drinking, I needed a warm friendly face to shine on me. My brother Dave and I were clearly licking our wounds from a crisis that hit us out of nowhere, and this man's smile made a difference. We went from feeling like complete failures to feeling a sense of optimism and hope. I will never forget it. I don't know the man's name, but the lesson he taught me that day changed the way I view life.

There I was feeling sorry for myself. The boo-hoo moment started to seem so pathetic after my interaction with that server. The $10 I gave him made him so grateful. What was $10 in the grand scheme of things to me? But to this man, it was a really generous tip for $6 nachos, a cerveza, and some water. To be honest, I actually think I meant to give him a $5 tip, but I was still reeling from the night before and my eyesight might have been blurred.

In any case, the gratitude and positive energy that this man gave me that day was all I needed for my *Sports Centre* turning point. Perhaps that man really needed the extra money and my act of generosity (intentional or not) was the universe conspiring in his favour. Perhaps it was the universe conspiring in both our favours.

As soon as I got home, my brother Dave and I decided to open a company. After the heartache and loss we had suffered a few months earlier, we knew we would rise from the ashes and become stronger than we were. My younger brother's energy was infectious. He always had this chip on his shoulder to prove haters wrong. We both wanted to prove to ourselves that we were worthy and that building something from scratch would be the solution. My brother was the best skilled mechanic I knew and one of the hardest working people I knew. I, on the other hand could sell anything. Together, I thought we could really compliment each others skillset as we could learn from each other. We tossed around really cheesy names like Extreme Automotive Inc. because we came from extreme sadness to create something awesome. Or StreamLine Automotive, because we were streamlining our life moving forward. Or ultra cheesy and typical names like Phoenix Automotive, because we were like a phoenix rising from the ashes. Man, we had so many cheesy names. We ended up with VOSIER Inc.

Why VOSIER Inc.? For one, it sounded like a badass European name that shouted luxury and elegance. The real reason was that it came from my last name, which is Siervo. Regardless of what adversity I would go through, I would still be who I am. My values, work ethic, and heart-centred approach to life would not change. I didn't want to allow the external forces to permanently change me into something I didn't want to be, which was a drunken mess in Mexico for seven days. So I had to look inward.

I took my last name and moved the last two letters, *VO,* to the front of my name to spell *VOSIER.* The tagline I created was *Driven by Endless Beginnings* to inspire people to believe that even though you feel like you're at the end of your life or at the end of a chapter of your life, it's really just a new beginning.

That was more than fifteen years ago, and the crisis at the time was a major breakup with a long-term girlfriends. At that time, I thought my life would end. I didn't think I would find anyone like her. It hurt. I felt an immense amount of loss and failure. I was depressed and didn't have the same drive I once did because an external factor made me feel like I wasn't worthy. But here I am writing the conclusion of a book that I never thought I would ever write. Life is interesting like that. You hopefully evolve and grow into the person you are supposed to be. It is the highs and lows that allow that growth to happen.

After the initial fear, anxiety, depression, and sadness subside (and I promise you they will), life will offer opportunities to turn what once made you weak into something completely different, but only if you are able to spot those opportunities and pivot into something truly transformational. From failure, doubt, fear, and depression can come character, grit, confidence, resolve, and an unbreakable mindset. Life arms you with experience and skills needed to face any crisis, heartache, failure, or pandemic.

I'm not saying you will win every time. But if you can take the hit, pivot accordingly, learn from the experience, and take advantage of opportunities, you will give yourself a fighting chance.

Every adversity, every failure, every
heartache carries with it the seeds of a equal
or greater benefit.—Napoleon Hill

This pandemic has crippled the world physically, mentally and financially. It hurt and it hurt, and just when you thought things would get better, it hurt again. It has been a long road. However, at the time of writing, there seems to be some light at the end of the tunnel. Businesses are slowly opening up. Vaccinations are becoming accessible worldwide. And the world seems more woke than ever. People are listening to each other. Families are eating dinner together. Business are learning to collaborate. In a sense, there has been a necessary reset that perhaps is the silver lining behind the pandemic. We were moving too fast. We were chasing shiny objects that only provided a fake sense of worth. We were due for a change.

If you're reading this, you didn't die. You are still alive, which means you have a fighting chance to pivot and pursue whatever it is that you want. This is not the last crisis you will face. It is simply another chapter in your amazing story of life.

Like so many stories throughout this book, you are narrating your own awesome comeback story. You can either say, "Shit, this is the end and I'm done," or "Fuck it. Let's pivot and turn this thing around!" I hope that you gained some skills, ideas, tips, or at the very least motivation from others to remind yourself that you got this. You can pivot and adjust regardless of any situation.

We started his book by going back in time to see how society has evolved from bartering to exchanging money to perhaps dealing in cryptocurrency in the future. Evolution is inevitable. The question is, how will you evolve?

Realize that your business is not your greatest asset. *You* are your greatest asset. *You* are the business. *You* are the brand. *You* can change the circumstances. Whether it's embracing opportunities to leverage skills around the world in the gig economy or pivoting to provide services to others looking into the gig economy, you can gain value and add value.

You can change your mindset and replace the word *sell* with *influence*. You can build real influence to highlight how you can add value and change the lives of others in a positive way. You can look back on the countless tips in this book about going digital, branding yourself, extending beyond your comfort zone, and really embracing a mindset of abundance. You can leverage social media and reach more people than ever before in history. It's exciting to be alive. It's exciting to be you.

The pandemic has also brought you the opportunity to recalibrate toward something more meaningful. Perhaps you lost money, friends, or family, but if you have read this far, you may have gained hope, skills, and an appreciation for life. Perhaps your pivot is to slow the fuck down and start living. Maybe it is to get out of the business completely and do something that makes you happy.

Regardless of what your pivot is, you are the one controlling the direction your life takes you moving forward. You are the master of your domain, captain of your ship, and author of your book. Now go pivot and turn that frown upside down. Turn fear into optimism. Turn extra time into new skills. Turn closing doors into opening opportunities. Turn being reactive into being proactive. Turn surviving into thriving.

Turn, spin, duck, or weave. Do whatever you have to do to own your situation rather than having it own you. In the end, it's you and only you standing in the ring of life. Your coaches, mentors, friends, and family are on the sidelines cheering you on. But they can't fight your battle. They can't throw a punch for you. It's you alone staring life in the face. It's you alone who took life's best shot and got up before being counted out.

Just remember, your toughest day so far has already happened, and you're still standing. So fuck it. Let's pivot into greatness and walk out like the champion I know you are.

Think Big

Be Brave

Live Bold

You got this!

Michael Siervo
Entrepreneur, Speaker,
Ambassador of Positivity
www.michaelsiervo.com

RESOURCES AND BOOK RECOMMENDATIONS

I HAVE TO ADMIT THAT I HAVE ALWAYS BEEN A SPONGE WHEN IT comes to self-improvement. However, this pandemic turned me into a hermit. That's not entirely a bad thing. I have never read more books, listened to more podcasts, and spoken more to people going through the same challenges as I have. Areas such as technology, graphic design, project management, and social media were areas in which I needed to improve if I was to survive in this new reality.

I've listed a few books and resources that gave me confidence and knowledge to not only pivot in my personal and professional life but to write this book. To dig deeper into many of the topics I discussed, feel free to explore these resources below.

Books that feed my brain

- *Think and Grow Rich* by Napoleon Hill
- *7 Habits of Highly Effective People* by Stephen A. Covey
- *As a Man Thinketh* by James Allen
- *Rich Dad, Poor Dad* by Robert Kiyosaki
- *The 4-Hour Work Week* by Tim Ferris
- *Relentless* by Tim Grover
- *Own the Day* by Aubrey Marcus
- *Start with Why* by Simon Sinek
- *Crushing It* by Gary Vaynerchuk
- *Harvard Business Review*
- *10X Rule* by Grant Cardone

- *One Million Followers* by Brendan Kane
- *The Social Media Marketing Workbook* by Jason McDonald
- *Hit Makers* by Derek Thompson
- *Millionaire Booklet* by Grant Cardone
- *Lean Startup* by Eric Ries

Podcasts that inspire me

- *The Joe Rogan Experience*: I love his raw and honest conversations with some of the greatest minds and personalities in the modern world.
- *The Tim Ferris Show*: Tim inspired me to explore the world of side hustles and the gig economy. His book *The 4-Hour Work Week* changed my life and view on business.
- *The Daily Stoic with Ryan Holliday*: Ryan Holliday is one of the best modern-day stoic philosophers. His teachings have kept me grounded and level-headed.
- **Ready, Set, RISE** with Michael Siervo: I'm biased here, because I know the host and think he's super-cool, but the guest are amazing. His conversations with (R)eal (I)ndividuals (S)haring (E)xcellence are inspirational.
- **Ready, Set, SELL** with Michael Siervo and Donny Wong: Hands down, one of the best 11-minute podcasts with super-sales-person-extraordinaire Donny Wong. Raw and high energy info for the busy salesperson.
- **Mind Your Business** with James Wedmore: I enjoy this dose of positive energy, manifestation, mindfulness, and increased performance.
- **Entrepreneurs on Fire** with John Lee Dumas: Award-winning podcast focusing on entrepreneurial journey, tips, and hacks

Apps that make my life easy

- **Canva**: Stand out on social media and at least look like you put in effort on your social media posts. Lots of templates for any business that wants to level up its social media game.
- **Studio**: One of my favourite apps that I use on my iPhone. Almost every logo, Instagram, or Facebook post runs through this app. Amazing designs to level up your posts.
- **Lightroom**: Thinking about adding animation, special effects, and eye-catching content to bring your socials to life? Check out Lightroom.
- **Salesforce**: Hands-down the top client-management system I use. Keep your contacts and funnels in order by streamlining your database.
- **Hootsuite**: So much value out of Hootsuite. They put all social media content under one manageable platform. The value-added advice, templates, guides, and tips are helpful for any business that wants to grow its social media.
- **Honeybook**: This platform is a great one-stop shop for client invoicing, documentation, sales-funnel tracking, and overall organization. Simple way to collect and track payments from customers.
- **Trello**: This free app is great for project management. Many of the virtual assistants I work with abroad use this to keep our projects organized.
- **Telegram**: Love this encrypted communication platform. I use this almost exclusively for managing communication with my team around the world. Simple, reliable, and easy to use.
- **Calm**: Pivoting is tough. I believe that meditation truly allows me to clear my mind so that I can make the best decision possible. This app helps me calm the monkey brain from jumping around to much

ABOUT THE AUTHOR

Michael Siervo is an entrepreneur, public speaker, published author, community leader, investment professional, certified coach practitioner, and philanthropist. Born and raised in an immigrant family in Toronto, he quickly saw how his family had to adjust and pivot throughout his life. At a young age wanted to be a teacher, however he realized that business was a great way to connect people, add value and positively impact the world.

After graduating from the University of Toronto with a degree in management and economics and a minor in sociology, he quickly advanced in the financial services industry. At that time he became the youngest district vice president in Western Canada for the largest wealth-management firm in the country. He has held roles as district vice president and director for several Fortune 500 companies and has been the CEO of his privately held companies.

He has owned businesses including financial services, real estate investing, restaurants, clothing and apparel, strategic coaching and consulting, media production, and digital marketing. He is the host of the *Ready, Set, RISE* podcast. He has been featured globally as a public speaker from Canada, to the Philippines to Africa. He has been awarded the order of merit and sales awards for two of the largest investment firms in Canada. He was recognized by the True Beauty Foundation as a community leader recipient, and Empowered Media TV as community ambassador. He is the first and only two time award winner of the Golden Balangay Awards, which recognizes the top Filipinos across Canada, wherein he won the World Vision Community Leadership Award and the GBA Executive of the Year Award.

He is the one of the co-founders and inaugural chairman of the board for the Filipino Chamber of Commerce Alberta. He is an ambassador for Gems for Gems (Canada's largest charity focusing on victims of domestic abuse), Founding Leadership Ambassador and Leadership Committee for The United Way. Michael continues to work with leaders and entrepreneurs as a coach and mentor. During the pandemic he created The KIND Project which focuses on raising fund for literacy and education in improverished countries. He is often seen travelling, working out, cold water plunging or enjoying nature with his family.

Follow Michael on social media at:

- Instagram: @iam.michaelsiervo
- Facebook: www.facebook.com/mr.michaelsiervo/
- Twitter: @michaelsiervo
- LinkedIn: linkedin.com/in/michaelsiervo
- Website: www.michaelsiervo.com
- Email: info@michaelsiervo.com
- YouTube: www.youtube.com/c/readysetRISE

Contact Michael for public-speaking engagements or coaching on sales, strategic business planning, or personal self development.

Register for Michael's Free Newsletter on Productivity, Performance and Passion and stay tuned for his upcoming online courses on personal self development.

ACKNOWLEDGEMENT

EVERY DAY I WAKE UP WITH A SENSE OF GRATITUDE AND appreciation. You see, being able to pivot has a lot to do with the way we perceive our current state in life and whether we can improve our future situation. It's a mindset shift that all starts with gratitude. Being able to see the sun rise in the morning is a reminder that I have another chance at making things better. It wasn't always like this way. There were mornings that started with depression, anxiety, and regret. Things have changed drastically since those days. Perhaps this pandemic forced me to pivot in more ways than one. Perhaps it was the catalyst of what was building up all these years. Failure, stress, and disappointment can break people however diamonds are formed from immense heat, pressure, and time.

If it wasn't for the many people who impacted my life, maybe I would still be a lump of coal waiting to transform into something greater. This sense of gratitude fills my heart as I am not who I am today without the support, words of encouragement, positive nudges to keep trying or the honest advice from a friend who has the courage to say the things that hurt but knows it is for the best. I am truly grateful.

First and foremost, I am grateful for God, The Universe, Source Energy, The Big Guy, whatever you may call it that has blessed me with the opportunities and fortune I have today. I could be anything in this world but I ended up being me. Thank you for blessing this simple human with the skills, ability, luck of environment and mindset to do what I am doing. I am truly grateful.

Thank you to the Siervo Family. To an immigrant family who taught me the power of hard work and high standards, I am thankful. To my father Lou Siervo, your sacrifices and tough love approach were not always understood growing up, but I know it now. I see what you were doing and respect the example you set for me. Thank you, dad. To my big brother Alfred, I don't have many role models, but you were my first. Thank you for always believing in me and showering your little brother with praise at my accomplishments. You are humble and a true example of a family man. I have learned so much from you. To my younger brother Dave, thank you for supporting me in the early years of business. You are one of the hardest, most determined people I know. I appreciate the lessons on grit and effort. Whether you knew it or not, you were always teaching me things and reminding me to be better. I hold myself to a higher standard because you expected that of me. I am excited to see you grow. To my mother Alicia Siervo, a kid can't have confidence if he has no one rooting for him. Thank you for being my first and biggest cheerleader. You are a kind soul who constantly inspires me to grow at any age, give with a full heart and love unconditionally. You are my first hero who taught me gentle patience and unconditional love. Thank you for giving me the building blocks of virtue and character.

Thank you to my Mother-in-law Alou for being the one of the most understanding people I have ever met. You have taught me to be at peace with certain situations and be strong and stubborn with others. Most of all thank you for teaching me about forgiveness. I appreciate you. To my brothers in law, Dexter and Woody. Surprisingly, you have taught me a lot about maturity and to let things go. Thank you for always being there in both your quirky and hilarious ways.

To my father-in-law Dr. Portugal, words can't express how much I miss you. Thank you for being an amazing mentor and role model. Your generosity, kindness, humour, and curiosity are traits that l try my best to emulate. Thank you for always listening to me and sharing sage words of wisdom. I know that this book would not be possible if it wasn't for the many lessons you taught me. You are the master at Pivoting and this book embodies you. The thought that you are looking down with pride as I continued to overcome adversity, fuelled me to keep pushing forward. Thank you so much for everything. I miss you.

Thank you to my dear close friends, Norman John, Maurice McFarlane & Johnny Sheard. I honestly don't know where my life would be after university if it wasn't for you guys. From supporting each other with stupid antics to having real conversations about life, I appreciate your friendship and wisdom.

Thank you to my aunties Eva Brunelleschi and Elvira Ardena. Thank you for always making me feel like I could do anything. I appreciate the honest conversations and advice you shared with me growing up as it helped me be the man I am today.

Thank you to my cousin, Regina Sosing. You continue to inspire me. From humble beginnings to attaining your masters to running a successful company, you have taught me that we are unstoppable if we put our minds to it. Thank you for your wisdom and support.

Thank you to my adopted aunties Alma Armada and Judith Barran. During difficult times while away from family, you were there for me. You are the closest people I have to aunties, mentors, and advisors in Calgary. Thank you for teaching me to ignore the bullshit, focus on what's important, be true to your vision and to love with a genuine heart. I don't know if I would have been able to get through some dark times without your guiding light. I am grateful for you.

Thank you to all the other authors, entrepreneurs, and hustlers in my inner circle. Your words of encouragement and support mean so much to me. We are all trying our best to create things that add value and that the world can appreciate. We consistently put ourselves out there to be ridiculed, targeted, mocked, and embarrassed when we fail yet we continue to try. Thank you for teaching me bravery.

Thank you to my design team, Jon Michael (JM) Acuna and my photographer Jesse Tomayo. Thank you for helping me bring to life my brand, my vision and my energy. JM, Thank you for the many late night hours working on our projects. I appreciate you.

Thank you for random shit storms, unforeseen adversity, fake people, poor choices, financial hardship, friends for a season, friends for a reason, heartbreak, health concern, recessions and this long drawn-out pandemic. Because of you, I was reminded that I am strong, resilient, and unbreakable. You can't stop me and I am grateful for your efforts to try. It only makes me better.

Thank you to the Toronto Raptors Organization. From being an underdog team that no star player would want to play for to winning an NBA Championship in 2019, you inspire me. Countless nights I felt like giving up but found a mental escape in watching a game. I forgot about my problems while yelling, screaming, and cheering at the screen! You taught me to root for others rather than feel sorry for yourself. Within us all is grit, determination, and the ability to be a champion. I am grateful you and that high energy Raptor Mascot.

Thank you to my wife Vivienne Siervo. It takes a very strong person to ride the highs and lows that come with being with me. Thank you for always showing me the kindness that exists in the world regardless of the darkness that can sometime envelop it. Thank you for debating with me and showing me other perspectives when I am stubbornly closed minded. Thank you for teaching me that life is about finding your own peace, driving at your own pace, dressing with your own style, connecting with your own spiritual path and living on your terms. Thank you for your constant support and for cheering me on when everyone else has left the building. Thank you for showing so many levels of love and how deep it can go. I appreciate you. I am grateful for you. I love you.

Finally, thank you to my 7 year old self. When you were a kid you were shy but told people you would be the President of Canada. Little did you know that Canada has a Prime Minister and not a President. However, technicalities never stopped you from dreaming and being ambitious. Thank you for believing in superheroes and that regular humans can make a difference. Thank you for standing up to bullies when you were a kid and ignoring bullies as an adult. You have better things to put your energy towards. There were some dark times when tomorrow seemed like a coin flip and getting up deserved a gold medal. Thank you for never giving up. Thank you for believing in yourself. Thank you for giving yourself a fighting chance regardless of the situation. Thank you to my future self for waiting for me. The journey has been tough but I'm coming.

To everyone who has ever meant something to me, or to anyone trying their best to live their best lives, thank you. I see you. I hear you. I am truly grateful for you.

Think Big. Live Brave. Be Bold.
-Michael Siervo

Printed in the United States
by Baker & Taylor Publisher Services